IMAGES
of America

RIVERDALE

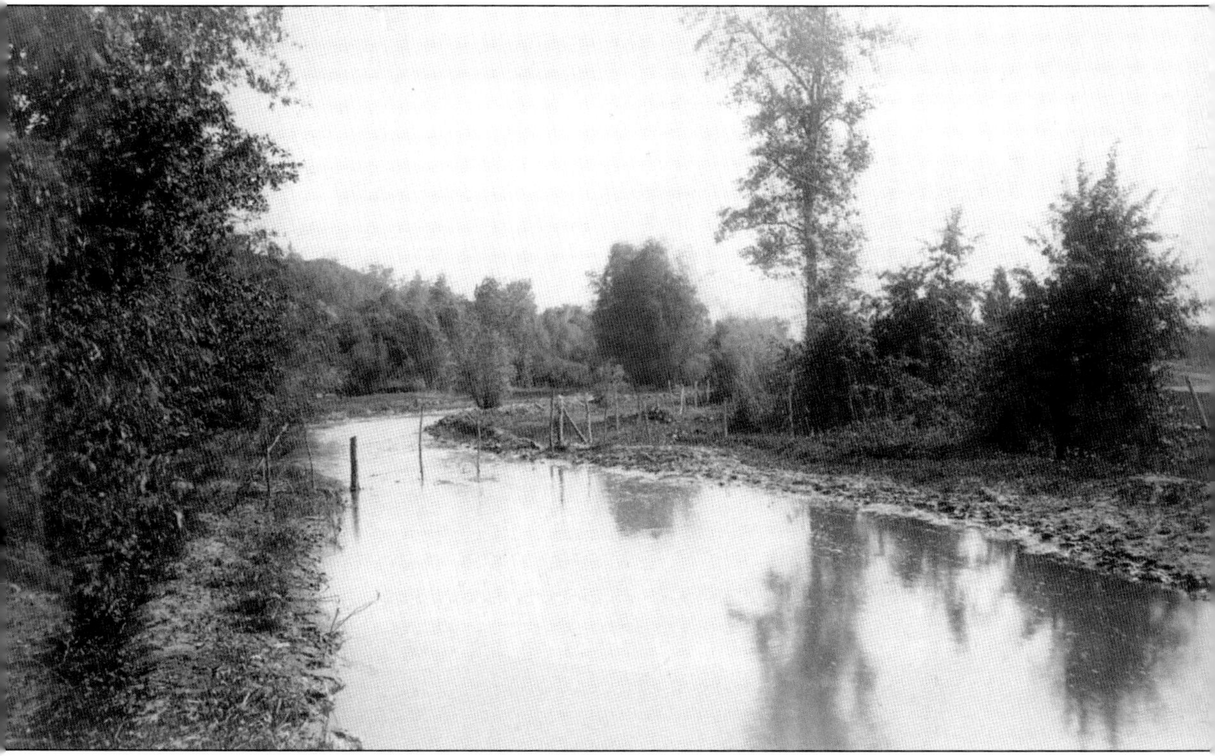

WEBER RIVER AT RIVERDALE, c. 1902. The Weber River, a landmark for which Riverdale is named, has been important to the community since the beginning of the settlement. Over the years, it has been used to water crops and power the mill and for recreation, such as tubing, swimming, kayaking, and ice-skating. The river also served as a baptismal site for early members of the Church of Jesus Christ of Latter-day Saints. (Courtesy of the Ogden Union Station Collection, 05490-11.)

ON THE COVER: FRUIT FARMER DON ELLIS, 1954. Carrying a 12-foot ladder and cherry bucket, Don Ellis is seen here in the family orchard. Ellis held a master farmer diploma from Weber College and was active in the Weber County Young Farmers Association, where he served as president. The Ellis family has farmed the west bench of Riverdale since Don's father, Alma, moved to Riverdale in the early 1900s. The family harvested Bing, Montmorency, and Lambert cherries, as well as peaches and apricots. (Courtesy of the Don and Ardis Ellis family.)

IMAGES
of America

RIVERDALE

Camee Ellis

ARCADIA
PUBLISHING

ISBN 978-1-4671-2852-0

Published by Arcadia Publishing
Charleston, South Carolina

Printed in the United States of America

Library of Congress Control Number: 2017954558

For all general information, please contact Arcadia Publishing:
Telephone 843-853-2070
Fax 843-853-0044
E-mail sales@arcadiapublishing.com
For customer service and orders:
Toll-Free 1-888-313-2665

Visit us on the Internet at www.arcadiapublishing.com

To everyone who has a special place in their heart for Riverdale, Utah.

Contents

ACKNOWLEDGMENTS

After launching the Remember Riverdale campaign in summer 2017, I gathered nearly 2,200 images from 75 sources, along with accompanying personal reminiscences, life histories, family trees, and newspaper articles. Thank you to all who made contributions. The best of care was taken to compile an accurate history of this special community.

I express thanks to my father-in-law, Brent Ellis, a lifelong Riverdale resident and current city councilman. His desire to preserve the city's history through historical markers sparked the inspiration for this project.

Thank you to Mayor Norm Searle for incredible support from the moment I presented the idea for this book and throughout the process. Thanks also to Riverdale City administration, staff, and city council for support, assistance, and contributions.

I appreciate the help of historians Gary Boatright Jr. and Judy B. Anderson for sharing all they have learned about Riverdale with me, Lee Witten of the Ogden Union Station Library for lending his expertise of the railroad in the Ogden area, and Janet Gibby Cox for her contributions.

Thanks to the Riverdale Utah Stake of the Church of Jesus Christ of Latter-day Saints, Riverdale Elementary School, the Weber School District Foundation, and the Weber County Daughters of Utah Pioneers Museum for their contributions.

I also thank the staff of Weber State University's Special Collections for helping to scan photographs submitted by residents at the Remember Riverdale scan days and for providing photographs from their collection.

I wish to thank all who reviewed the manuscript, and Arcadia Publishing for making local histories important and readily available.

I am grateful for the following people who recorded Riverdale's history over the years: Warren Gould Child Sr., Warren Gould Child Jr., Andrew Jensen, Alexander Carlsen, Lucille Child Judkins, Verla R. Hull, Cora S. Bingham, Doris Woodbury, Ralph E. Porter, William W. Terry, Milton R. Hunter, Richard W. Sadler, Richard C. Roberts, Glenna Jones Stump, Chris R. Stone, and the *Ogden Standard-Examiner* newspaper.

Finally, my greatest appreciation goes to all of my family—to my husband for his encouragement and amazing help, my daughter for her excitement for this book, my sons for their suggestions to add a photograph to the book every time they saw anything old, and my parents for their help and support.

I sincerely hope this book will help current and future generations to remember Riverdale.

Introduction

When most people think of Riverdale, Utah, Riverdale Road comes to mind—a successful, yet busy, six-lane highway lined with restaurants, shopping centers, and car dealerships. While these businesses offer many necessities and conveniences to residents of Weber County, they stand in contrast to what Riverdale once was—a quiet, rural, farming community full of little lanes.

Riverdale began as a favored site for Native Americans, who camped in the valley. The topography and river created a microclimate allowing temperatures to be 10 degrees warmer in the winter and 10 degrees cooler in the summer.

Many natural springs are known throughout the area. Blue Springs, located just west of present-day Gibby Floral, served as the water source for a Native American campsite. Wagons traveling between Salt Lake City and Brigham City also camped at the site and utilized its water supply.

James Graham built a simple log cabin for his family in Riverdale in 1850. Other early settlers included Rufus Allen, Adam Fife, John Richards, William Stimpson, James Mitchell, Hugh Findlay, John Lonson Child, Warren Gould Child Sr., John Crow Thompson, Richard Dye, William C. Parker, Thomas Slater, James Shupe, Solomon Freeman, Alexander Patterson, and Gordon Beckstead.

Known as Weber in its early days, the community changed its name to Union in 1862. By 1864, the majority of homes in the settlement were strung out along the main road (present-day 4400 South) and along the east side of the Weber River, giving the community the name Stringtown. Some referred to the community as Jack Thompson's Settlement. By 1868, a post office was established and the settlement was named Riverdale, derived from it being a dale, or valley, near the Weber River. However, the 1870 US census record simply referred to it as the Weber River valley.

In about 1853, Daniel Burch constructed a gristmill on the east side of the Weber River. John Taylor, an apostle and later president of the Church of Jesus Christ of Latter-day Saints (LDS), purchased the mill and the site became known as Taylor's Mill. With the coming of the Transcontinental Railroad in 1869, the mill found itself adjacent to the railroad line, which Riverdale residents helped construct. The first railroad stop in the Ogden area, known as Taylor's Mill Station or Taylor's Switch, was located in Riverdale. A grand celebration was held when the first train reached the Ogden area on March 8, 1869. As with other areas, the coming of the railroad increased land prices near the mill and transformed Riverdale into a lively place. This glory was short-lived as the main railroad junction later moved to Ogden City.

The Weber River has played a significant role in the community as a water source for irrigation and powering the mill. Additionally, it served as an LDS baptismal site. An early settler, Warren Gould Child, constructed a ferryboat to provide access for travelers crossing the river. Over time, many bridges and viaducts have been built over the Weber River and the railroad tracks.

Settlers found the soil in Riverdale ideal for growing crops. Canals were dug from the Weber River to irrigate nearby land, which was soon filled with farms and orchards. Crops grown in Riverdale included wheat, oats, barley, corn, alfalfa, sugar beets, potatoes, tomatoes, peas, beans, onions, cabbage, apples, peaches, apricots, cherries, and plums.

In 1858, a log building with dirt for both the floor and the roof served as the schoolhouse. Students sat on seats made of split logs at this first school site, located on the south side of present-day 4400 South near the Parker Drive roundabout. In 1862, a larger log schoolhouse replaced the original structure. In 1865, Warren G. Child and John C. Thompson built a cobble rock schoolhouse where an LDS meetinghouse now stands at 1056 West 4400 South. The community also used this building as a church and for local gatherings. In 1900, a new meetinghouse was built for the Riverdale Ward, followed by a new schoolhouse in 1911 at a location known as School Hill. Over the years, the school was used as both an elementary and junior high school. Unfortunately, fire destroyed the building in 1966. A new building, the current Riverdale Elementary School, was built on the same location in 1967.

Present-day 4400 South was once the main road in Riverdale and an original part of the territorial road connecting Ogden and Salt Lake City. With the advent of the automobile, Riverdale found itself on the route of the historic transcontinental Lincoln Highway. Horseback riders rode side by side with automobiles, and hitching posts remained in town for many years. With all the travelers, a tourist cabin court was built on the main road. The W.J. Greaser Store across the street provided all the supplies a traveler needed.

Other businesses dotted the community, including blacksmith shops, creameries, canneries, dairy operations, and a pea vinery. Telephone service came to Riverdale in 1883, and state prisoners paved the main road with concrete in 1916. It was paved with tar in 1918 by the state commission. As traffic increased from 1940s war efforts, the narrow bridge over the river on 4400 South became a bottleneck. Planners designed and built an impressive new viaduct to the south of the main road, helping to create what is now Riverdale Road. In 1955, streetlights illuminated the community, and a sewer system was added in 1957. The national interstate highway system reached Riverdale in the 1960s, bisecting the community and its farmlands despite pleas to change the location of the planned roads.

In an effort to make civic improvements, residents held a meeting and Riverdale, unincorporated for nearly a century, was formally incorporated as a town on March 4, 1946. On July 9, 1956, Riverdale became a third-class city. The cover of the 1960s Lions Club city directory dubbed Riverdale "The Future Hub of Weber County." This visionary statement has come to fruition as businesses began to fill the area and continue to do so today.

Residents believed Riverdale to be an idyllic place to live, with its farms and fine people. The community has also enjoyed many entertainment options in Riverdale—two drive-in movie theaters, nightclubs, the Cinedome 70 theater, Classic Skating, Schneiter's Riverside Golf Course, a boys' swimming hole called "Old Soapy," the Weber River Parkway Trail, and four parks. Additionally, local civic organizations including the Lions Club, Riverdale Ladies Club, and Riverdale Jaycees provided opportunities to socialize and engage in the community.

Many features in the community serve as reminders of the city's rich history. Old barns, farm equipment, remnants of orchards, the school's rock wall, and a few historic homes still dot the landscape. Many descendants of Riverdale's original settlers still call Riverdale home, and street names are reminders of the past—Carter Drive, Ritter Drive, Parker Drive, and Cozy Dale Drive.

Riverdale has become what it is today as a result of those who built this great city. Mayor Norm Searle (2014 to present) has said, "The 'face' of Riverdale has changed significantly since the first settlers arrived and many changes are still taking place, but the future is bright!"

One

Early Settlement

Stringtown and Residents

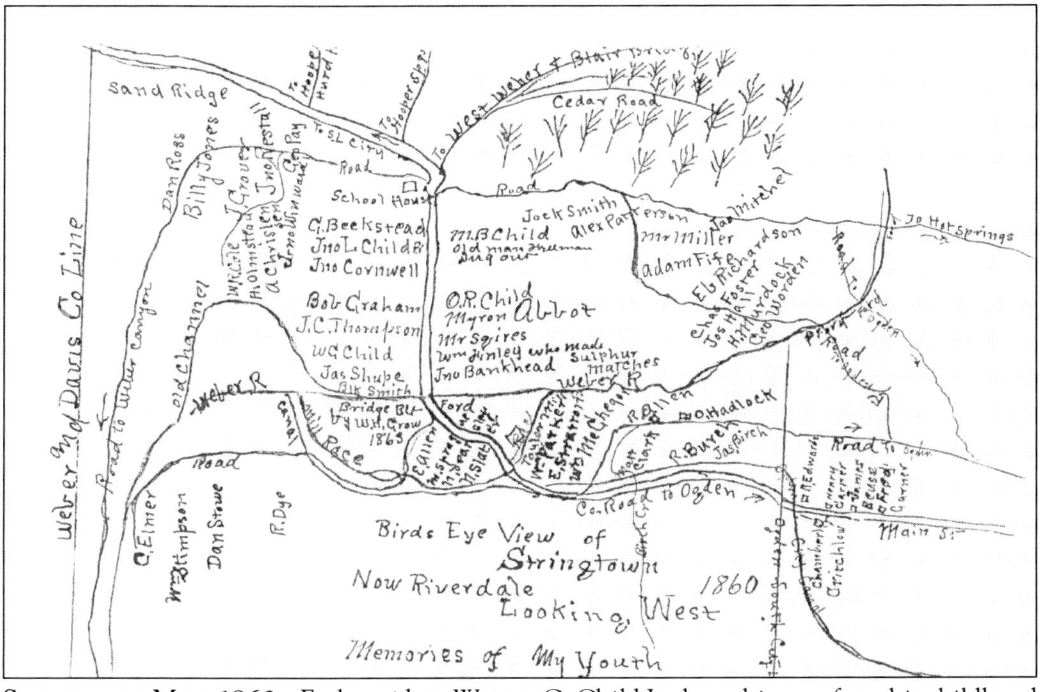

Stringtown Map, 1860s. Early resident Warren G. Child Jr. drew this map from his childhood recollection of Riverdale in the 1860s when the community was called Stringtown due to the homes being strung out along the main road. The map depicts orchards, the first schoolhouse, James Shupe's blacksmith shop, the Weber River bridge, Taylor's Mill, and the locations of early residents' homes. (Courtesy of Riverdale City.)

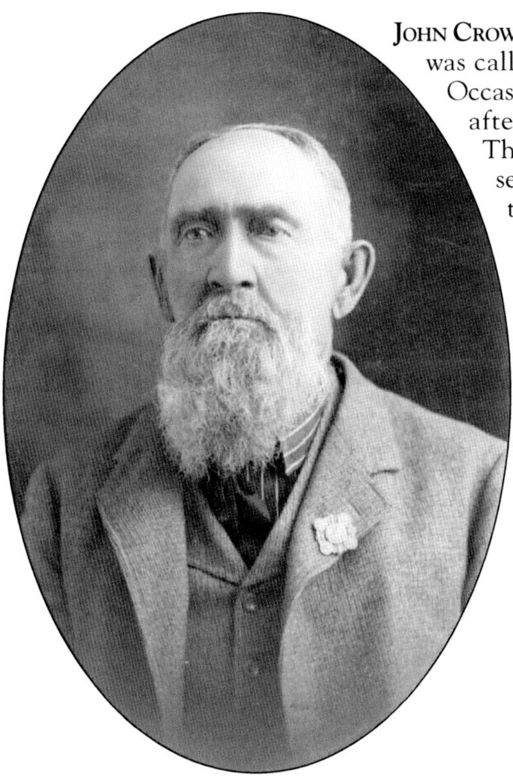

John Crow Thompson, 1897. In its early days, the settlement was called Weber, then Union, and later, Stringtown. Occasionally it was called Jack Thompson's Settlement after prominent citizen John Crow Thompson. Thompson was a member of the Mormon Battalion, served the community as a tanner, first counselor to Riverdale Ward bishop Sanford Bingham, postmaster, and deputy sheriff. He was contracted to build the cobble rock schoolhouse in 1865 along with Warren G. Child Sr. (Courtesy of the Slade family.)

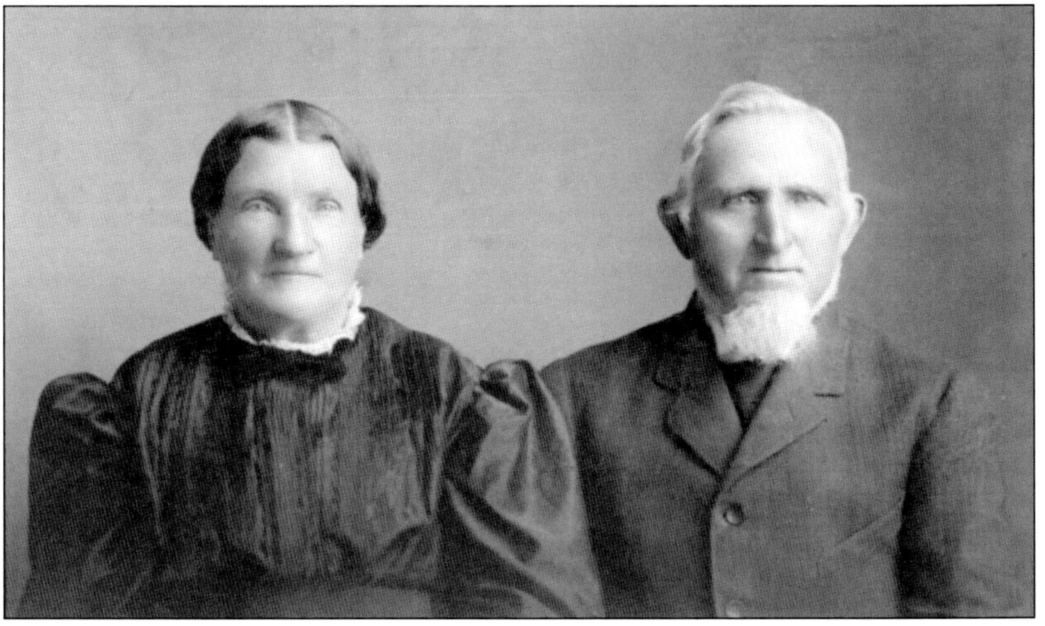

Mary and Richard Dye. Richard Dye and Mary Malden Peek Dye moved to the settlement in 1860. Richard oversaw the canal and served as justice of the peace, school trustee for the Riverdale School District, superintendent of the Riverdale Ward Sunday school for 31 years, and ward chorister for 40 years. Mary served as the Relief Society president for 19 years. (Courtesy of Brett Rawlins.)

WARREN G. CHILD SR. Born on February 21, 1835, in New York, Warren G. Child immigrated to the West in 1852 and moved to the settlement in the spring of 1860. Child kept a journal, which provides details about the settlement. In 1866 and 1868, he built and operated a ferry for travelers to cross the Weber River. In 1869, he helped grade two miles of land for the Union Pacific Railroad. (Courtesy of the Lucille Child Judkins family.)

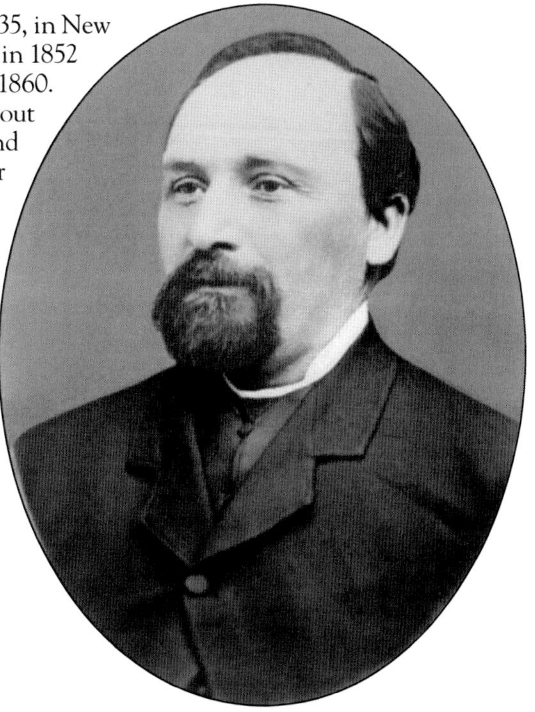

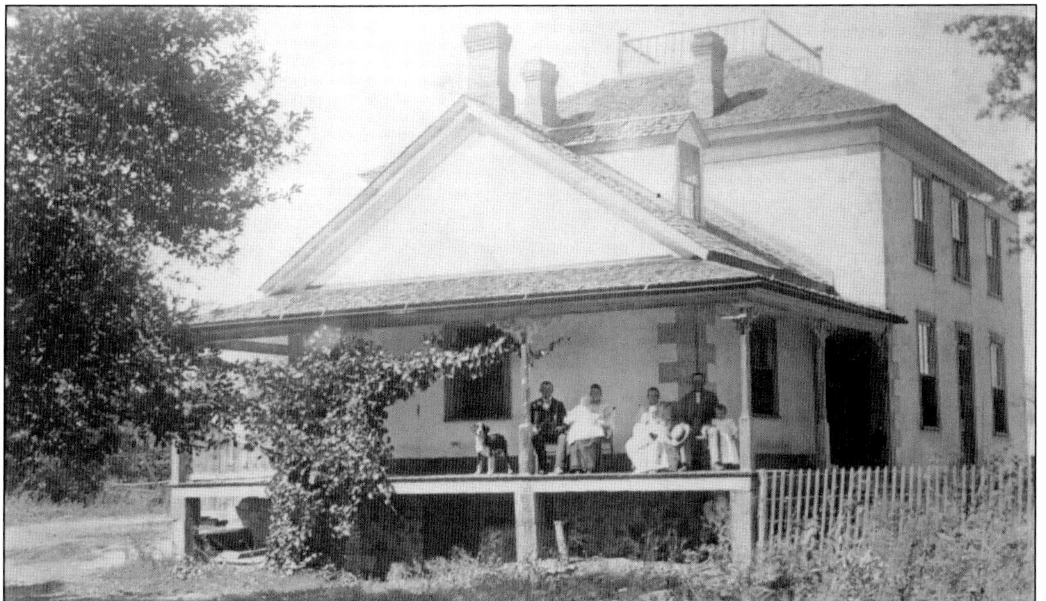

WARREN G. CHILD HOME, C. 1894. Warren G. Child Sr. and his wife, Hannah Austin Wilder, built their first home in Riverdale in 1852, their second in 1853, and their third (pictured) in 1876. Adam Aranthon Bingham, and later Charles and Emma Mitchell, occupied the home that stood at 791 West 4400 South. From left to right are Jesse Alexander Child (Warren and Hannah's son), Elizabeth Stratton Child, Jesse Edward Child (baby), Annie Stratton Bingham (Elizabeth's sister), Aranthon Bingham (baby), Adam Aranthon Bingham, and Adele Bingham. (Courtesy of E. Garry Judkins.)

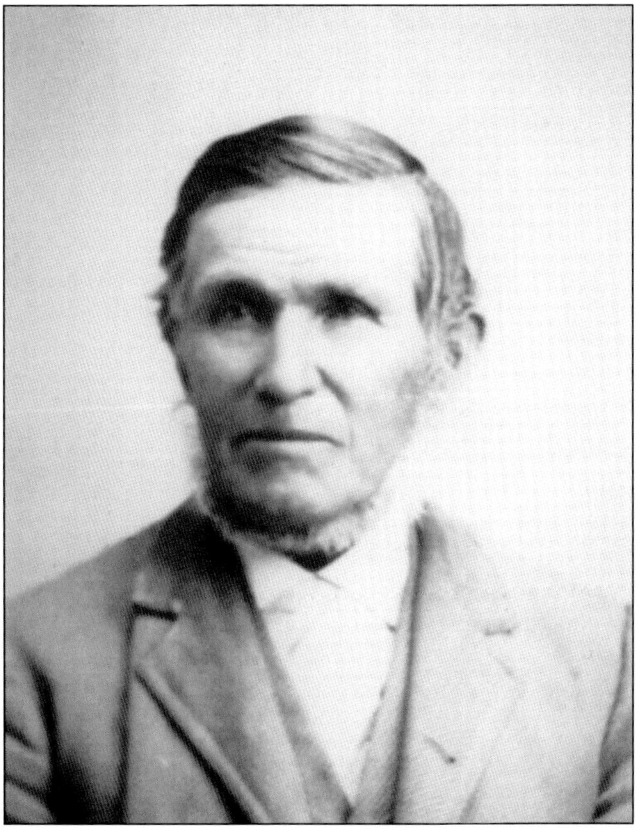

WILLIAM STIMPSON SR. Born in England in 1821, William Stimpson joined the Church of Jesus Christ of Latter-day Saints in 1849. He left England in 1856, immigrating to Utah by rail and handcart. The next year, Stimpson moved to the Riverdale area. He was married to Rebecca Lubbock, Edna Hinchcliff, and Ann Mary Pedersen, and had a large posterity. (Courtesy of Kathleen Cevering.)

WILLIAM STIMPSON JR. HOME. William Stimpson Jr. was born in Riverdale on April 27, 1859, on the east side of the Weber River. From left to right are Verna Stimpson (granddaughter), Annie Rebecca Bybee Stimpson (wife), Murrelle Hunter (granddaughter), and William Stimpson Jr. (Courtesy of Kathleen Cevering.)

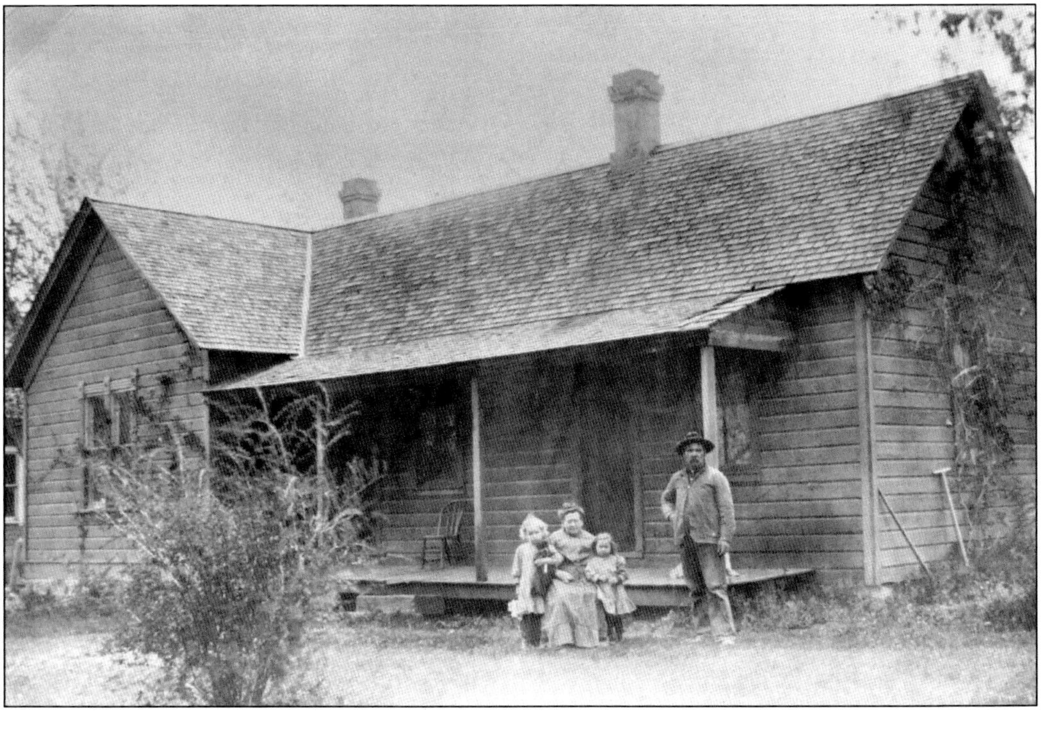

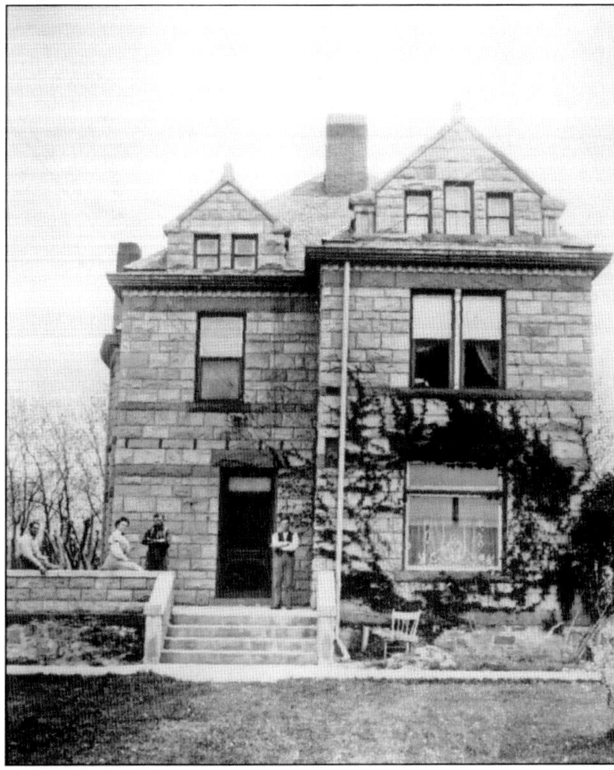

RITTER MANSION. Listed on the Utah State Historic Register, this home was built from 1890 to 1895 by John Thompson Ritter and his wife, Martha Lewis Ritter. The mansion was constructed from stones quarried from Park City and Coalville, which were transported to Riverdale by horse and wagon. Located at 5038 South 1150 West, it still stands. As a farmer, dairyman, and lifelong Riverdale resident, John and his wife lived on 60 acres and sold the fruits and vegetables grown on their land. In addition to their crops, they produced 250 pounds of butter each day from a creamery in the basement. The home served as the location for many church socials. Riverdale Utah Stake patriarch Chauncey Burton, who also lived here, gave blessings in the parlor room to church members. (Courtesy of Judy B. Anderson.)

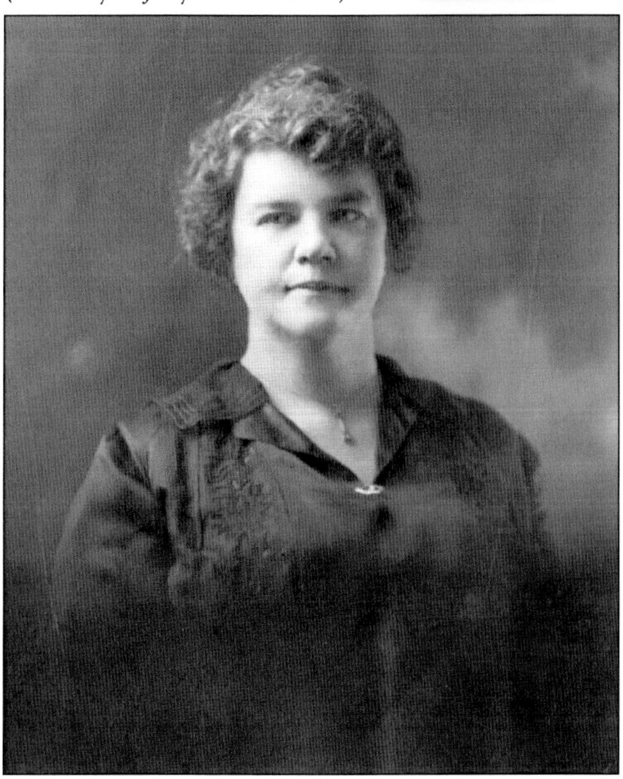

MARTHA LEWIS RITTER. Born in Coalville, Utah, on June 1, 1875, Martha Lewis Ritter attended the Agricultural College of Utah (now Utah State University) in 1892. She served as superintendent of religion classes, first president of the Riverdale Farm Bureau, and as county matron, assisting youth and the poor in Weber County. Active in social welfare, she worked with the Red Cross and was the first captain of the Riverdale Daughters of Utah Pioneers camp. (Courtesy of Weber State University Special Collections.)

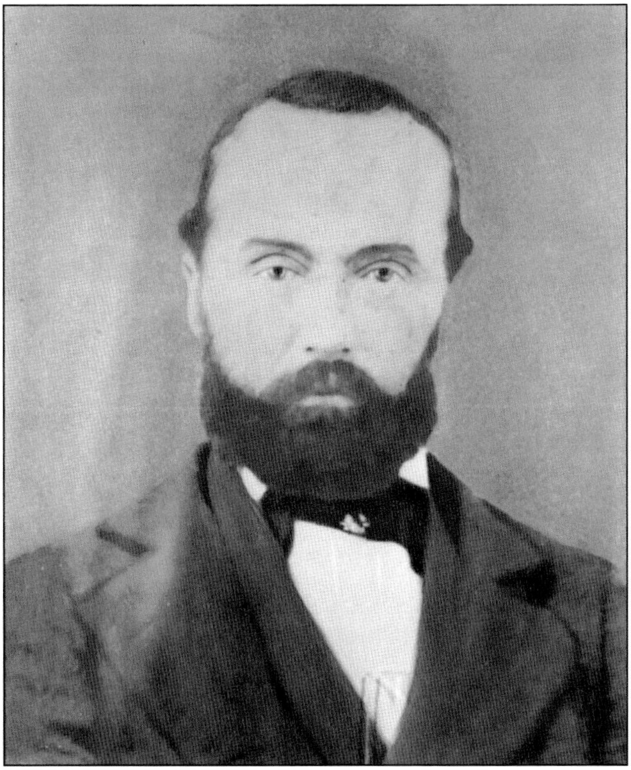

Sanford Bingham. Born on May 3, 1821, in Vermont, Sanford Bingham married Martha Ann Lewis in 1847 in Nebraska and the couple moved west. After living in various areas of Ogden, they purchased a farm in Riverdale in 1862. In 1863, he married a second wife, Agnes Fife, and had a total of 24 children. Bingham served as justice of the peace in the Riverdale Precinct, was a member of the board of trustees in the Riverdale School District, and designed the cobble rock schoolhouse. In the spring of 1868, the territorial legislature appointed Bingham to build a bridge over the Weber River. That same year, he was appointed bishop of the Riverdale Ward, a capacity he served in for 25 years. He passed away in Riverdale on November 21, 1910. (Courtesy of the Weber County Daughters of Utah Pioneers Museum.)

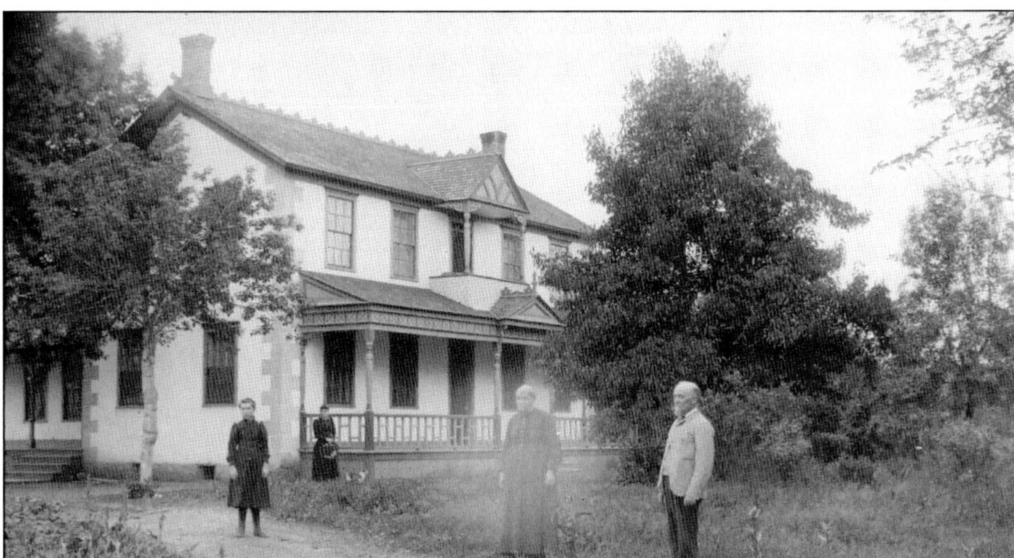

Sanford and Martha Bingham Home. The Binghams' home was located at approximately 961 West 4400 South. Bingham Canyon copper mine was named after Sanford and his brother Thomas. They discovered copper there in 1848 while grazing their cattle. Brigham Young advised the men against pursuing mining operations. Establishing communities and survival were more important at that time. From left to right are two unidentified girls, Martha Ann Bingham, and Sanford Bingham. (Courtesy of Jan Petersen.)

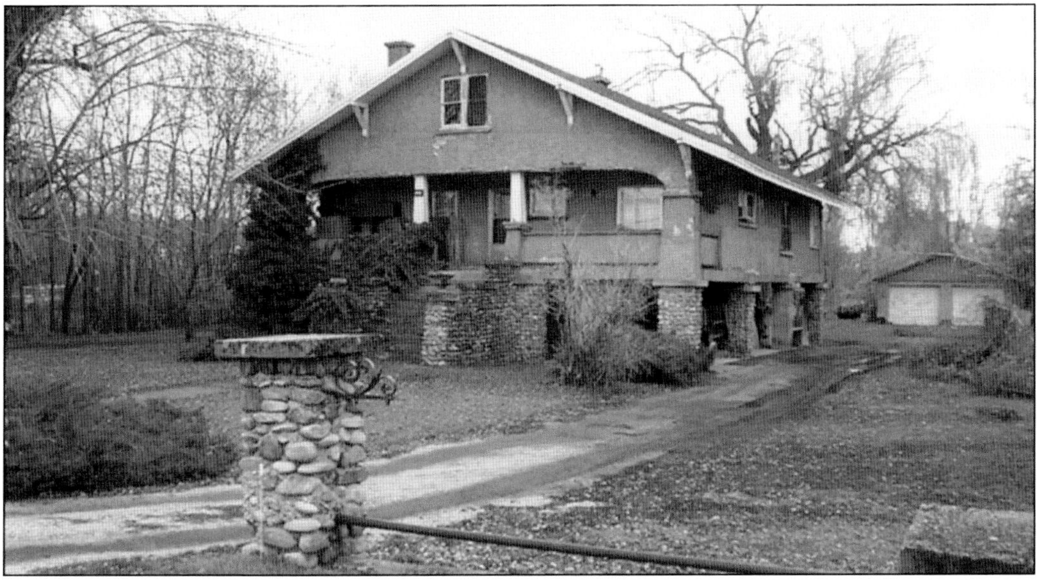

TANNERY REMODELED INTO HOME. John C. Thompson built a tannery out of rock, which John A. Stimpson later remodeled to be his home. Stimpson sold the home in 1919 to Frank McBride, a prominent stockman in Jackson Hole, Wyoming. The Virgil Hosler family later lived here. The home, known as "the Dell," was among the most modern and picturesque residences in the area, with beautiful waterways in the yard. (Courtesy of Judy B. Anderson)

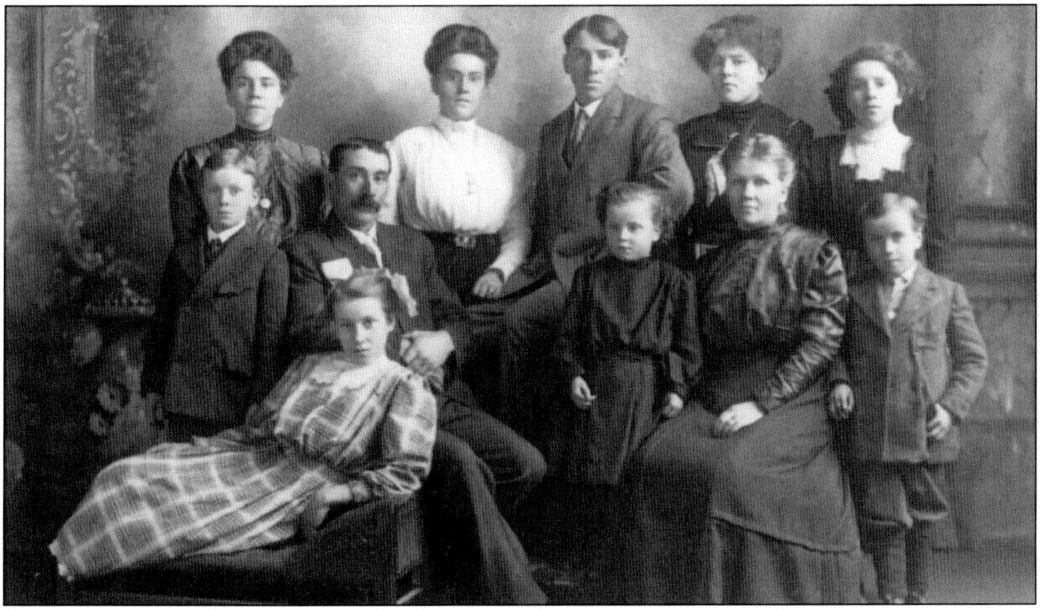

JOSEPH AND LUCINDA PATTERSON FAMILY. Joseph Fife Patterson was born in a little log cabin in Riverdale in 1865 to an industrious Scottish pioneer family. He served as president of the Riverdale Bench Canal. Joseph married his wife, Lucinda, in 1885. From left to right are (first row) Blanche Patterson (Grose) (on bench); (second row) David Frank Patterson, Joseph Fife Patterson, Cora Patterson (Hill), Lucinda Spaulding Patterson, and Adam Patterson; (third row) Mary Ann Patterson (Hopson), Edith Lucinda Patterson (Stark), Joseph Alexander Patterson, Ellen Patterson (Staker), and Ada Patterson (Child). (Courtesy of the Joseph R. Patterson family.)

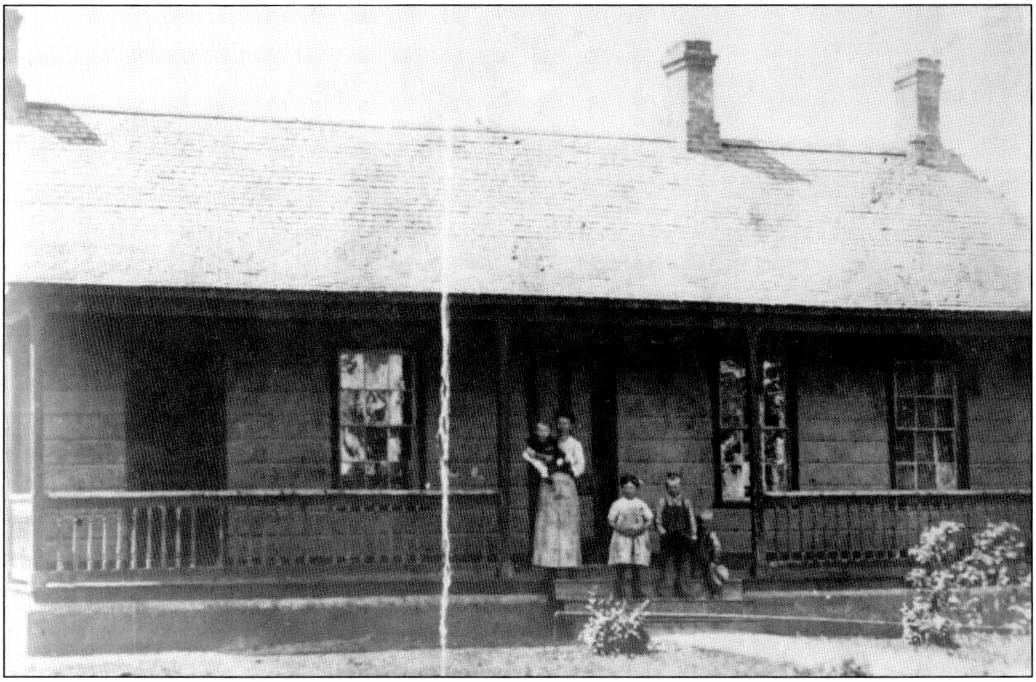

Pauline Cobia and Children, 1917. Built in 1875, this home is located on the south side of 4400 South, about one block east of the Riverdale 1st and 7th Wards meetinghouse. Pictured are Pauline Kunzler Cobia and her children. (Courtesy of the Lucille Child Judkins family.)

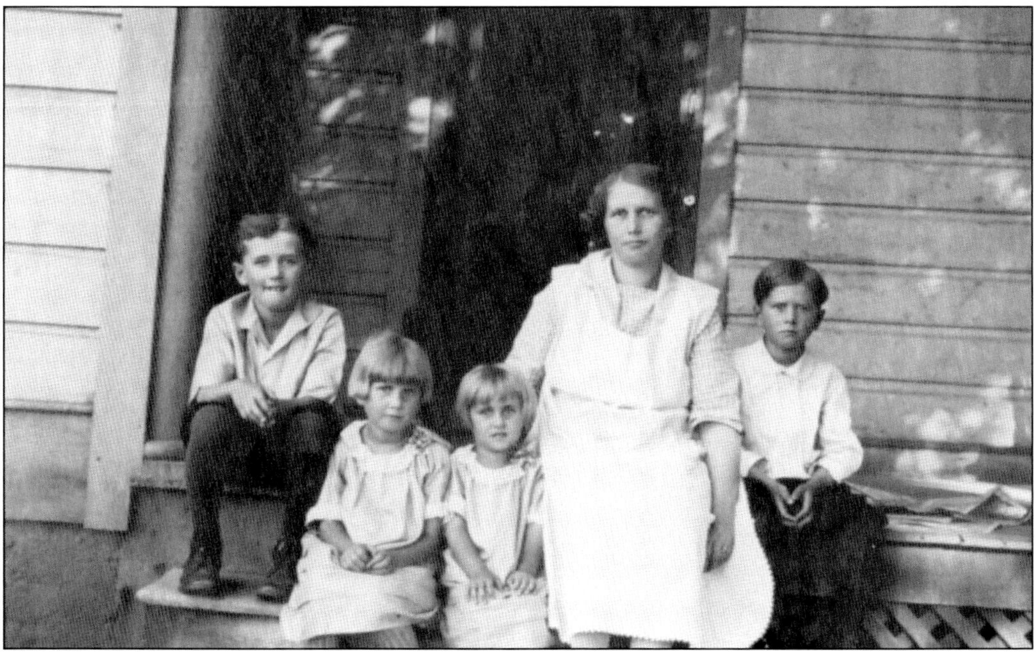

Mary Emeline Allen Stimpson. Between 1915 and 1921, Mary and her husband, Joseph Henry Stimpson, lived in Japan where her husband served as the LDS Japan Mission president. Several of their children were born during their time in Asia. From left to right are Allen, Inez, Mary, Mary Emeline Allen Stimpson, and Eldon. (Courtesy of Barbara Porter.)

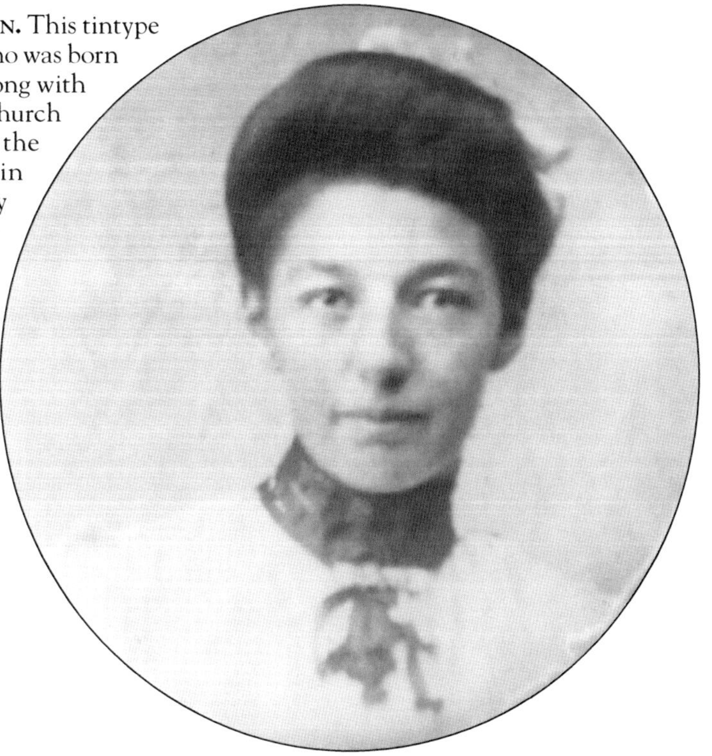

GERTRUDE TER BRUGGEN ROMAN. This tintype shows Gertrude ter Bruggen, who was born in Amsterdam in 1859. She, along with her family, joined the LDS Church in Holland before coming to the United States. Well known in the Ogden area, her obituary states that she "was looked up to by all as a woman of sterling qualities." (Courtesy of Roy and Edith Purkiss.)

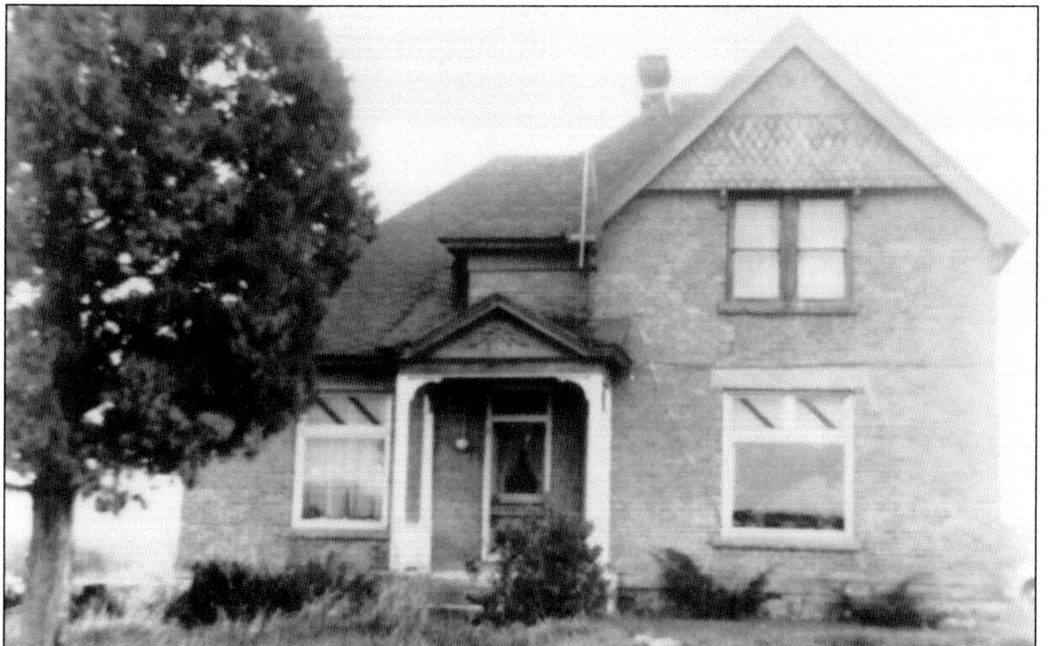

DANIEL AND GERTRUDE ROMAN HOME. Born in Italy in 1851, Daniel B. Roman married Gertrude ter Bruggen in 1880. Together, the Romans conducted a mortgage business and sold produce from their 34-acre farm. The Romans' beautiful home at 4258 South 1000 West still stands in Riverdale. (Courtesy of Kathleen Nielson.)

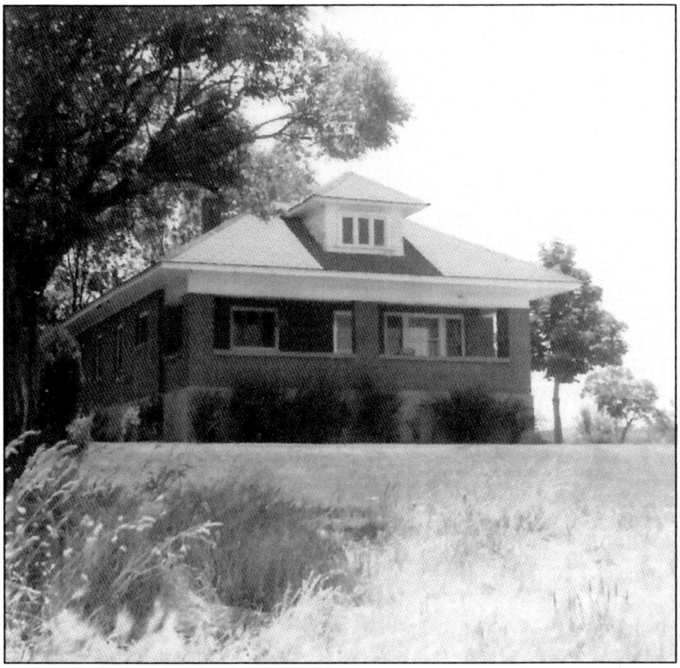

John and Drusilla Thompson Home. The Thompsons lived in Riverdale in a large, one-room cabin southwest of this home. As more children were born to the couple, they outgrew the cabin and built this house in 1918. A natural spring ran through the yard encased in a cement wall, where there was always a cup hanging for a drink. It was said to be the best tasting water. In 1935, the Thompsons installed an indoor bathroom; they were the first in Riverdale to have the luxury of indoor plumbing. Neighbors visited just to see the toilet flush. (Courtesy of Judy B. Anderson.)

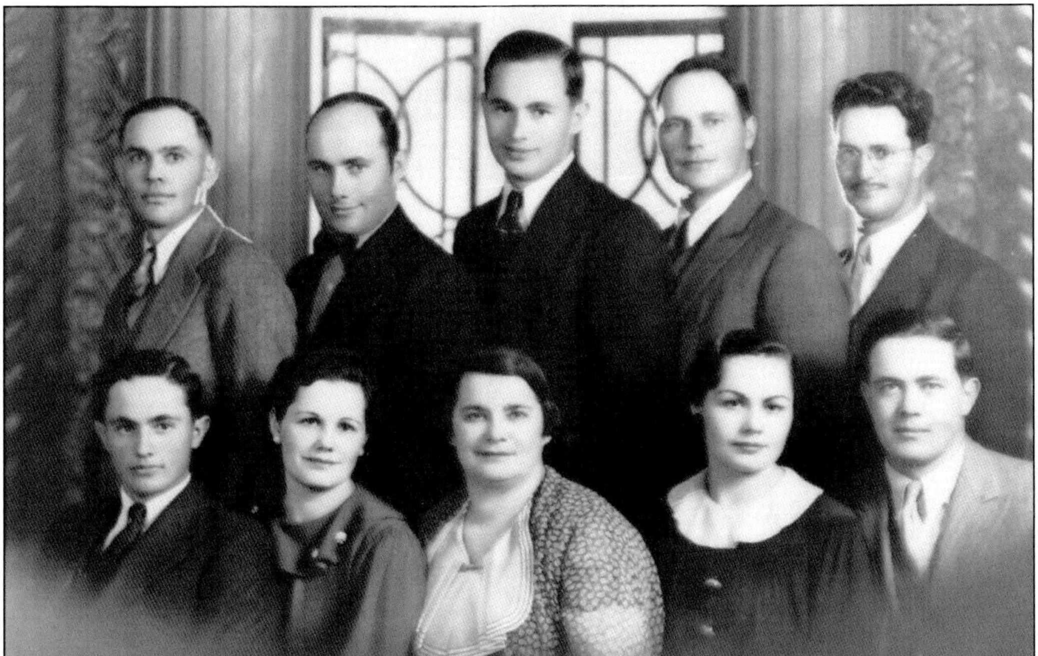

Drusilla Thompson and Children, 1936. Drusilla Hutchinson met her husband, John Randolph Thompson, in Riverdale when she worked as a caretaker for an elderly woman. She met John as he chased a cow through the woman's yard and could not help but laugh at him. This family photograph was taken at John's funeral. From left to right are (first row) Woodrow, Louise, Drusilla, Fay, and Henry; (second row) Harvey, Joseph "Smith," John, George, and Karl. (Courtesy of Joseph M. Thompson and Judy B. Anderson.)

Two

FAITH

ROOTED IN RELIGION

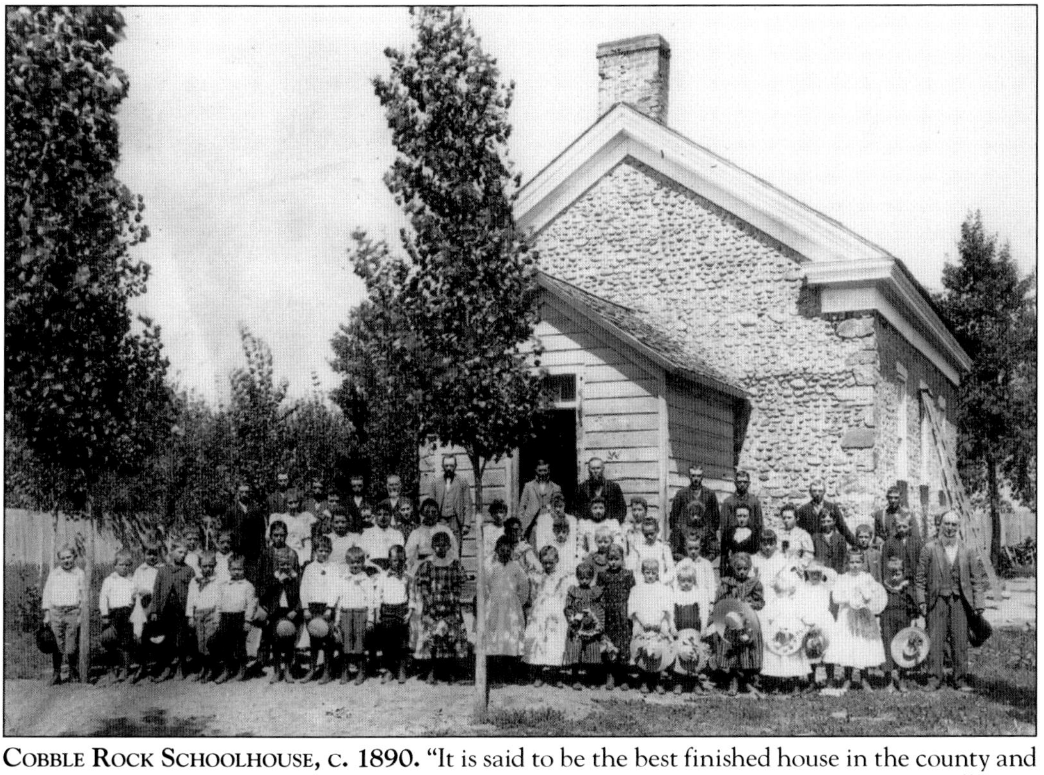

COBBLE ROCK SCHOOLHOUSE, C. 1890. "It is said to be the best finished house in the county and done in the shortest time," Warren G. Child Sr. wrote in his journal of this one-room schoolhouse. Used as a meetinghouse, a school, and for community gatherings, the structure was 33 feet by 23 feet and had a 12.5-foot ceiling. Completed on November 3, 1856, it was built by Warren G. Child and John C. Thompson as contracted for $4,000. One teacher taught all the grades. Later, the first through fifth grades met in the rock structure, and a brick addition was added to the front, where the sixth through eighth grades met for class. The building stood approximately in the same location as the current Riverdale 1st and 7th Wards meetinghouse at 1056 West 4400 South. Individuals identified in the photograph include William Cope Parker (far right), John Randolph Thompson (back row, second from left), and George Peery Thompson (right of door). (Courtesy of Judy B. Anderson.)

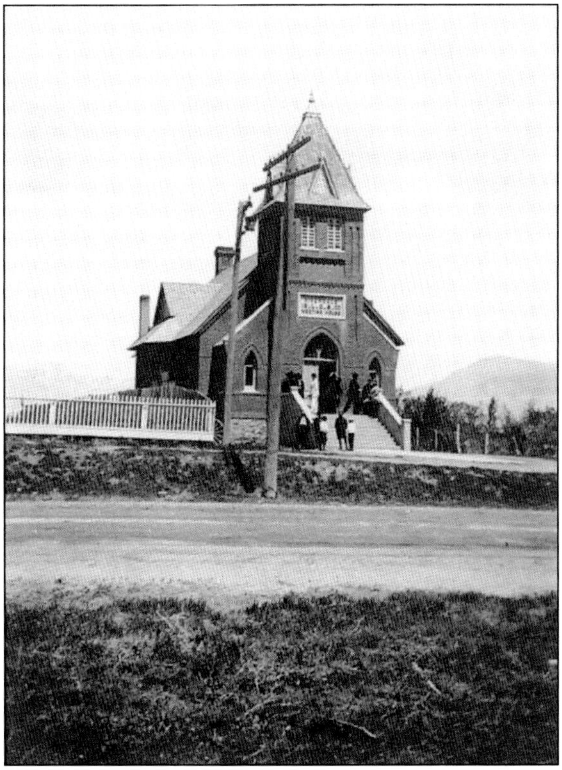

Riverdale Ward Meetinghouse, 1900. Dedicated on September 16, 1900, this LDS meetinghouse was built and furnished in 90 days. It was located at the northwest corner of 1000 West and 4400 South, which is now the east parking lot of the current Riverdale 1st and 7th Wards meetinghouse. It stood here until sometime between 1933 and 1946. (Courtesy of Judy B. Anderson.)

Sanford Bingham and Sons, c. 1900. Sanford Bingham served as the bishop of the Riverdale Ward from the day of its organization on June 14, 1877, until 1902, when he became a patriarch. He is pictured here with his sons. From left to right are (first row) Adam Aranthon Bingham, Sanford Bingham, and Walter Bingham; (second row) Andrew Bingham, Enoch Bingham, Sanford James Bingham, and Norman F. Bingham. (Courtesy of Riverdale City.)

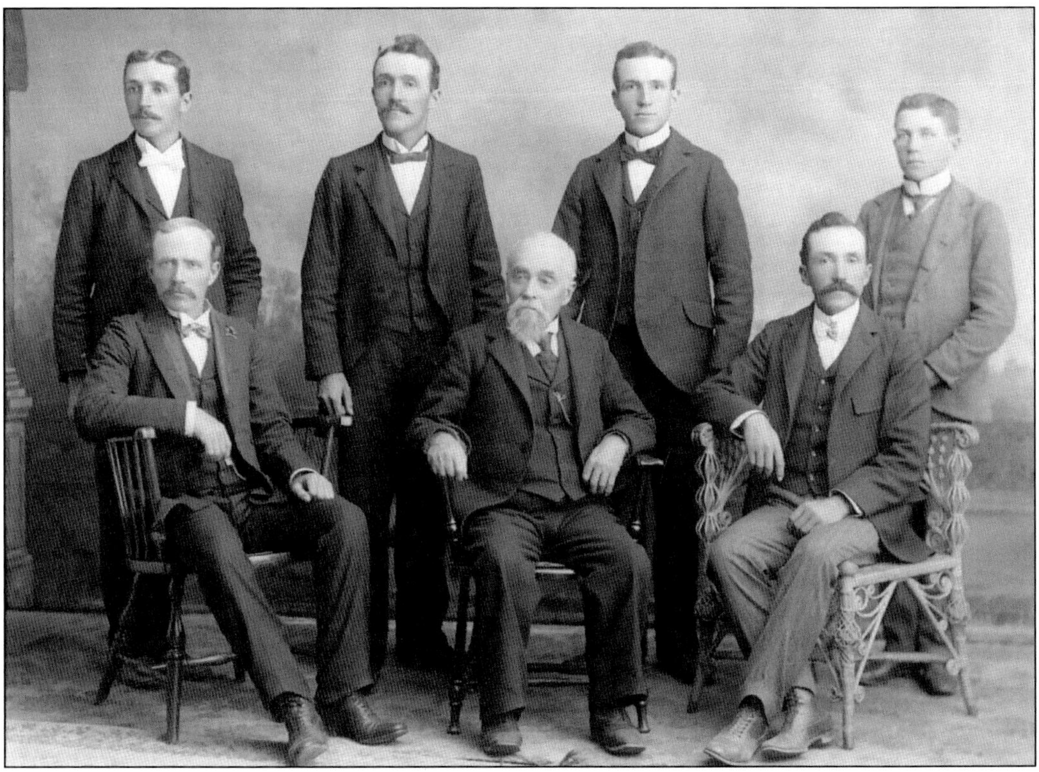

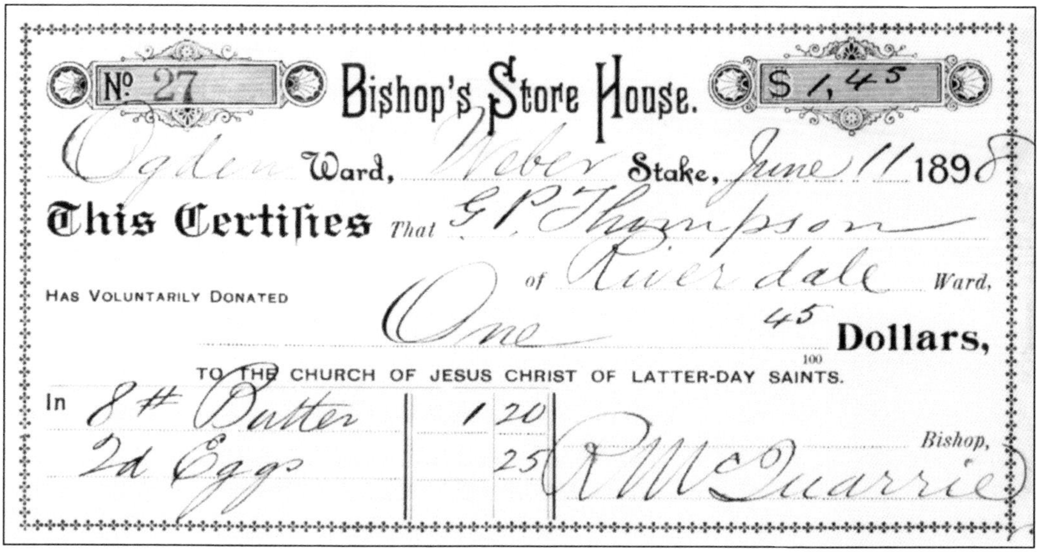

No. 27 **Bishop's Store House.** $1,45

Ogden Ward, Weber Stake, June 11 1898

This Certifies That G. P. Thompson of Riverdale Ward,

HAS VOLUNTARILY DONATED One 45/100 **Dollars,**

TO THE CHURCH OF JESUS CHRIST OF LATTER-DAY SAINTS.

In		
8# Butter	1	20
2d Eggs		25

R M McQuarrie Bishop.

BISHOPS' STOREHOUSE RECEIPT. This receipt from Bishop R.M. McQuarrie documents a donation from George Peery Thompson to the Bishops' Storehouse on June 11, 1898. His donation consisted of eight pounds of butter and two dozen eggs. Other donation receipts show Thompson donated hay, wheat, dried fruit, and chickens. Donations such as these helped the poor and needy in the area. (Courtesy of Judy B. Anderson.)

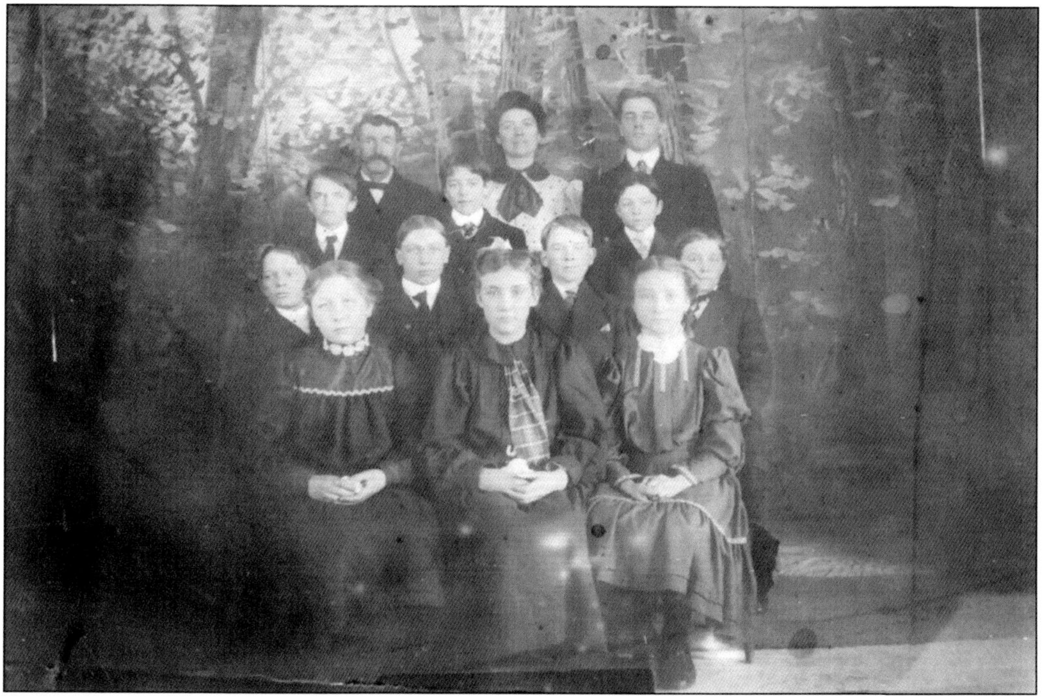

BOOK OF MORMON CLASS, 1907. This Book of Mormon class was taught in the Riverdale Ward. From left to right are (first row) Polly Child, Katie Fife, and unidentified; (second row) Alexander Carlsen, Edward Child, Wilford Bingham, and Aranthon Bingham; (third row) John Ballantyne, Gus Roman, and Arthur Stratton; (fourth row) William Allen, Nettie Russell, and Thurval Carlsen, who all taught the class. (Courtesy of the Lucille Child Judkins family.)

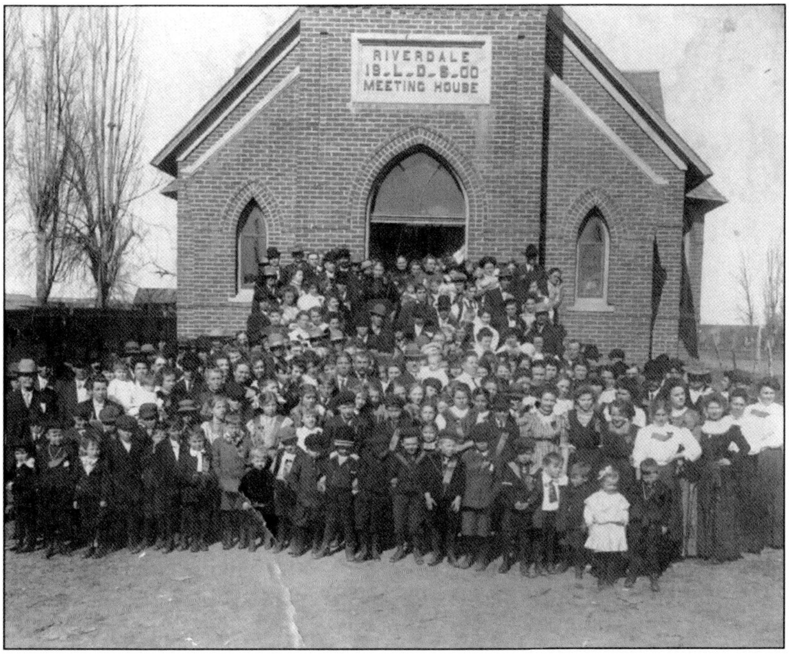

Riverdale Ward Meetinghouse. A place of gathering and worship, the meetinghouse was also used for many community events. The people pictured here are gathered for an unidentified occasion. The area behind the meetinghouse shows the rural nature of the community at that time. (Courtesy of Riverdale City.)

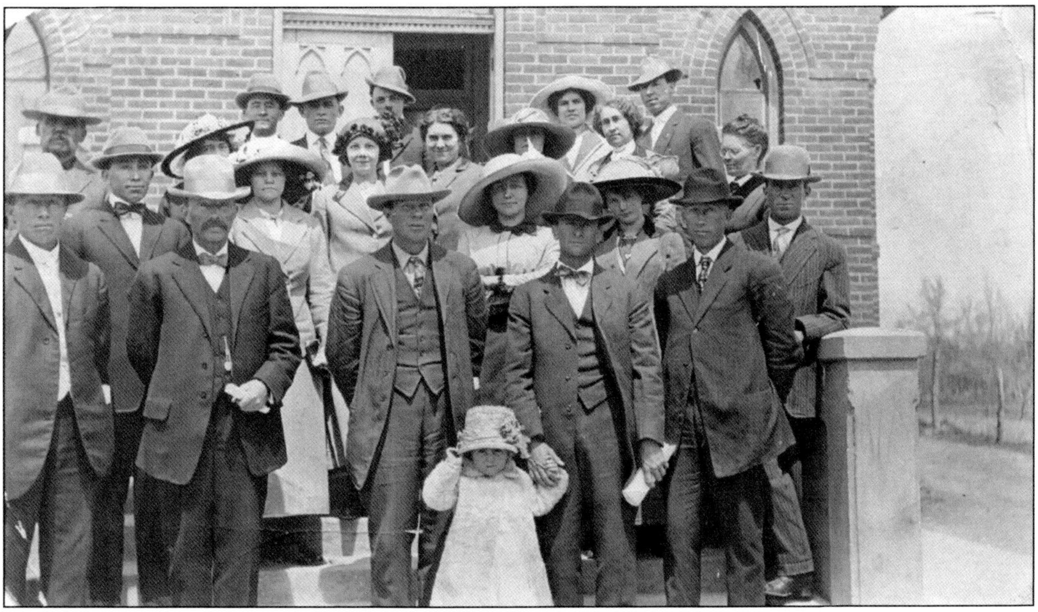

Sunday School Officers and Teachers, c. 1913. Pictured at the Riverdale Ward meetinghouse are, from left to right, (first row) Jesse A. Child, Adam Aranthon Bingham, Joseph Brockbank, Emma Jacobs (child), Murray Kimball Jacobs, and George C. Child; (second row) Frank Bybee, Margaret (Bingham) Jacobs, Maria Bingham (Campbell), Mary Allen (Stimpson), and James Bingham; (third row) William Stimpson Jr., Eva Campbell (Bybee) (partially hidden), Belva Dawson (brimless hat), Mora Wadsworth, unidentified (hidden face), Margaret Stimpson, and Mary Campbell (glasses); (fourth row) Briant Jacobs, Alex Carlsen, Arthur Stratton, Polly (Stimpson) Staker, and Herbert Staker. (Courtesy of the Lucille Child Judkins family.)

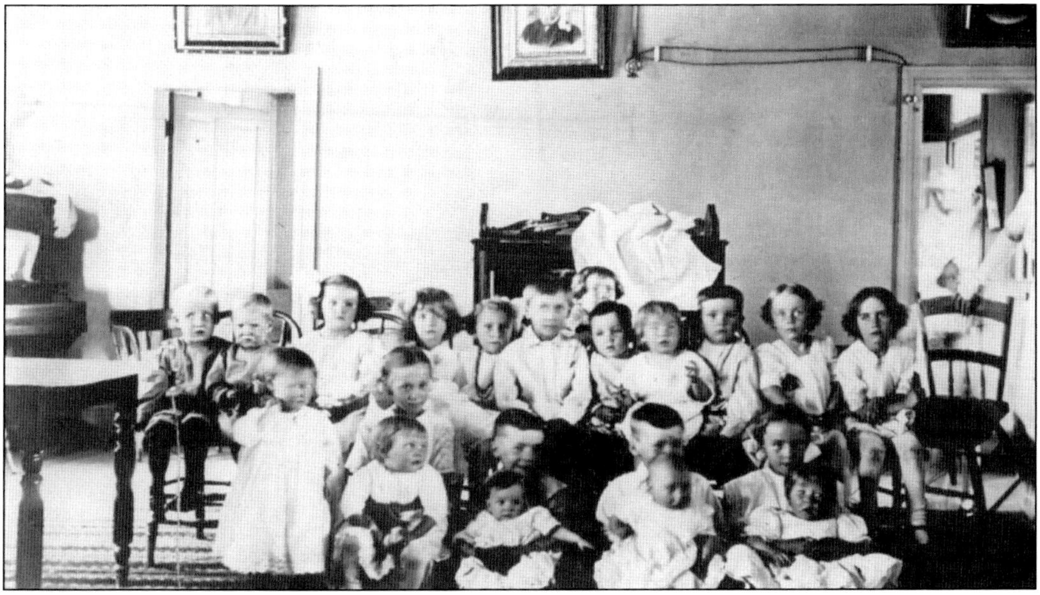

Children in the Meetinghouse. This photograph provides a view of the interior of the meetinghouse. On the wall behind the children are three framed portraits, likely the bishopric of the ward. The center portrait shows Bishop Sanford Bingham. (Courtesy of Kathleen Cevering.)

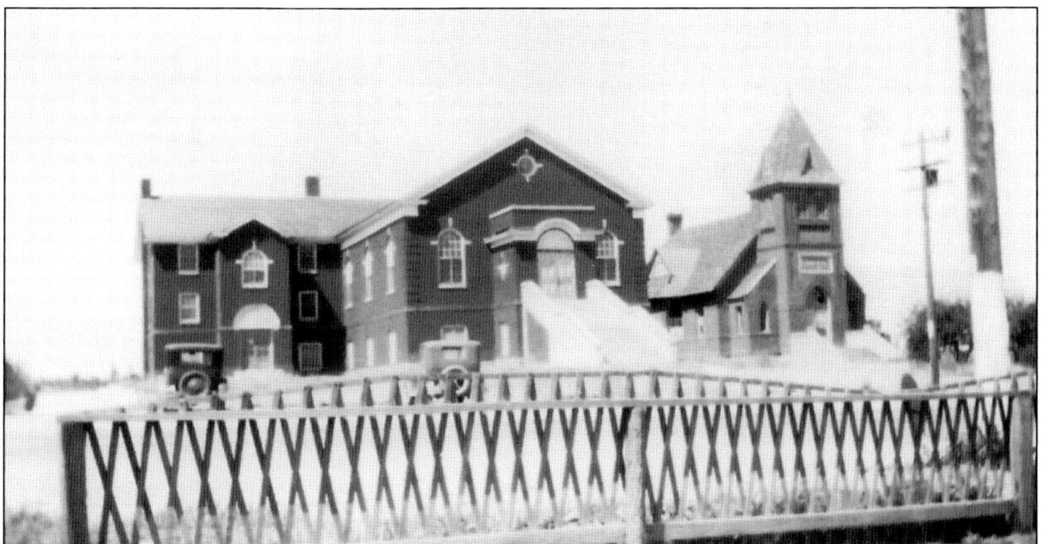

1925 and 1900 Riverdale Ward Meetinghouses. The Riverdale Ward constructed a new meetinghouse in 1925 for $39,000. Church president Heber J. Grant dedicated the building on December 13, 1925. The two meetinghouses stood side by side until sometime between 1933 and 1947. The meetinghouse built in 1925 did not include a kitchen, so workers constructed a tunnel between the two buildings, and the kitchen facilities of the old meetinghouse were used. (Courtesy of Judy B. Anderson.)

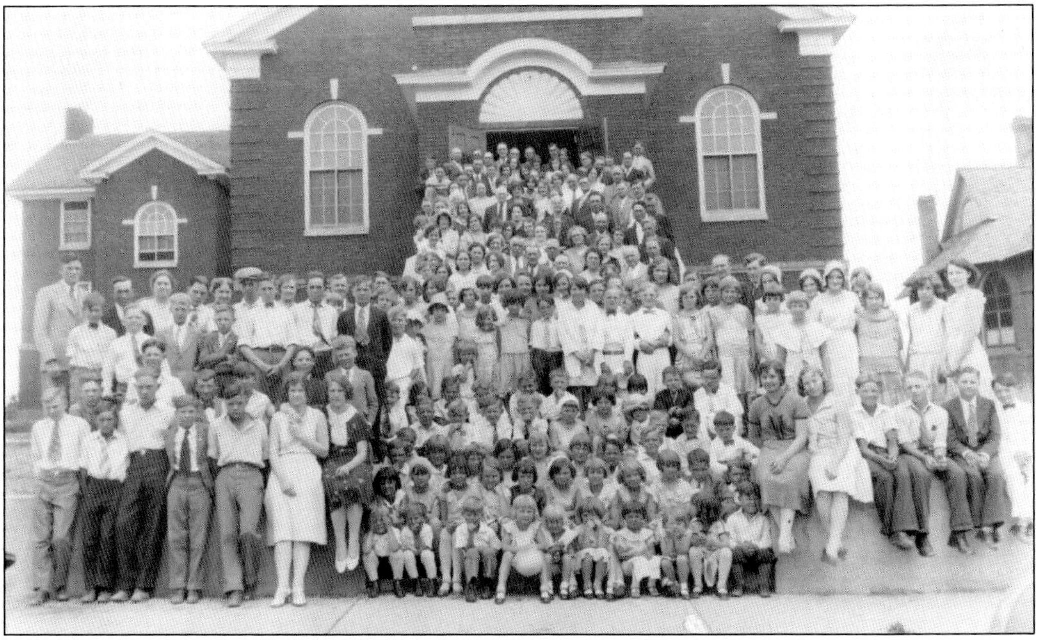

RIVERDALE WARD SUNDAY SCHOOL, 1933. This photograph shows the Sunday school on the front steps of the meetinghouse. Without air-conditioning, paper fans were often handed out at the top of the stairs to churchgoers as they entered the building. The door opened to the back of the chapel inside the meetinghouse. This section of the building was later walled off and changed to be the front of the chapel. (Courtesy of the Lucille Child Judkins family.)

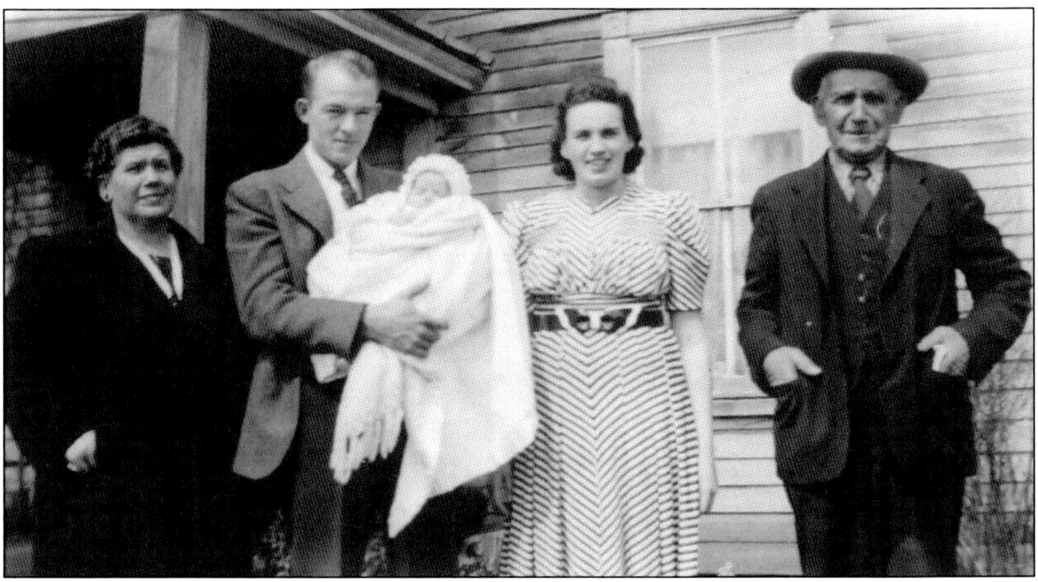

BABY BLESSING AND FOUR GENERATIONS. William Stimpson Jr. blessed his great-granddaughter Kathleen Cevering on March 30, 1941, at the Riverdale Ward meetinghouse. Pictured here at her grandmother's home are Ethel Hunter (grandmother), Everett "Afe" Cevering (father), baby Kathleen Cevering, Phyllis Hunter Cevering (mother), and William Stimpson Jr. (great-grandfather). (Courtesy of Kathleen Cevering.)

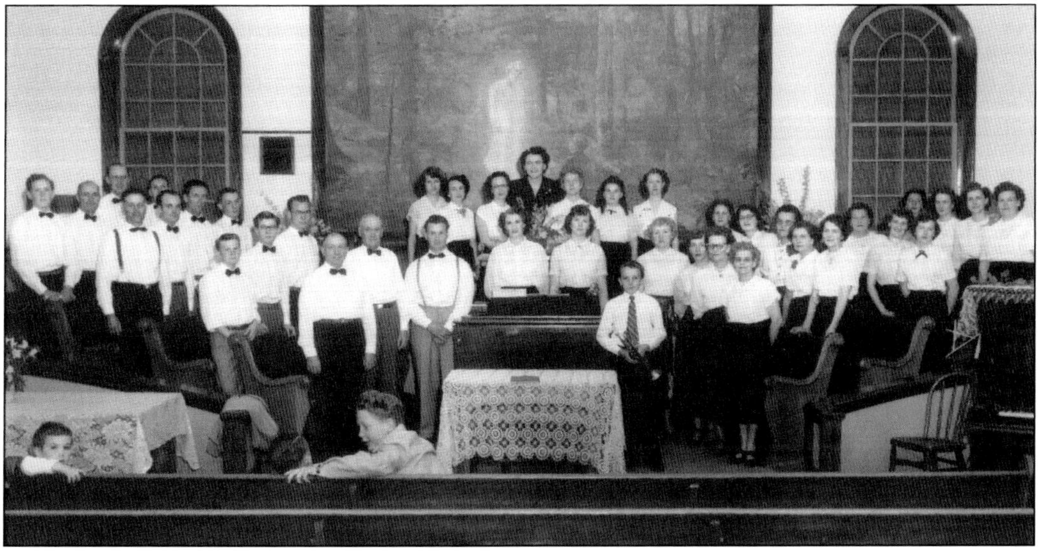

RIVERDALE WARD CHOIR, 1953. Male choir members pictured include Jack Frost, Joseph Smith Thompson, G. Edwin "Ted" Anderson, Waite Cash, Elmer Wesley "Wes" Woolsey, Jack Frost Sr., Jimmy Boswell, Johnny Marston, Edward Child, and Alma Ellis. Female choir members pictured include Virginia Mitchell, Lillian Froerer, Flossie Deem, Betty Coleman, Bessie Boswell, Bertha Child, Pearl Child, Pernecia Fiet, Mammie Dickson, Cleo Brough, Zola Marston, Hattie Johnson, and Marilyn Tubbs. Jimmy Jackson played the trumpet, and Roma Frost and Berneice Ellis played the organ. The painting by Lewis A. Ramsey seen behind the choir was titled "The Restoration" and depicted the angel Moroni showing the golden plates to Joseph Smith. The painting was not unique to the Riverdale Ward meetinghouse; Ramsey painted many copies for other LDS meetinghouses. (Courtesy of the Lucille Child Judkins family.)

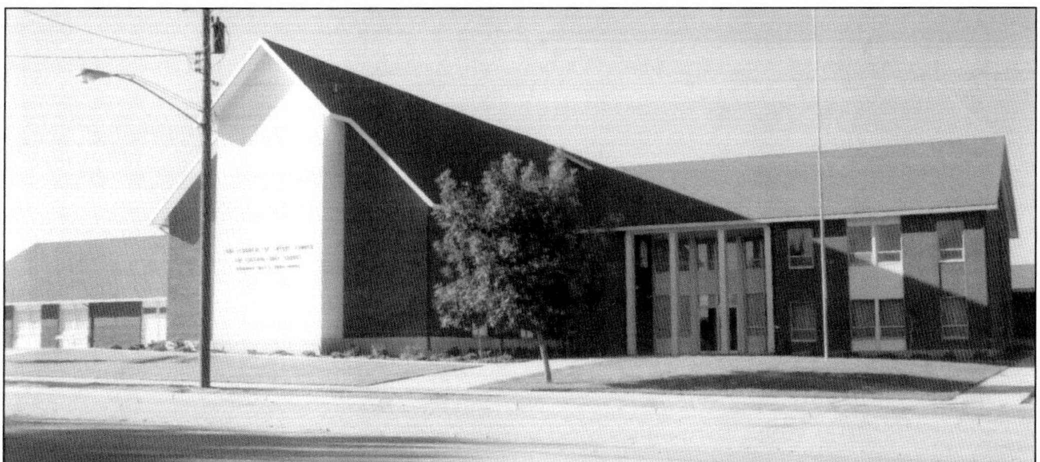

RIVERDALE WARD MEETINGHOUSE. The Riverdale Ward meetinghouse, also known as the "Red Brick Church," has changed since its original construction in 1925 through various additions and remodeling. In about 1962, the ward was assigned to build an addition for a recreation hall, Relief Society room, kitchen, classrooms, and furnace room, among other renovations. The long staircase to the main entrance was also removed. The building was rededicated on June 27, 1965, by Elder Spencer W. Kimball. Shown here is the building after more changes were made in 1973. (Courtesy of the Lucille Child Judkins family.)

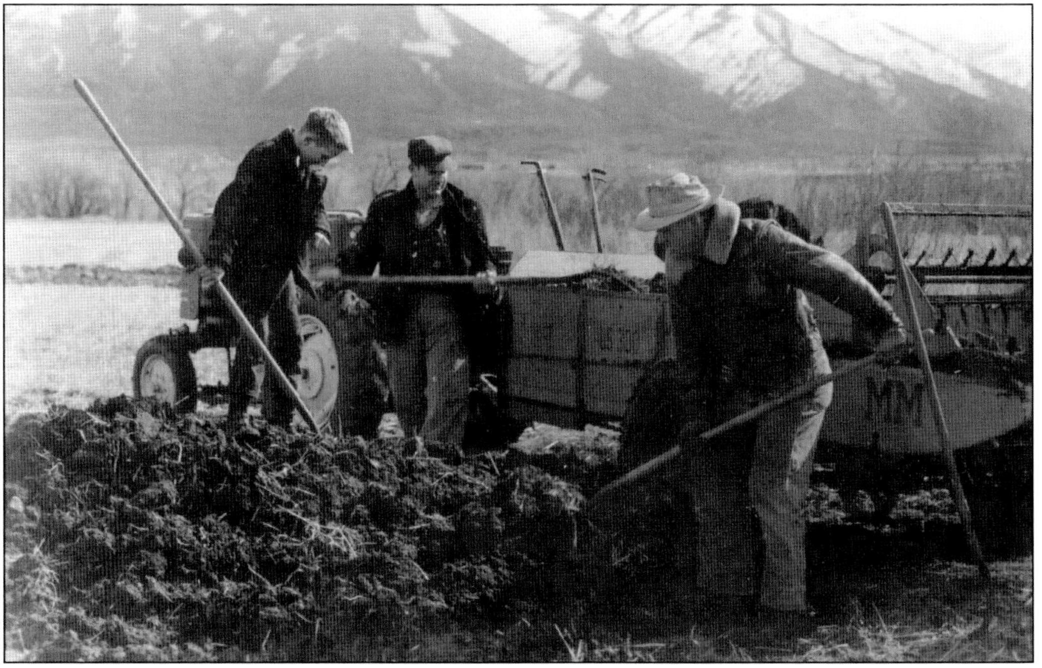

Welfare Farm. The Riverdale Ward managed a church welfare farm on the south side of Riverdale. Here, a boy and two men are shown working the farm. At one time there was also a Relief Society granary/tithing house near the meetinghouse. (Courtesy of the Lucille Child Judkins family.)

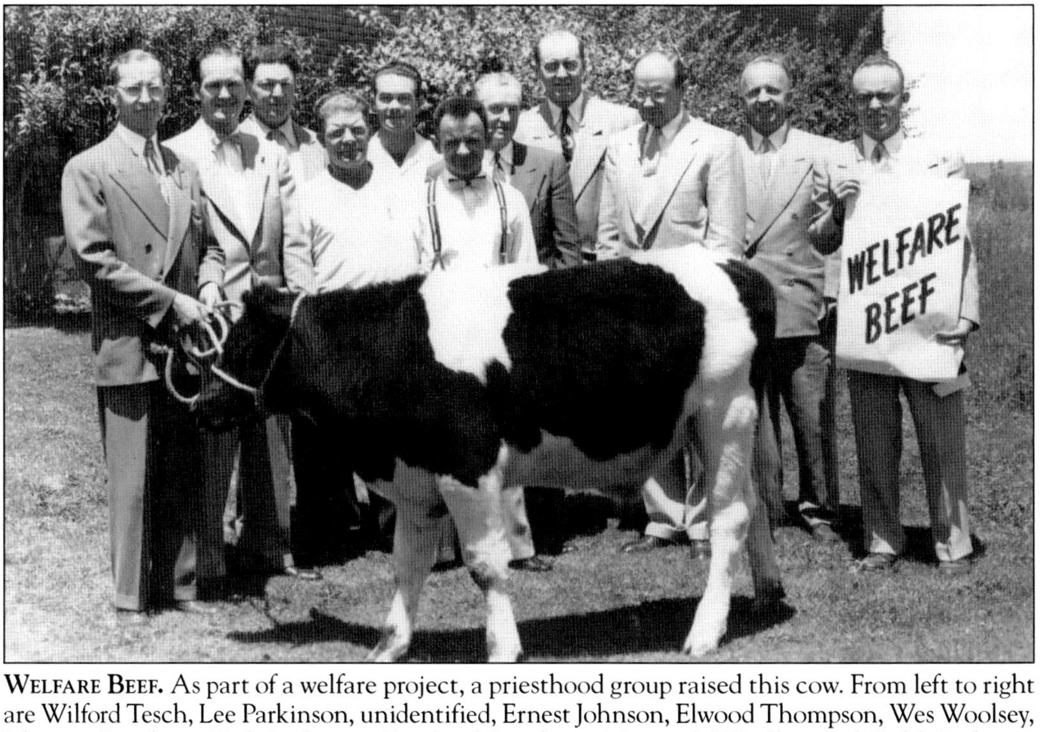

Welfare Beef. As part of a welfare project, a priesthood group raised this cow. From left to right are Wilford Tesch, Lee Parkinson, unidentified, Ernest Johnson, Elwood Thompson, Wes Woolsey, Thomas Bingham, Ted Anderson, Rowland Bingham, Monteith Woolley, and Dahl Crabtree. (Courtesy of the Lucille Child Judkins family.)

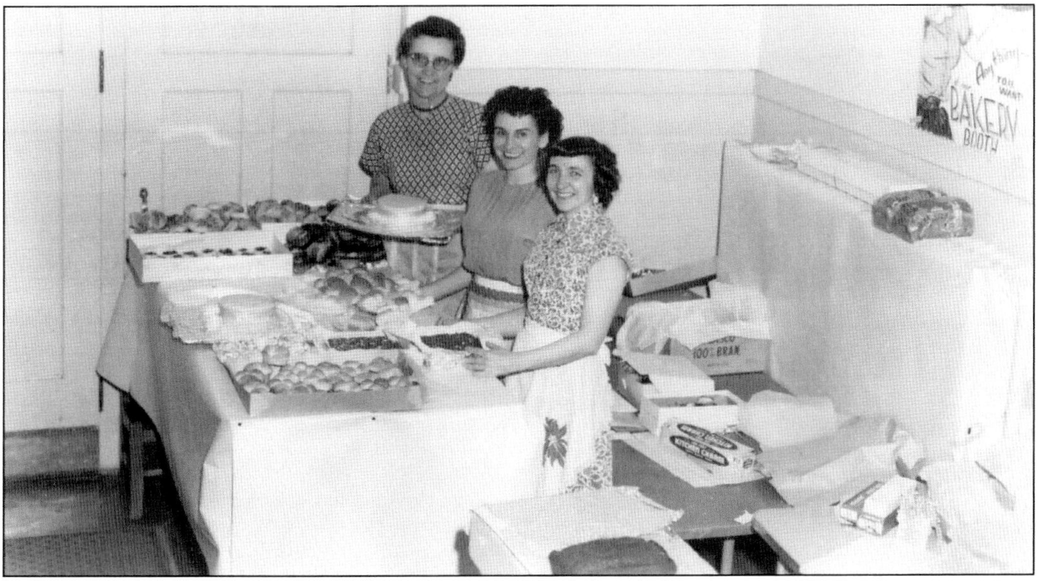

Bake Sale. The women of the church frequently held bake sales to raise money for church building projects, missionary funds, and other needs. From left to right are Cleo Brough, Lucille Stephens, and Cora Bingham. (Courtesy of the Lucille Child Judkins family.)

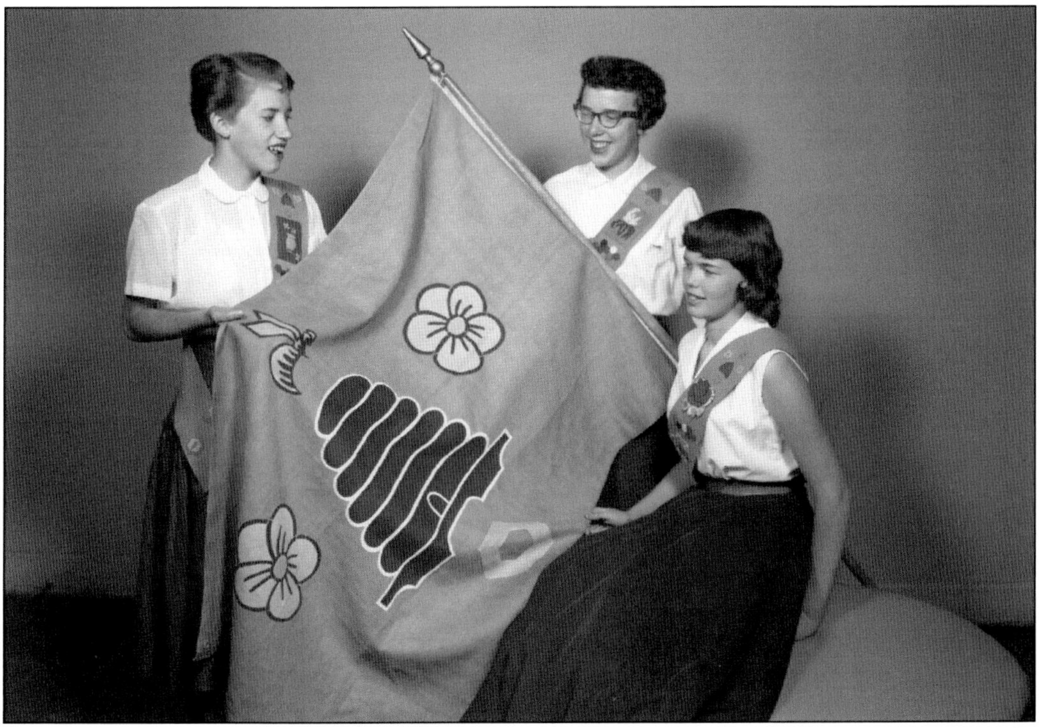

Beehive Swarm Day, 1955. The Riverdale Utah Stake held a Beehive Swarm Day as part of a program for the Young Women's Mutual Improvement Association (YWMIA). In attendance were 400 guests, including 175 girls, 44 of whom became honor bees in the YWMIA. Displaying a beehive banner are, from left to right, VerLayne Fowers, Kathryn Bench, and Connie McDougal. (Courtesy of Weber State University Special Collections.)

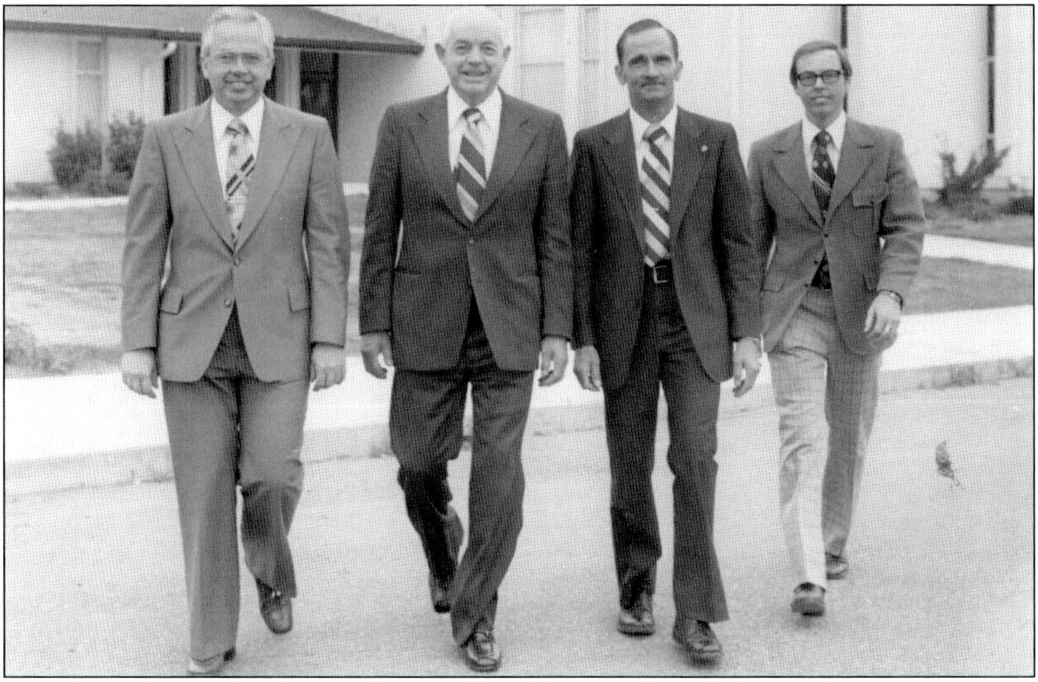

Riverdale Utah Stake Presidency. The Riverdale Utah Stake presidency at the time of the construction of the Riverdale Stake Center is shown here. From left to right are Ronald C. Hamblen (first counselor), Grant Gibby (president), Wes Barton (second counselor), and Danny Gibson (executive secretary). (Photograph by Donald Child; courtesy of Janet Gibby Cox.)

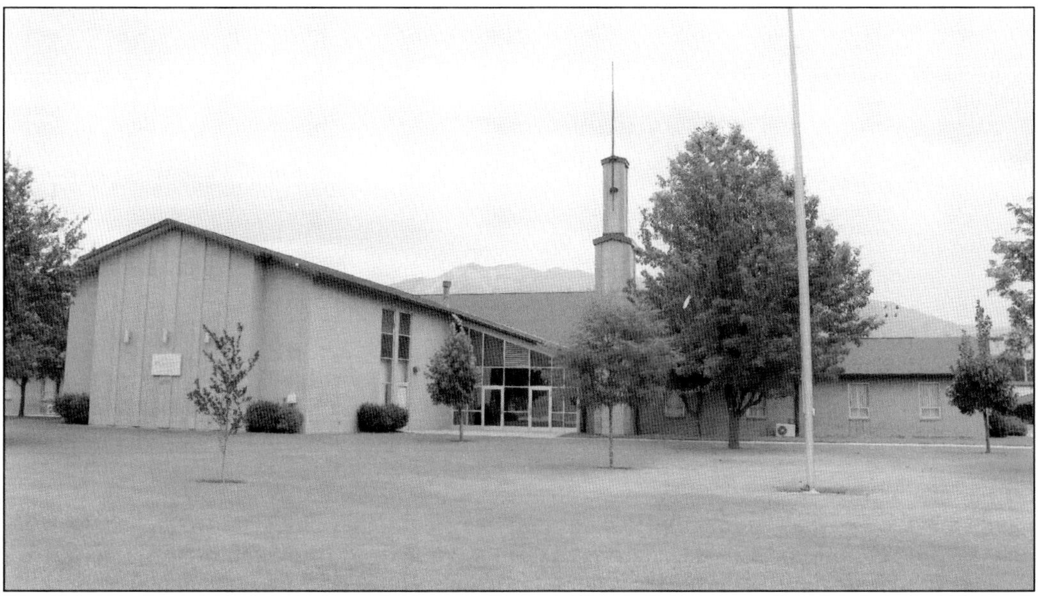

Riverdale Utah Stake Center. Local church leaders broke ground for the Riverdale 5th Ward and Riverdale Utah Stake Center on September 24, 1977. It was dedicated on June 3, 1979, by Elder Thomas S. Monson. Located at 4000 Parker Drive, the meetinghouse was designed by architect Verl L. Gessel and currently houses the Riverdale 5th, 6th, and 8th Wards and stake offices. (Author's collection.)

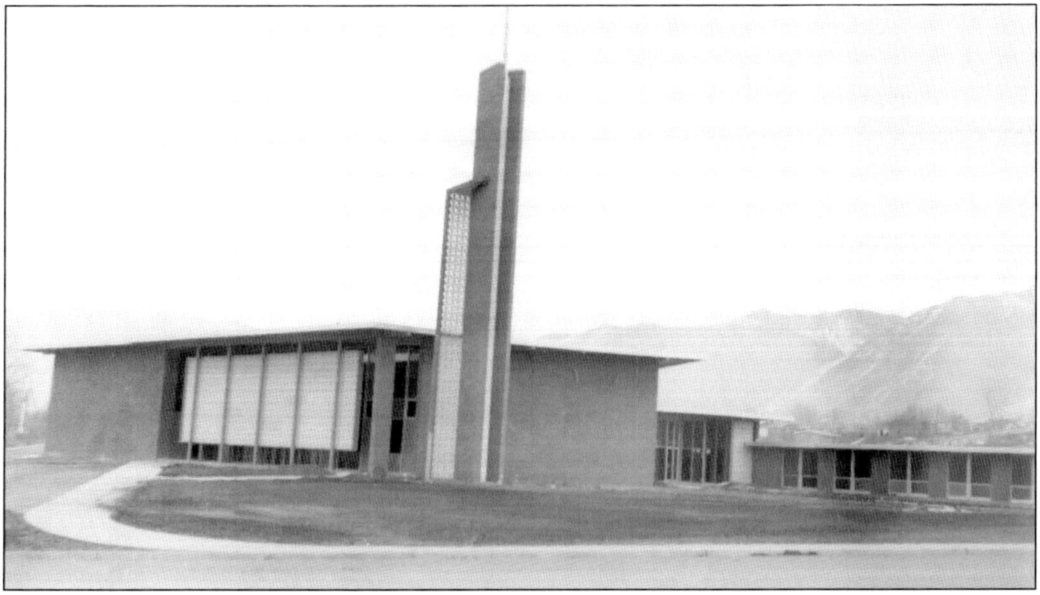

Ogden 49th Ward Meetinghouse. On September 11, 1955, the Ogden 49th Ward of the Riverdale Utah Stake was formed from part of the Ogden 32nd Ward and 270 members from the Riverdale Ward. This split the Riverdale Ward for the first time. The congregation met at Club Heights Elementary School until this building was completed in 1961. It was dedicated on July 13, 1969, by stake president Rudolph Van Kampen. This meetinghouse is located at 4210 South 300 West and currently houses the Ogden 49th Ward and Washington Terrace 1st and 2nd Wards. (Courtesy of Barbara Porter.)

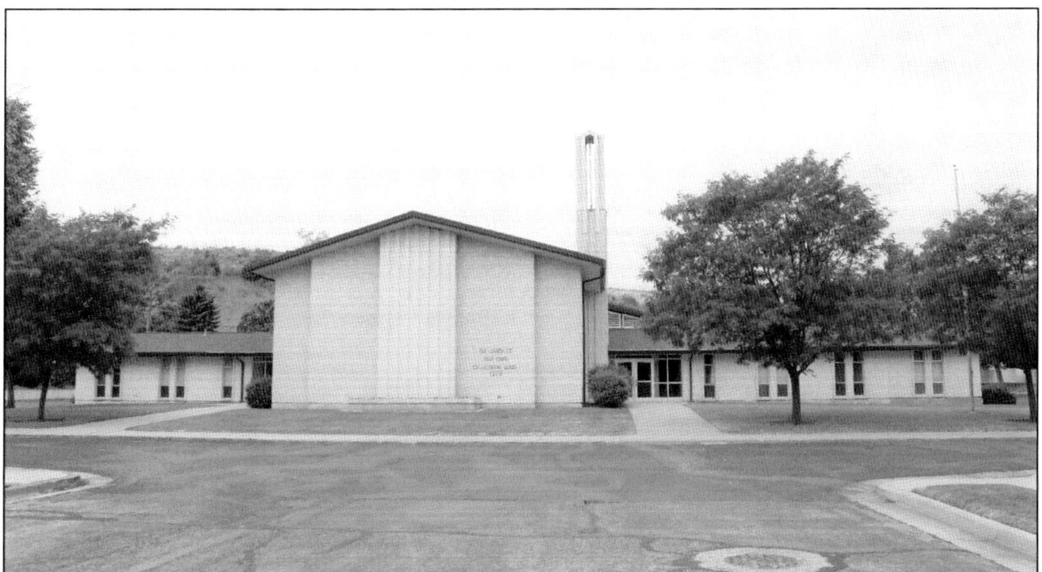

Riverdale 2nd, 4th, and Single Adult Wards. Located on the south side of Riverdale at 5500 South 1175 West, this building currently serves as the meetinghouse for the Riverdale 2nd, 4th, and Single Adult Wards. It was built in 1972 and dedicated on March 10, 1974, by Pres. Spencer W. Kimball. (Author's collection.)

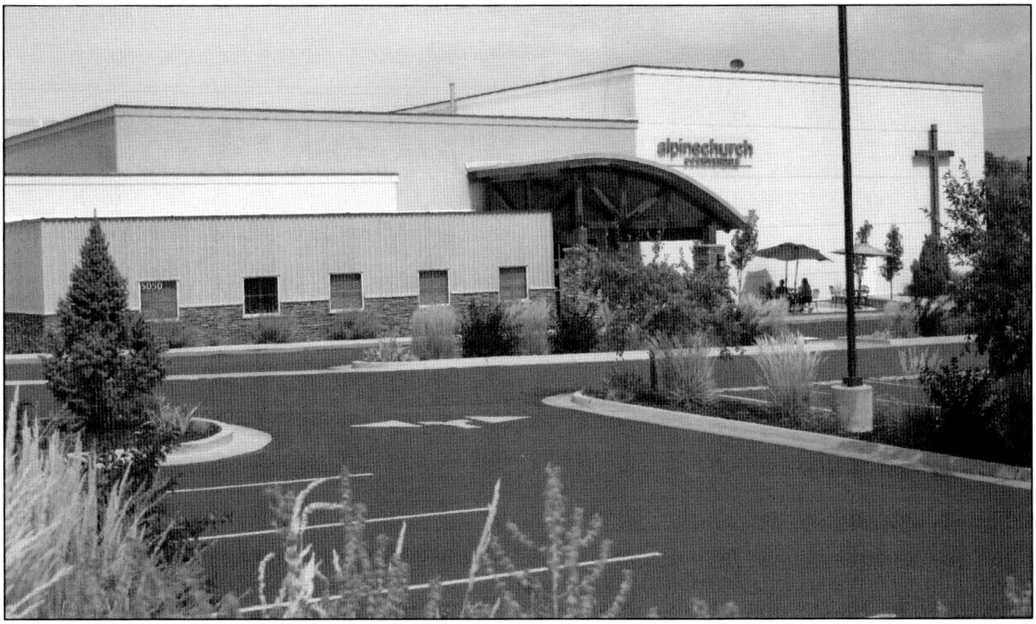

ALPINE CHURCH. Started in 2001 in Pastor Bryan Dwyer's backyard, Alpine Church has the goal of helping people to pursue God. The church's first permanent location, seen here, was built in Riverdale in 2007 and is located at 5050 South 1275 West. Since that time, Alpine Church has expanded to nine campuses in Utah. Pastor Tom Koehler serves as the leader of the Riverdale congregation with the assistance of his wife, Marina. (Courtesy of Alpine Church.)

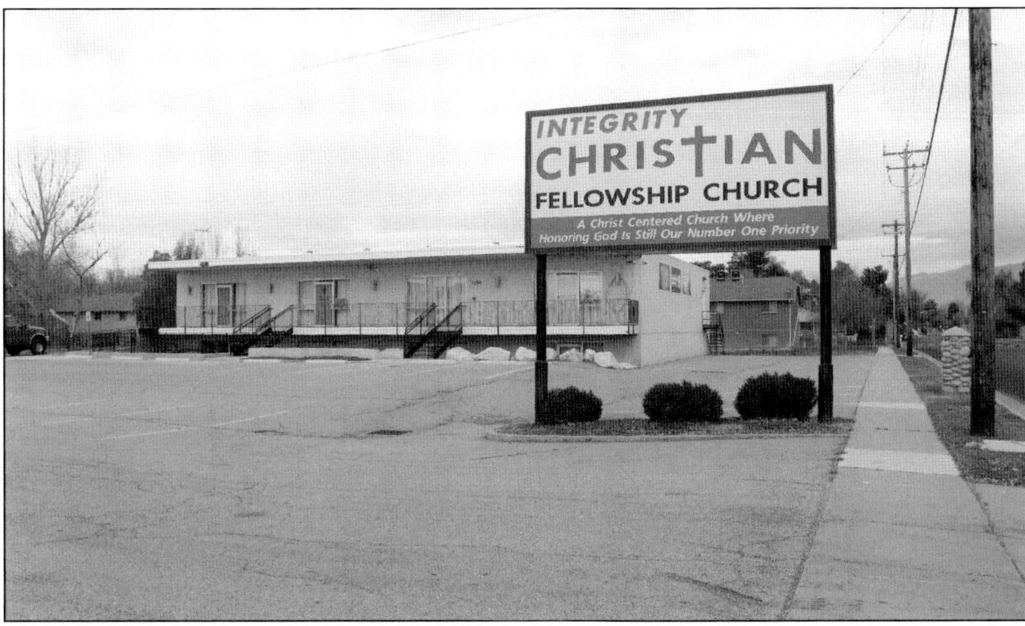

INTEGRITY CHRISTIAN FELLOWSHIP CHURCH. On April 3, 2016, Integrity Christian Fellowship Church held its dedication at 4762 South 1150 West. It relocated from Ogden to Riverdale after renovating the former Four Sisters Furniture building, which it now occupies. The church is a group of Christians from many backgrounds. It is led by Pastor Tim Henderson and his wife, Minister Vicki Henderson. (Author's collection.)

Three

Education

Learning atop School Hill

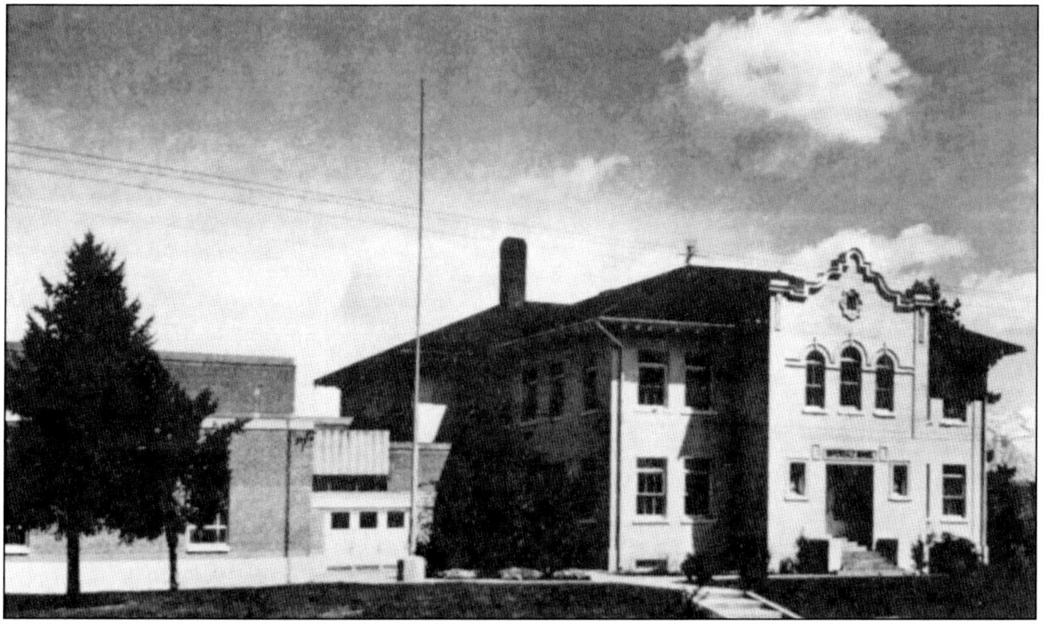

Riverdale School, Built 1911. The first organized schooling in Riverdale started in the winter of 1858. A 14-foot-by-12-foot log schoolhouse was built in the summer of 1859 at the location of the current Lions Centennial Park. The roof and floor were dirt, and the seats were made of logs. Students used slate tablets and had few books available to them. Hugh Findlay was the first teacher and also served as a school trustee along with William Riley Cole and Adam Fife. In 1862, a larger 16-foot-by-16-foot log schoolhouse replaced the first building. In 1865, classes moved to the newly constructed cobble rock schoolhouse (see page 19). The school pictured here replaced the cobble rock schoolhouse and was built in 1911 where the current Riverdale Elementary stands. The brick schoolhouse had four classrooms and was built on a site known as School Hill. A portion of the rock wall from this school is still visible today. For over 100 years, this site has served as a place of education for Riverdale students. (Courtesy of the Weber School District Foundation.)

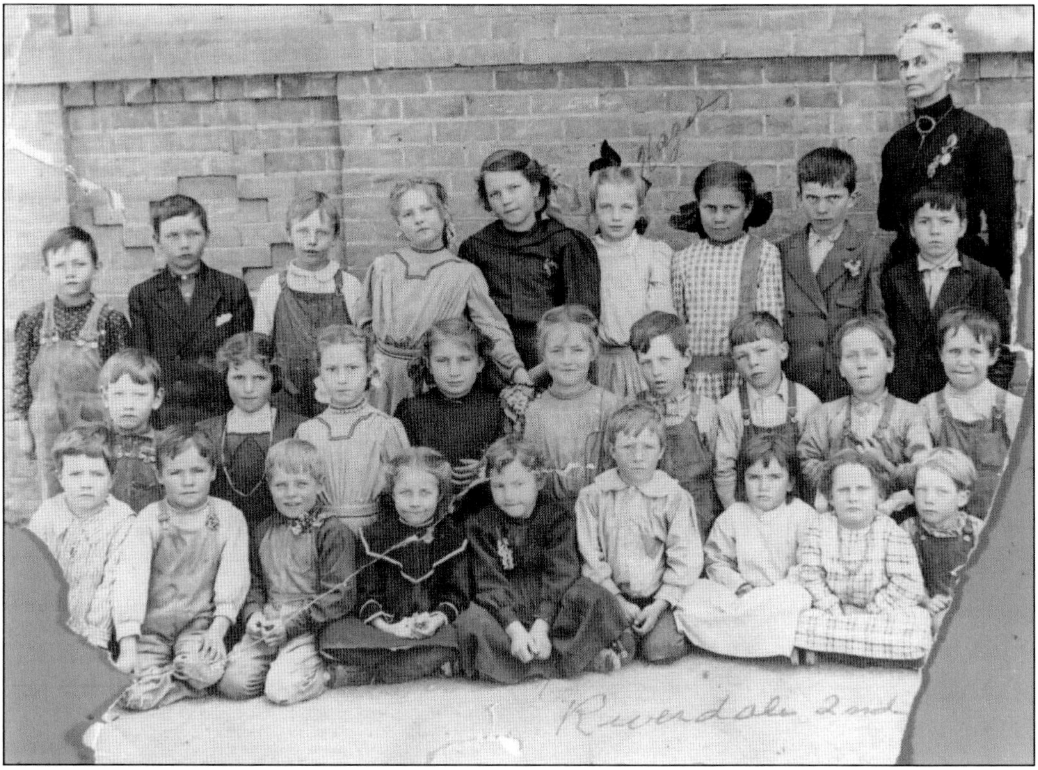

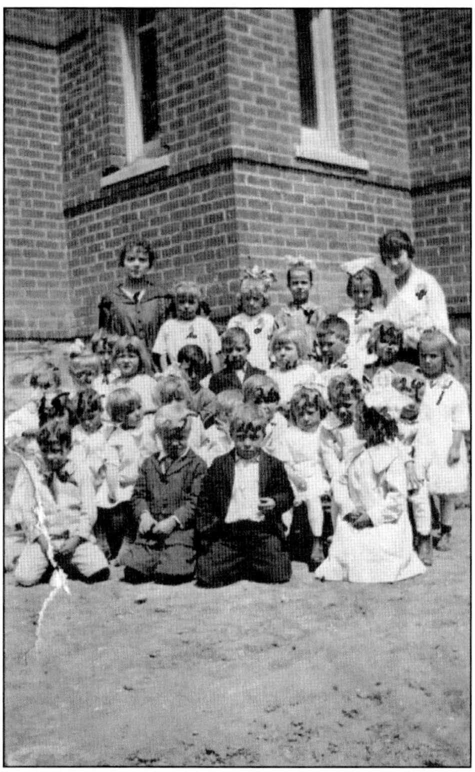

First and Second Grades, 1909. Due to overcrowding in the school, first- and second-grade classes were taught in the basement of the nearby Riverdale Ward meetinghouse. From left to right are (first row) Bert Child, Seymour Bingham, Joe Fife, Gladys Fife, Alene Fife, Francis Bingham, Cleone Ballantyne, Melba Jarrell, and ? Means; (second row) Glen Bingham, Agnes Bingham, Betsy Stoker, Jenness Child, Athalean Bingham, Vern Parker, Herman Child, Adam Patterson, and Harold Bingham; (third row) Lloyd Gunderson, George Thompson, Ralph Ritter, Golda Stoker, Edna Grover, Hazel Carlsen, Lillian Russell, Duane Taylor, Charlie Grover, and Mrs. Young (teacher). (Courtesy of the Lucille Child Judkins family.)

Kindergarten Class, c. 1919. Ethel Parker (Hess) (back left) and Laverne Bingham (Hillis) (back right) taught the students pictured here. Students identified in the photograph include Vivian Fife, Rita Jacobs, Stella Child, Lila Parker, Floyd Couch, Louise Shipley, Ruth Stimpson, Berneice Ellis, Lucille Child, Leah Child, Leo Child, Norma Pike, and Melvin Bingham. (Courtesy of the Lucille Child Judkins family.)

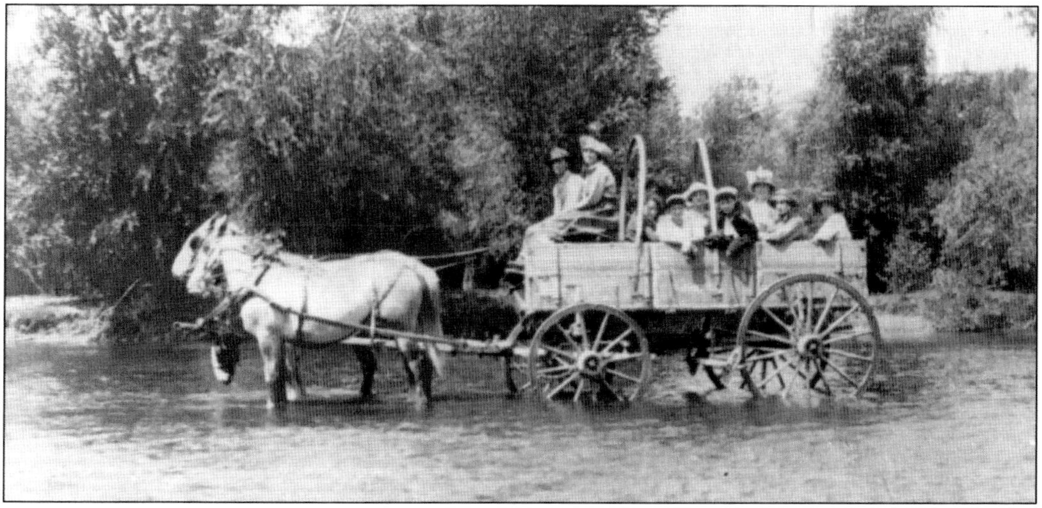

SCHOOL WAGON. Students traveled to school by walking, on horseback, or by a horse-drawn wagon known as the "school wagon" or the "kiddies' wagon." School wagons were used in Weber County until the mid-1920s, after which school buses transported students. Interested drivers submitted bids to the school district. The selected driver provided his own bus, fuel, and repairs. Arthur Bingham drove Riverdale students in his bus between 1937 and 1941. (Courtesy of the Weber School District Foundation.)

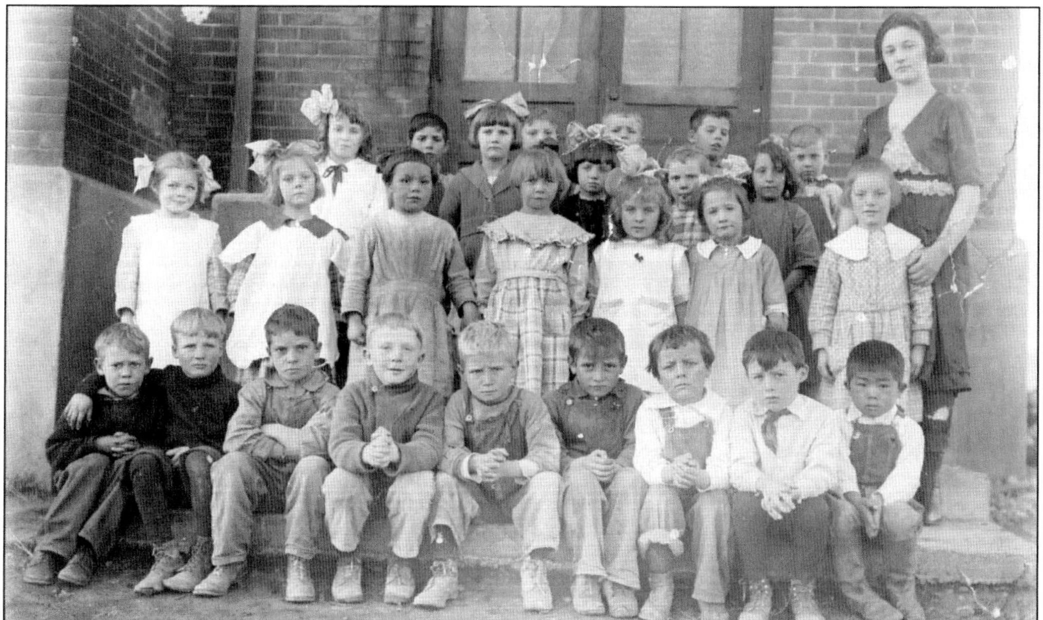

RIVERDALE SCHOOL FIRST GRADE, 1920–1921. From left to right are (first row) Delbert Pike, Willard Read, Frail Zito, Ray Brooks, Carl Cobia, Lewis Zito, Bryce Jensen, Floyd Couch, and Hideo Kato; (second row) Norma Anderson, Katherine Farr, Fay Thompson, Lucille Child, Margaret Bingham, Susie Jacobs, Naomi Campbell, and Virgie Zito; (third row) Beth Ellis, Amelio Zito, Virginia Taylor, Freeda Hunter, unidentified, Inez Stark, Virgie Zito, and Miss Reese (teacher); (fourth row) Henry Meibas, unidentified, Rocky Zito, and Clarence Jones. (Courtesy of the Lucille Child Judkins family.)

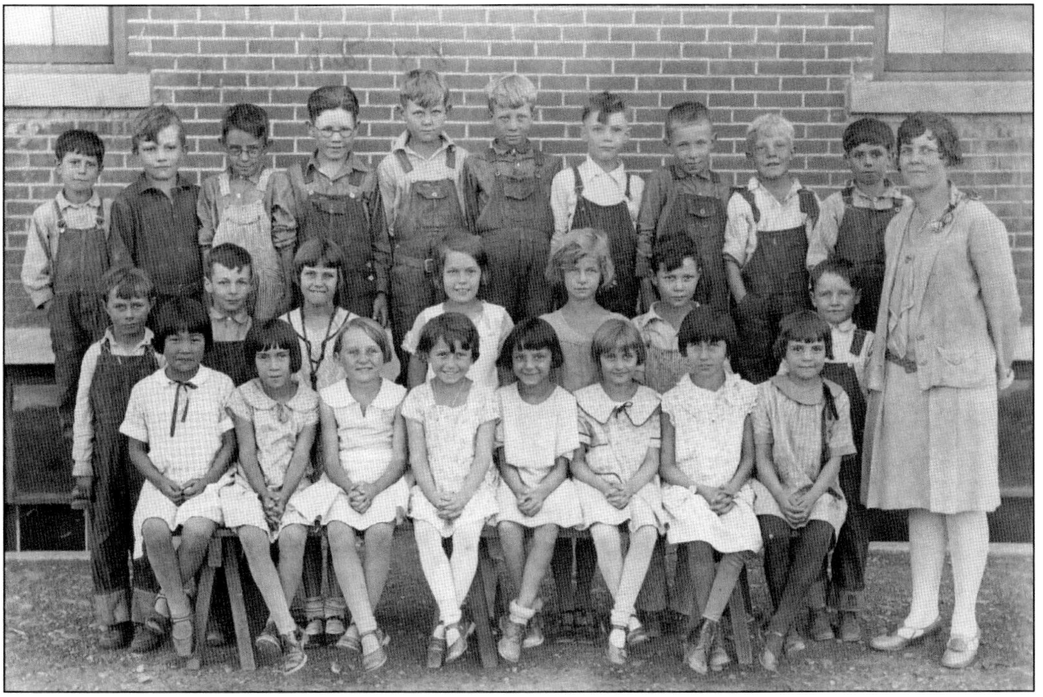

Riverdale School Third Grade, c. 1929. Miss Jensen, seen standing at far right, taught this third-grade class. Student Jeane Ritter (Knight) is in the first row, fourth from left. (Courtesy of the Wallace and Jeane Ritter Knight family.)

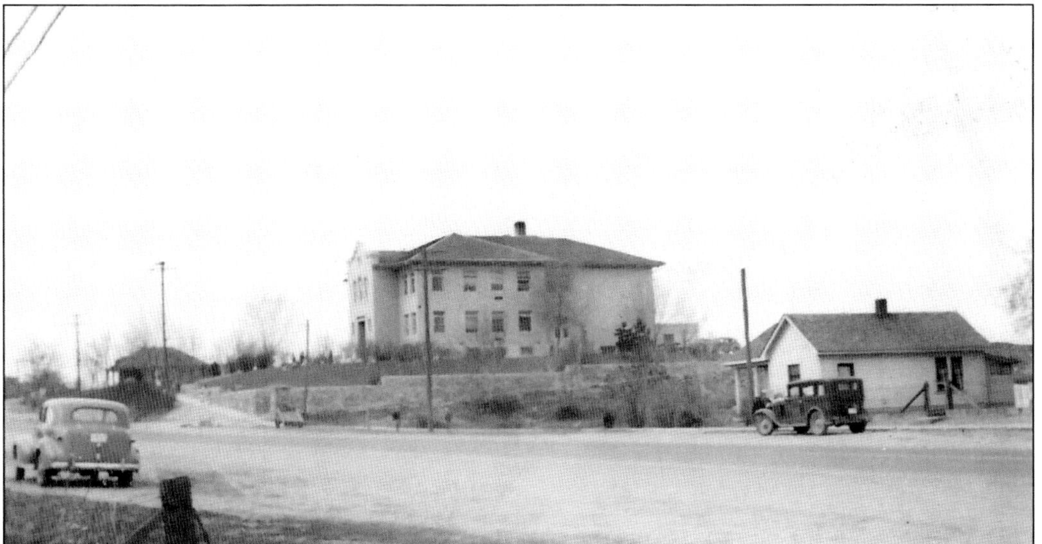

Riverdale School, 1930s. Riverdale School is seen sitting atop School Hill in this view looking west up 4400 South. A portion of the rock wall surrounding the school still stands at Riverdale Elementary School. In the early 1900s, the Riverdale Amusement Hall was located just west of the school. (Courtesy of Judy B. Anderson.)

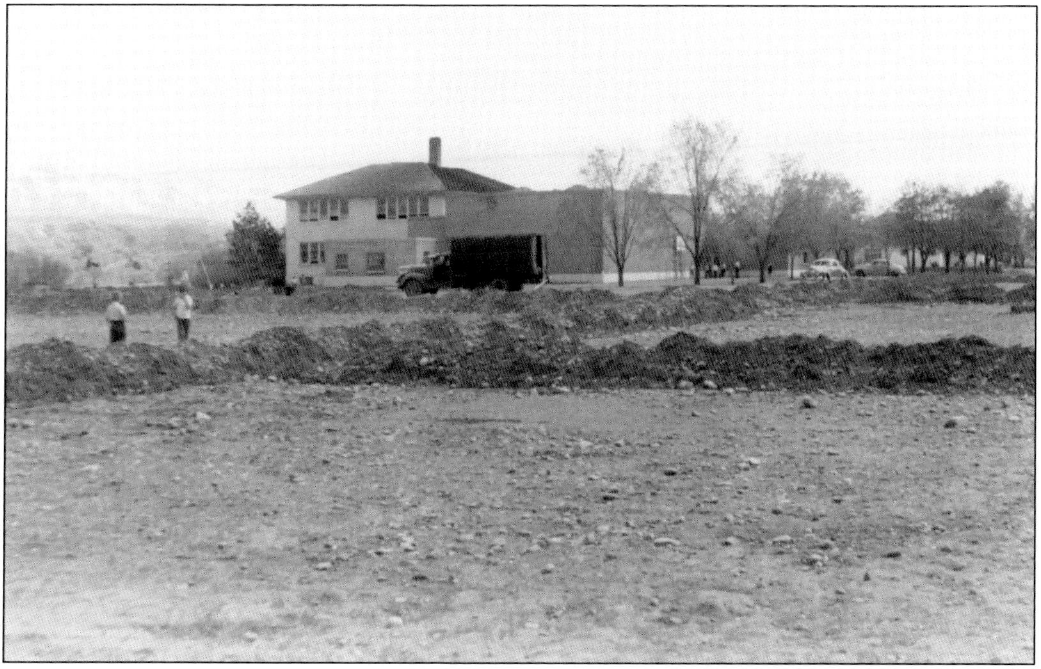

Back of Riverdale School. Looking south, this view shows the back of Riverdale School. On the left is the original building, and on the right and at the rear are additions to the school. (Courtesy of Riverdale City.)

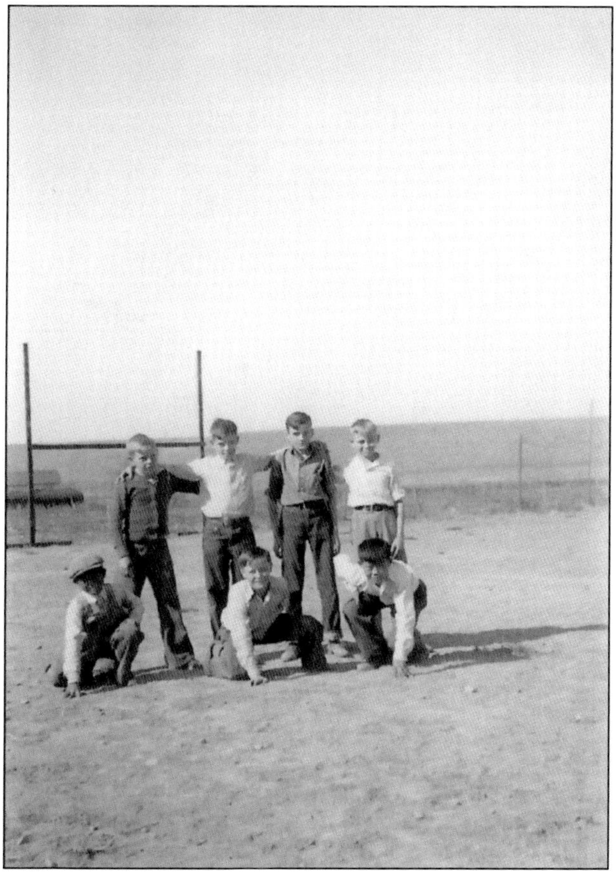

Football, 1936. This photograph shows one of the many activities held on school grounds. Howard Ellis is third from the left in the back row. (Courtesy of the Don and Ardis Ellis family.)

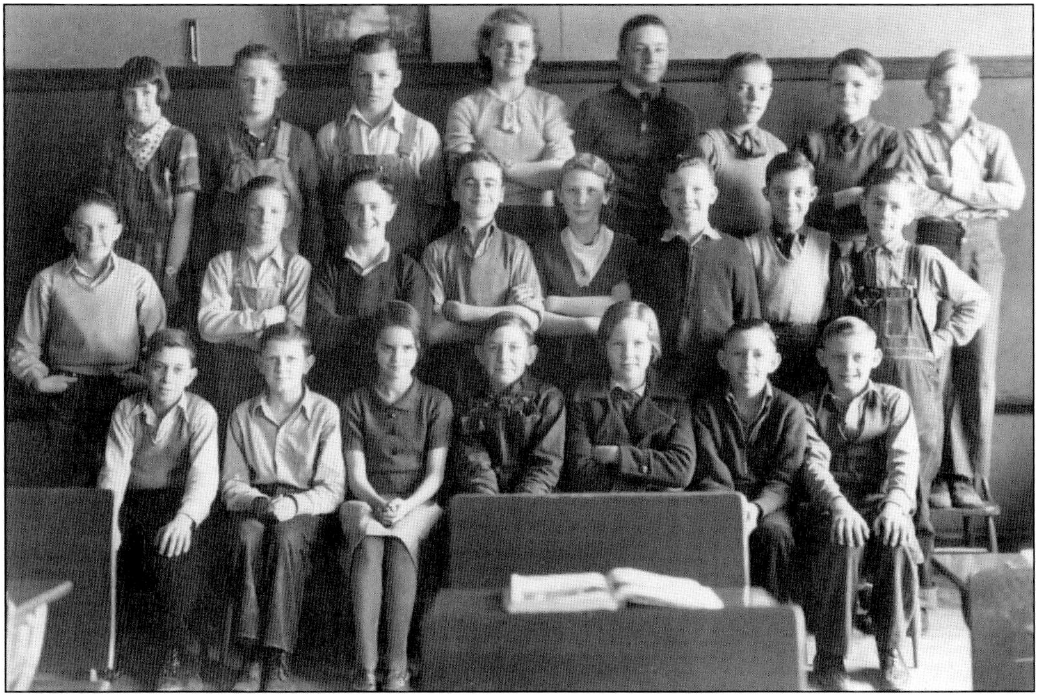

Riverdale School Seventh Grade, 1937. For a time, Riverdale School was used as a junior high school. Known students in this photograph include Joseph Patterson (first row, far left), Carl Pingree (first row, second from left), and Don Ellis (second row, fourth from left.) (Courtesy of the Joseph R. Patterson family.)

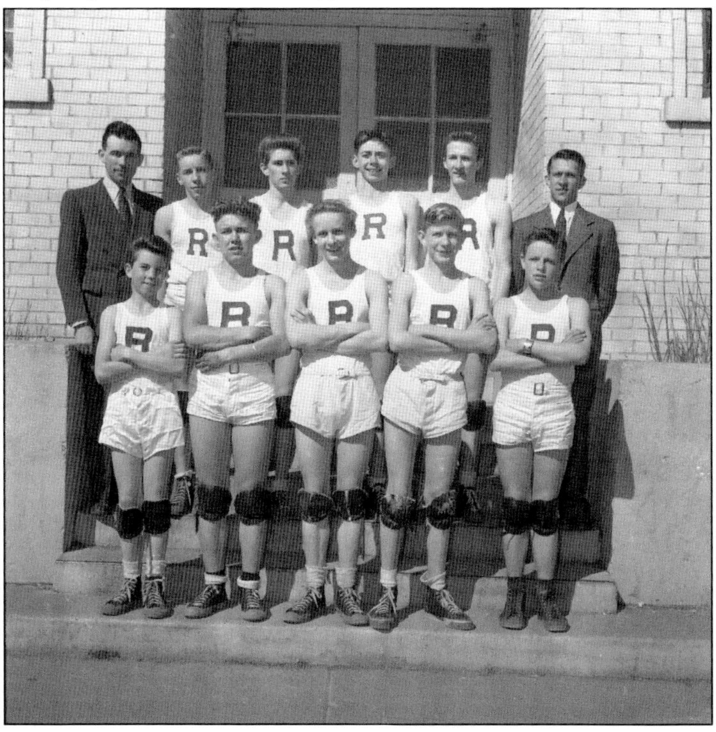

1947 Basketball Champions. The Riverdale Junior High basketball team won the 1947 county banner. Wallace Knight coached basketball and track at the junior high for seven years and was the principal of five local elementary schools. From left to right are (first row) Robert Steck, Floyd Manning, Eugene James, Ray Newey, and Bent DuBell; (second row) James McDougal (principal), Bob Colvin, Mark Hamblin, Pat Dougherty, Gary Elmer, and Wallace Knight (coach). (Courtesy of Weber State University Special Collections.)

Science Club, 1947. The Riverdale Junior High science club participated in the Thomas A. Edison centennial by replicating five of his inventions: the phonograph, ore separator, fuse, lightbulb, and storage battery. Ronald Heywood (left) is examining a replica of Edison's first phonograph, and Toshiro Shiba is working on a replica of Edison's first ore separator. (Courtesy of Weber State University Special Collections.)

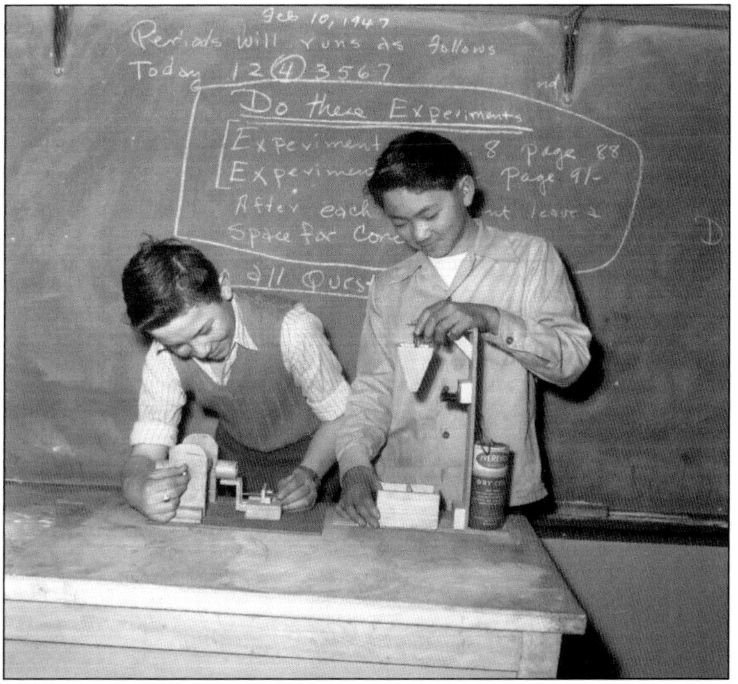

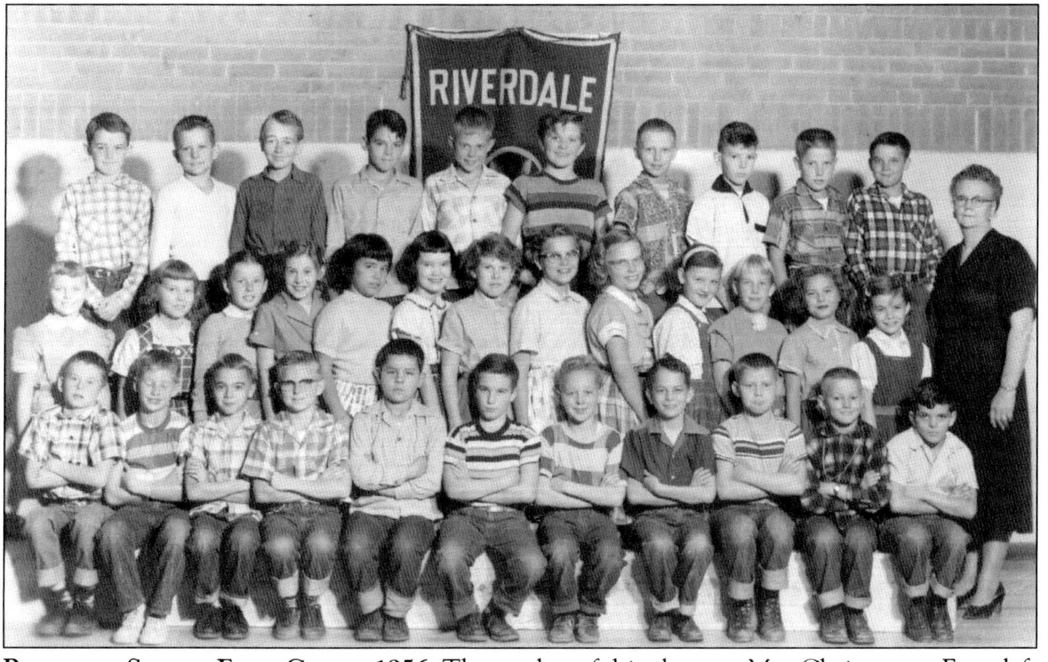

Riverdale School Fifth Grade, 1956. The teacher of this class was Mrs. Christensen. From left to right are (first row) Mike Garfield, unidentified, Brent Ellis, four unidentified, Kenny Nebeker, unidentified, Lynn Stimpson, and unidentified; (second row) Jill Smith, two unidentified, Patsy Blotchet, Mary Ann Cabrales, Carla Preece, Linda Crary, Kathy George, three unidentified, Ann Carlisle, Jean Knight, and Mrs. Christensen (teacher); (third row) Russell Child, two unidentified, Roger Bush, Bryant Cragun, Johnny Hull, two unidentified, Curtis Salisbury, and Richard Hughes. (Courtesy of Mary Ann Cabrales Woodbury.)

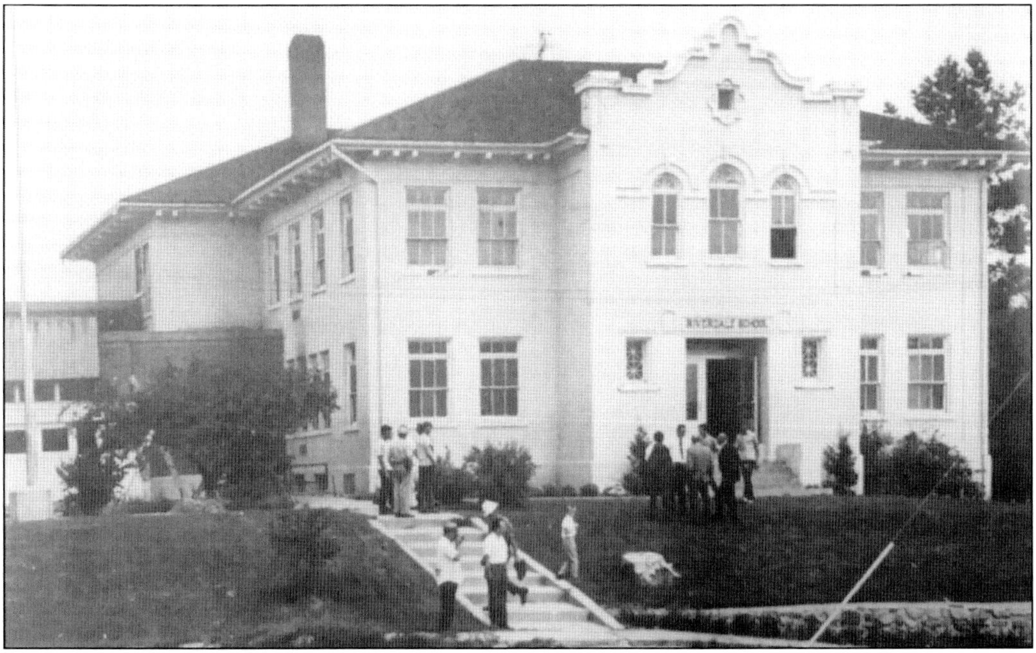

RIVERDALE SCHOOL. The school had two classrooms upstairs and two on the main floor. Around 1922, the school expanded to include four rooms on the north. The restrooms, furnace, and multipurpose room were in the basement. The room above the front entrance housed the office and later the library. After the addition to the school, kindergarten met in the basement; first, second, and third grades met on the main level; and fourth, fifth and sixth grades met in the top floor. The school's brick was painted cream. (Courtesy of Riverdale Elementary School.)

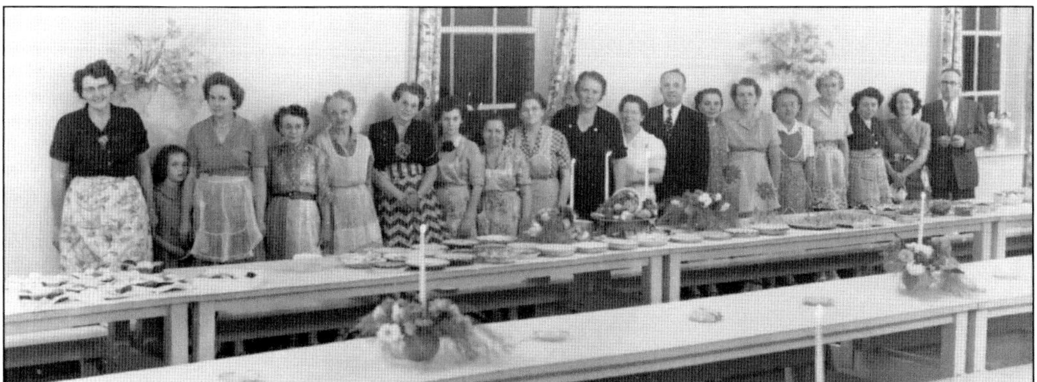

SCHOOL CAFETERIA, 1952. In the school's early days, local women took turns supplementing the children's sack lunches with soup, chili, rice, or hot chocolate. It was made in their homes and brought to the school every day at noon. Later, school lunch cost 25¢, and an extra carton of milk cost 2¢. In 1952, the Riverdale Ward held a dinner, prepared by those in the photograph, in the Riverdale School cafeteria. This photograph shows the interior of the cafeteria, which was part of the 1939 addition on the west side of the school. From left to right are Lillian Froerer, Joyce Ritter (young girl), Ruth Ritter, Ivy "Dolly" Child, Mabel Ellis, unidentified, Dorothy Applonie, Eva Applonie, three unidentified, Monteith Woolley, unidentified, Katherine Bingham, ? Hunter, Annie Adelphia Bingham, Lucille Child Judkins, Mary Child, and Dahl Crabtree. (Courtesy of the Lucille Child Judkins family.)

RIVERDALE SCHOOL FIRE. On Sunday, July 16, 1966, around 10:30 a.m., a fire started in the Riverdale School. Police chief Wes Woolsey reported that it may have been arson or caused by a pile of oily rags. More than 60 firefighters and 12 trucks from Riverdale, Washington Terrace, Roy, and Weber County fought the blaze for four hours. In the end, the walls of the school still stood, but the interior was extensively damaged. (Courtesy of Roland Child.)

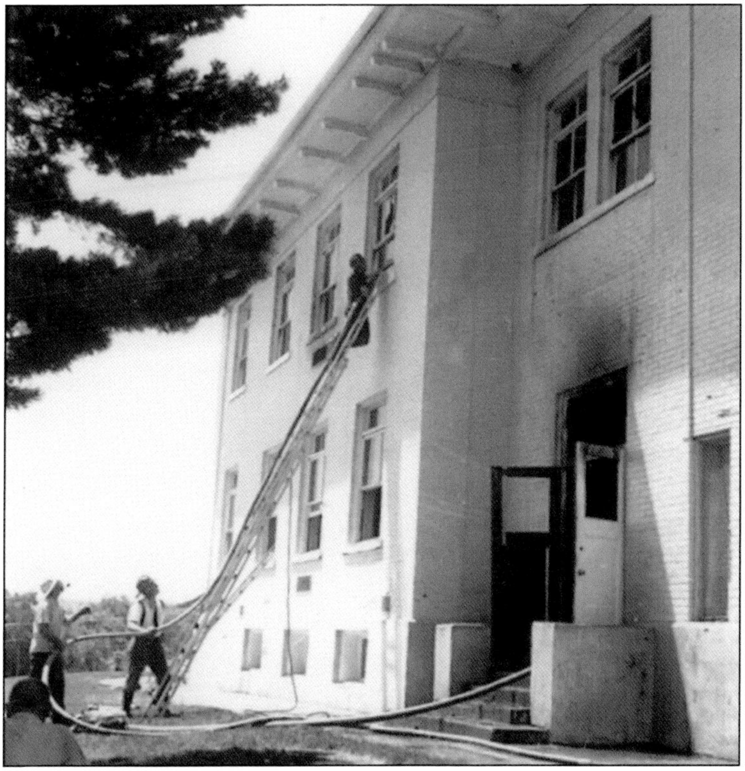

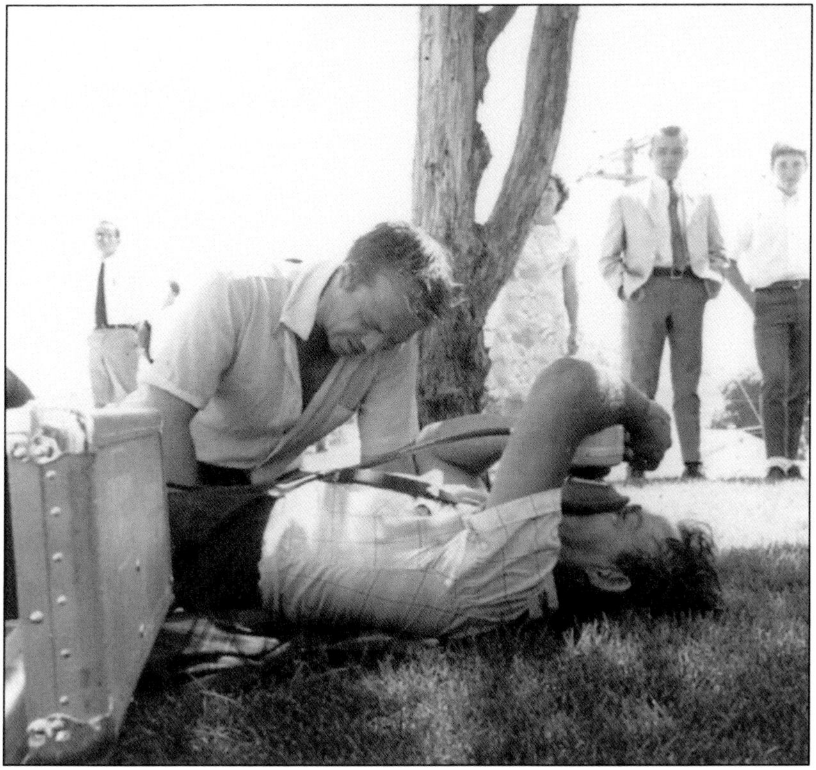

SMOKE INHALATION. After battling the blaze, Riverdale fire marshal Don Kirk was administered oxygen. Sitting next to him is fire chief Roland Child. Both men were transported to the hospital to be treated for smoke inhalation. (Courtesy of Roland Child.)

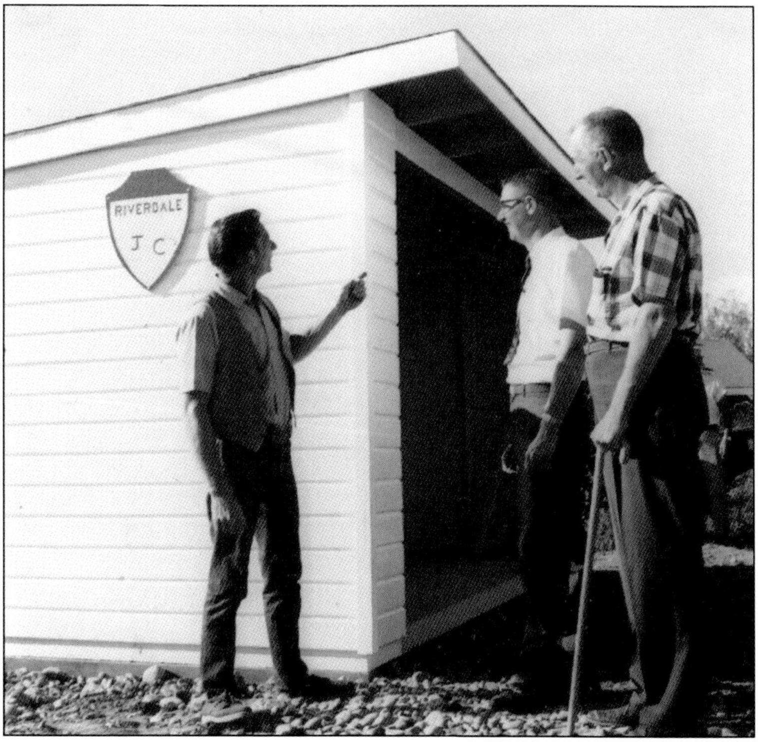

Bus Shelters, 1966. The school board decided to raze the 1911 schoolhouse and build a new school on the same site. Students were bused to four nearby elementary schools until the new school was ready. A service group, called the Riverdale Jaycees (see page 106), built six bus shelters for the schoolchildren. In the photograph, Chairman Norman Leishman (left) presents a bus shelter to Mayor Gail Sanders (center). (Courtesy of Norman W. Leishman.)

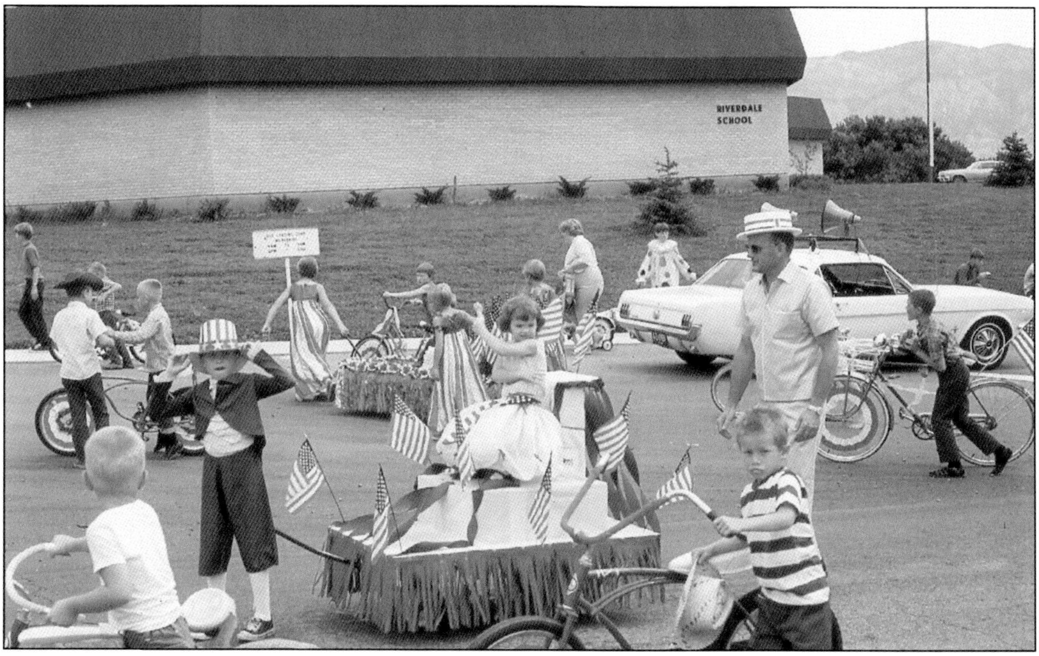

Riverdale School, Built 1967. Architect John L. Piers designed the new school constructed by Acord-Harris Construction Company. Opened for students in the fall of 1967, Piers designed the school for six grades. By 1976, it employed 40 staff members and taught 606 students. The new school can be seen in the background of this parade photograph as it looked before a 1977 addition was built for kindergarten. (Courtesy of Gail and Doris Sanders.)

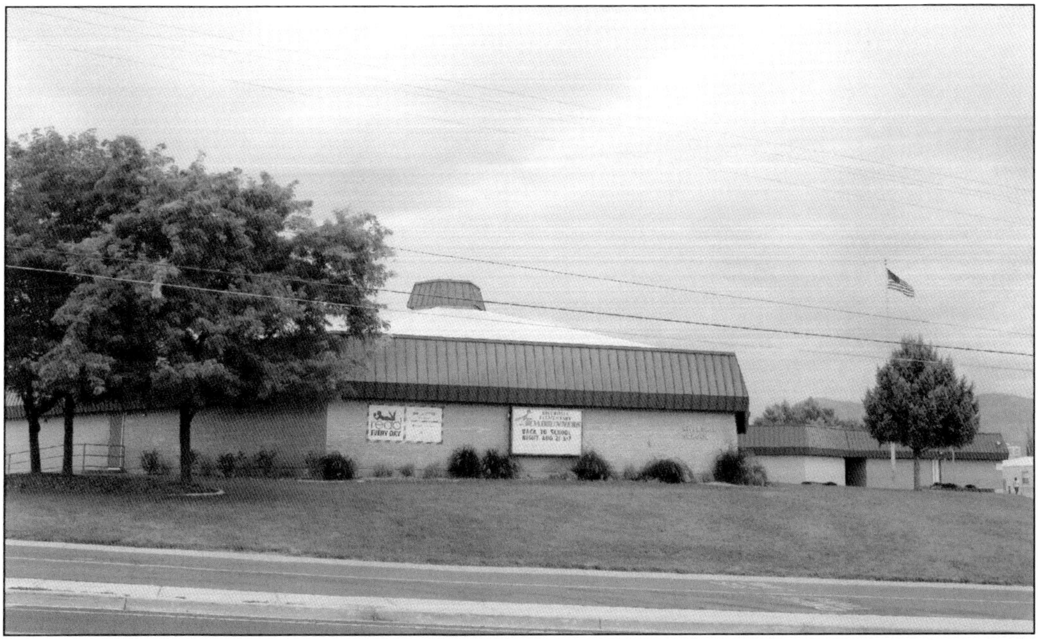

RIVERDALE ELEMENTARY, 2017. Today, approximately 550 students attend Riverdale Elementary School in the Weber School District. Kindergarten through sixth grade are taught here, with a staff of 54 working to meet the needs of the young students. The Riverdale Roadrunners proudly wear their school colors of purple and white. (Author's collection.)

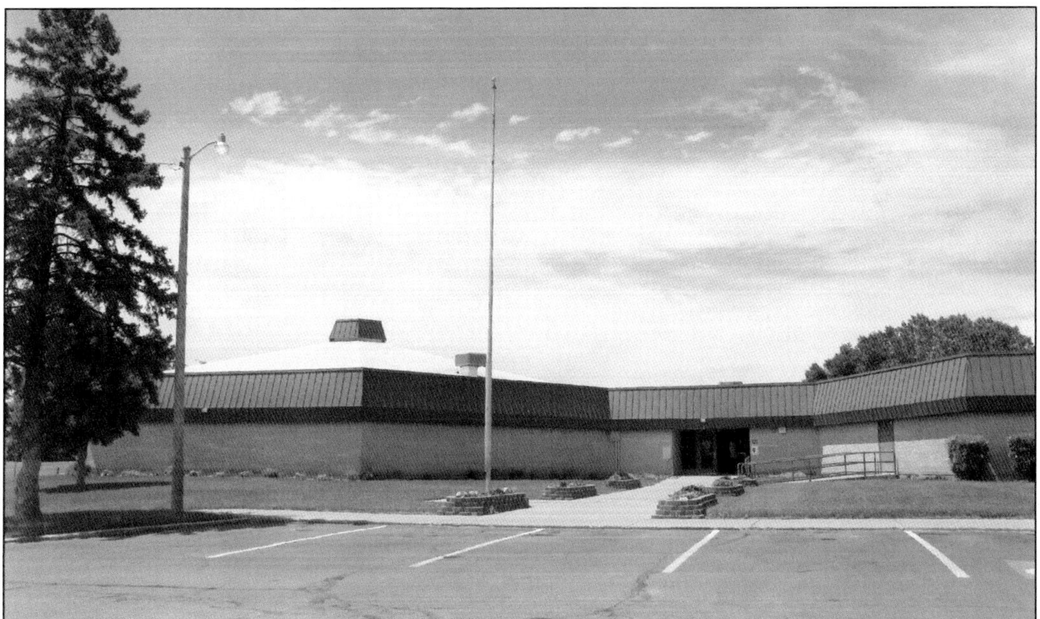

SCHOOL DAYS. The school's academic curriculum includes English, math, science, social studies, language arts, music, physical education, and art. The school, along with the help of the parent-teacher association, plans many fun events and learning activities for students and their families. Staff and teachers place a focus on encouraging the students to look forward to a college education. (Author's collection.)

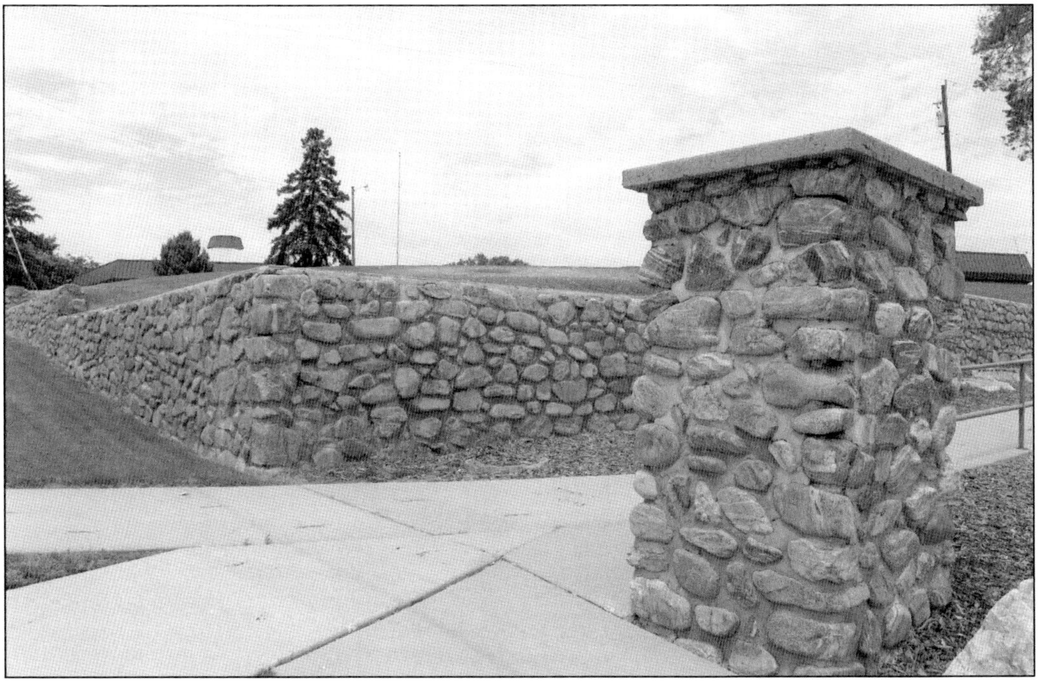

Rock Wall and Pillar, 2017. Though destroyed by fire, part of the original rock wall and a rock pillar from the 1911 schoolhouse remain at the site. The remnants are located on the south and east sides between the school and the lower parking lot. (Author's collection.)

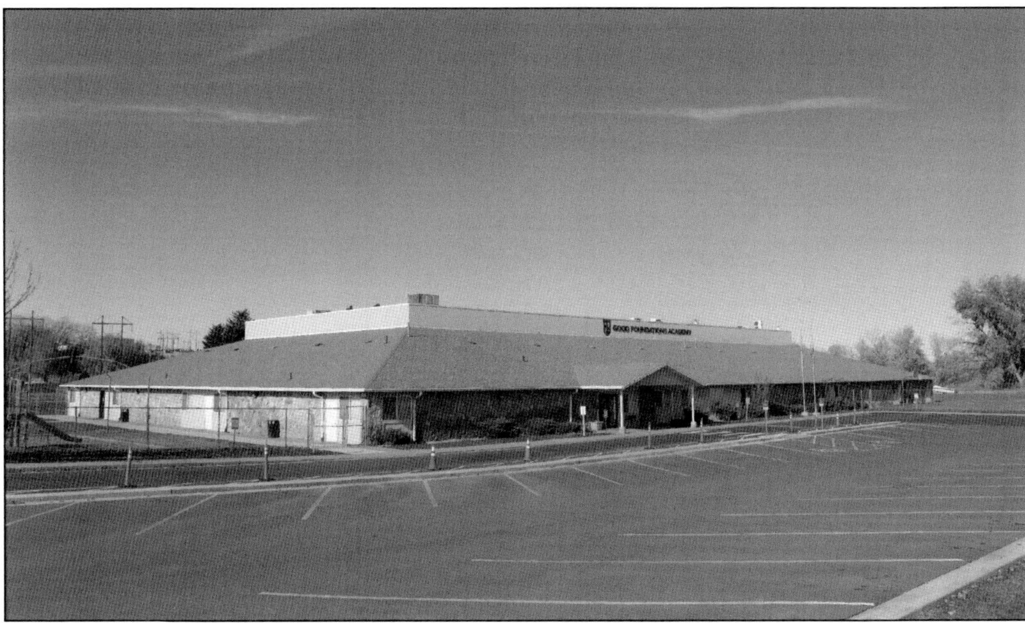

Good Foundations Academy. Originally the Christian Heritage School, this building is now home to Good Foundations Academy, a kindergarten-through-sixth-grade charter school offering an educational program emphasizing character and academic excellence. Over 500 students attend the academy. Located at 5101 South 1050 West, the school opened in August 2010. Other schools in Riverdale include the Utah Military Academy and Bravo Arts Academy. (Author's collection.)

Four

Agriculture

Taylor's Mill and a Land Filled with Crops

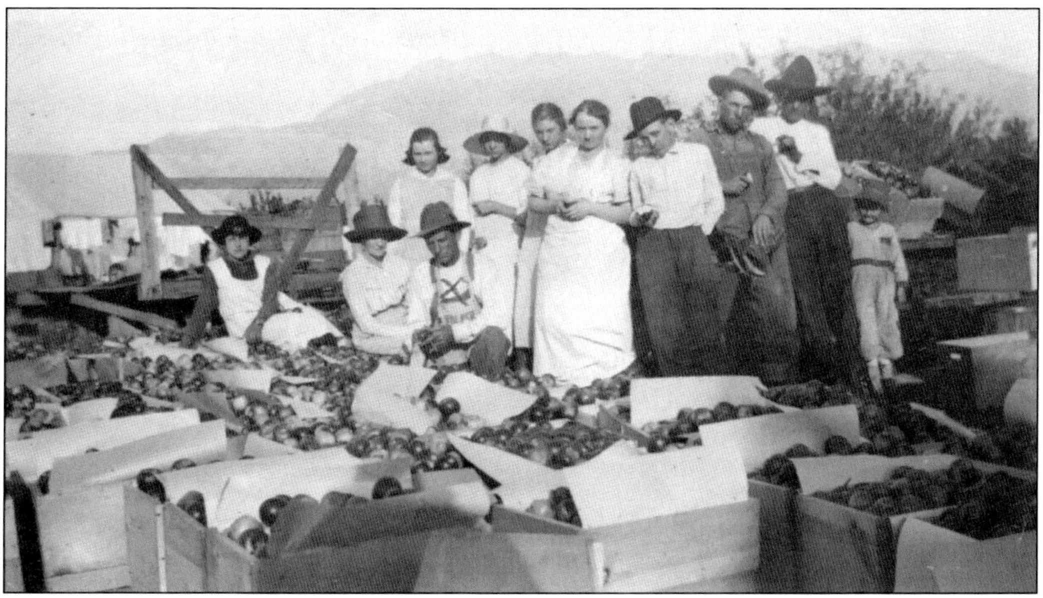

Pomona Orchard. Since its establishment, settlers found Riverdale to be an excellent place to farm. The first settlers dug a canal from the Weber River to irrigate the land. In time, Riverdale was filled with farms and orchards. This photograph shows Charles Taylor, his daughter Virginia (far right), and workers packing apples from Taylor's Pomona Orchard. The orchard land was later used for the Cinedome 70 theater and then for today's Larry H. Miller dealership, Cherry Creek Apartments, and Golden Spike Park. (Courtesy of Sandra Judkins.)

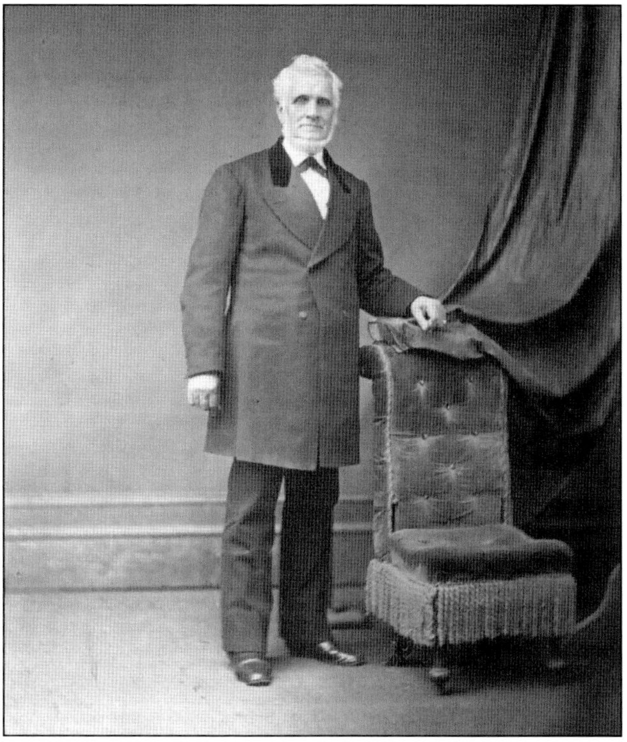

Pres. John Taylor. Daniel Burch came to the area in 1848 and built a sawmill just east of the Weber River in about 1853. Once located at 4287 Riverdale Road, the mill was later converted into a gristmill by Burch and his sons. Elder John Taylor, an LDS apostle, purchased the mill in 1858, two years after Daniel Burch's death. Taylor later became the president of the church. He made several improvements to the mill and added a carding machine. Richard Dye and Edward Stratton managed mill operations for Taylor. (Photograph by C.R. Savage; courtesy of the Lucille Child Judkins family.)

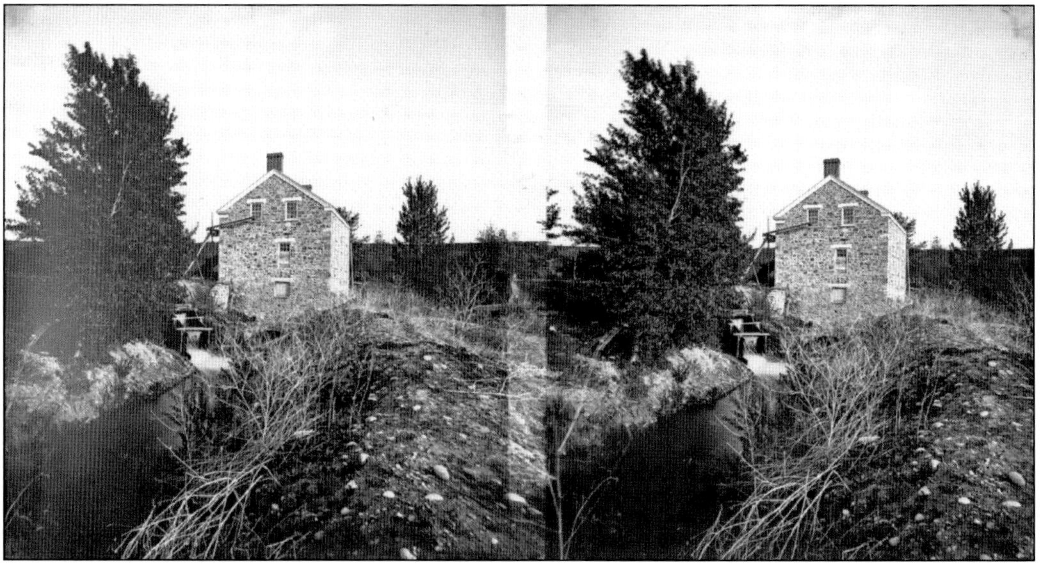

Taylor's Mill, 1869. Following John Taylor's purchase of the mill, it was known as Taylor's Mill. A landmark in the community for decades, the mill was made of stone and was 44 feet by 30 feet. A millrace built by Daniel Burch in 1853 carried water from the Weber River to power the mill and remained in use until 1945. The first railroad station in Ogden sat west of the mill and was known as Taylor's Mill Station and Taylor's Switch. In 1883, the mill had three operations—a gristmill, a sawmill, and a carding machine. This stereograph view was taken on a collodion glass-plate negative by Andrew J. Russell. The mill remained in the Taylor estate until 1890. (Photograph by Andrew J. Russell; courtesy of the Oakland Museum of California.)

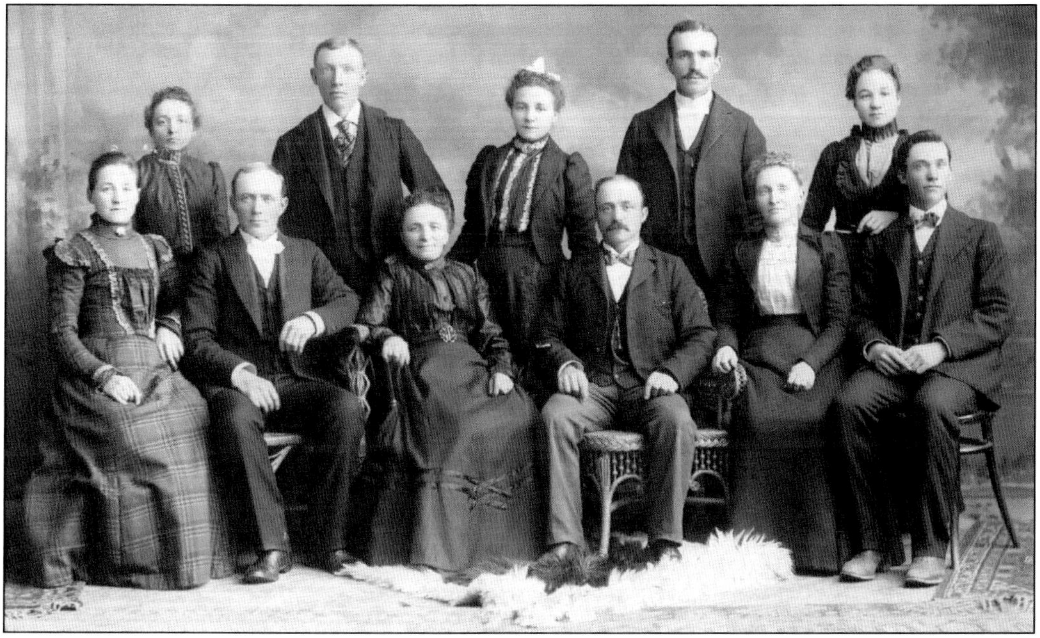

Adele Stratton and Children, 1905. Edward Stratton was introduced to his wife, Adele DeSaules, by John Taylor. Taylor and his family took Adele, a French-speaker from Switzerland, into their home when her grandmother passed away. Edward and Adele lived in the carding machine building at the mill when they were first married. Together, they had seven children. Edward passed away at age 33. Adele is pictured here with her adult children and their spouses. From left to right are (first row) Annie Stratton Bingham, Adam Aranthon Bingham, Adele DeSaules Stratton, William Arthur Stratton, Sarah Jane Firth Stratton, and John Fife; (second row) Elizabeth Stratton Child, Jesse A. Child, Sophia Stratton Bingham, S. James Bingham, and Adele Stratton Fife. (Courtesy of the Lucille Child Judkins family.)

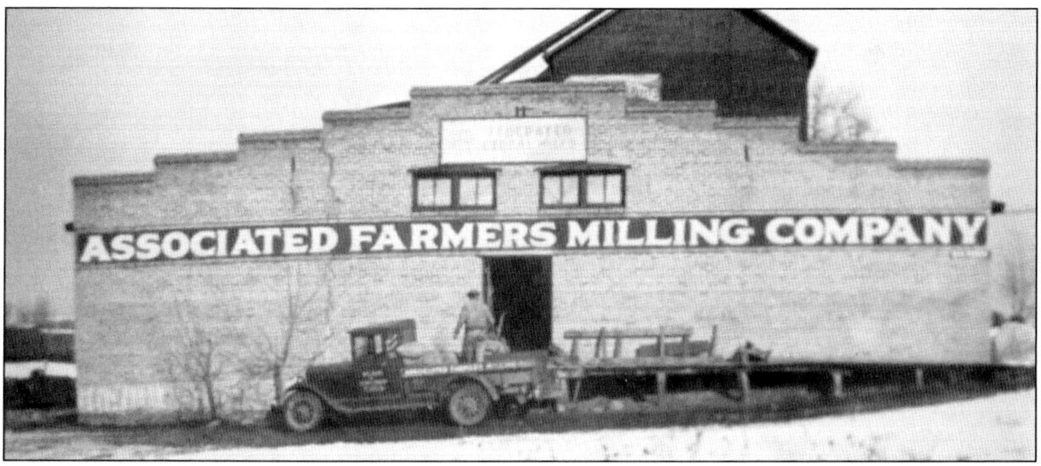

Associated Farmers Milling Company. As operations grew, the mill building expanded over the years. Additions included a timber wall extension, receiving dock, equipment shed, warehouse, and offices. Ownership transferred from Taylor's estate to the Ogden Milling and Elevator Company on May 2, 1890. Later known as Associated Farmer's Milling Company, the small sign in the photograph reads "Federated Cereal Mills." Residents remember it most recently as the All-O-Wheat Cereal Company. (Courtesy of Riverdale City.)

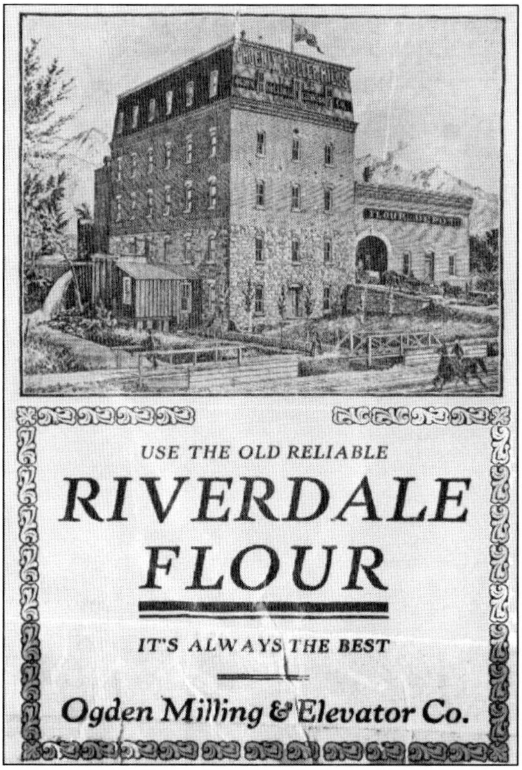

RIVERDALE FLOUR ADVERTISEMENT. The whole-grain flour produced at the mill in Riverdale was said to be the finest flour produced west of St. Joseph, Missouri. This Ogden Milling and Elevator Company advertisement touted Riverdale Flour as "always the best." The mill in the illustration is the Phoenix Roller Mills, once located at 1430 Washington Boulevard in Ogden. It also was operated by the Ogden Milling and Elevator Company. (Courtesy of the Ogden Union Station Collection, 03439.)

ALL-O-WHEAT CEREAL COMPANY. As the name suggests, the mill only made whole-wheat products. In 1982, the mill was listed in the National Register of Historic Places through the efforts of Weber County historian William W. Terry. In his book *Weber County Is Worth Knowing*, Terry wrote, "This mill, constructed in 1853, was in continuous operation longer than any other mill in the State of Utah." (Courtesy of Weber State University Special Collections.)

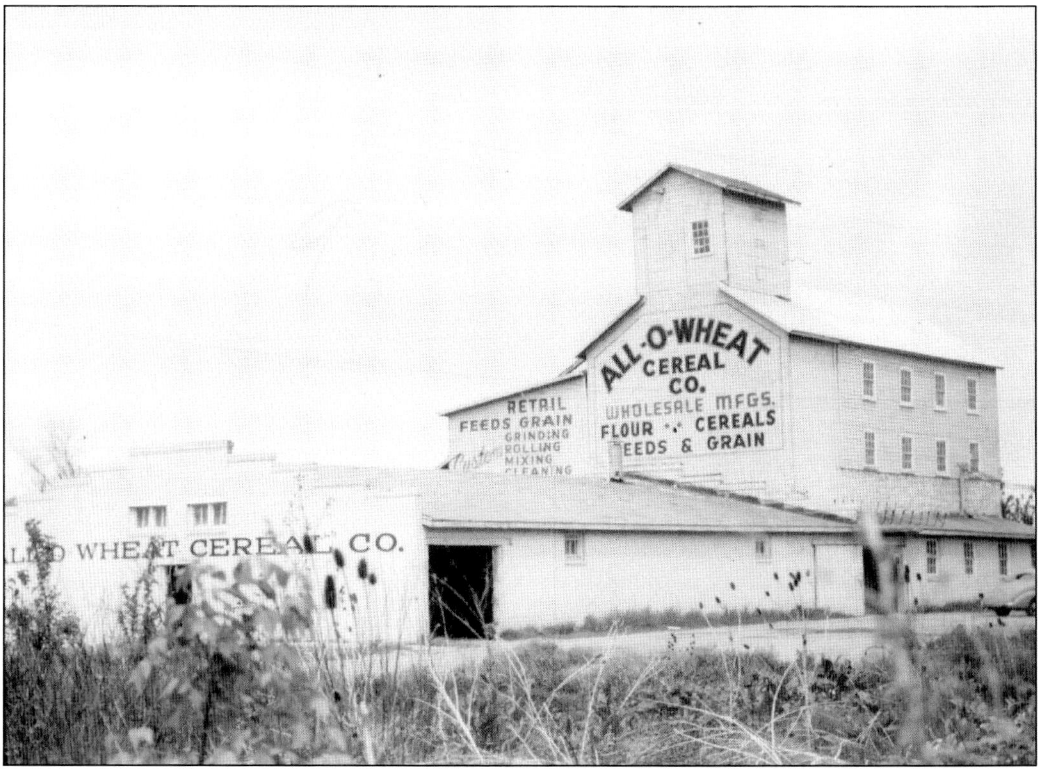

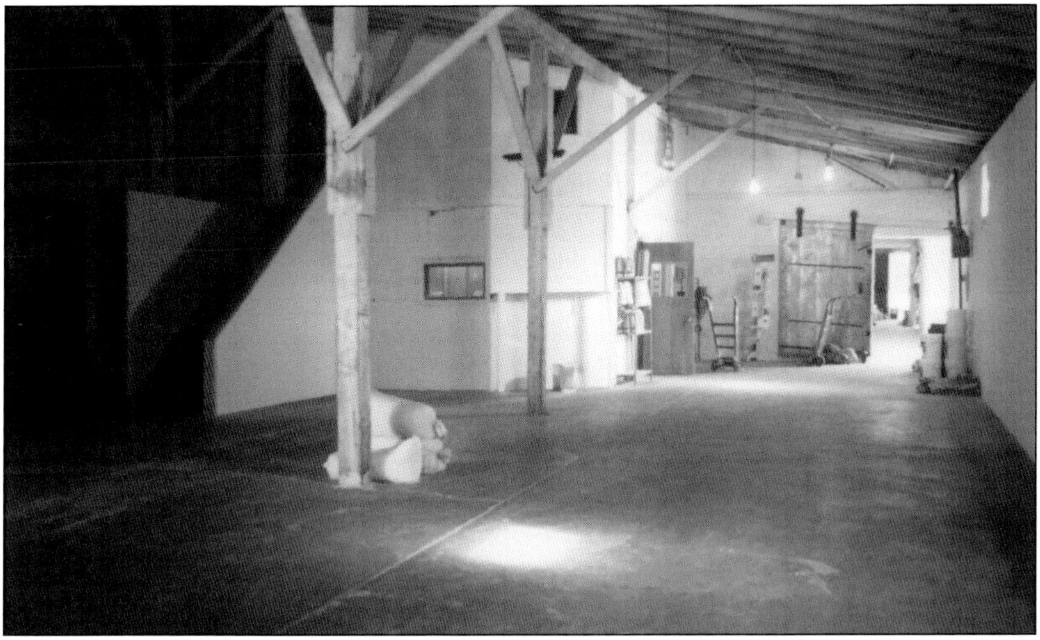

Interior of Mill. This photograph shows an interior view of one of the mill's additions. In operation until the mid-1980s, the mill fell into disrepair and was considered a health and safety hazard. After a nuisance abatement hearing, the mill was demolished by its owner on October 28, 1997. Many residents still mourn the loss of this historic landmark. (Courtesy of Riverdale City.)

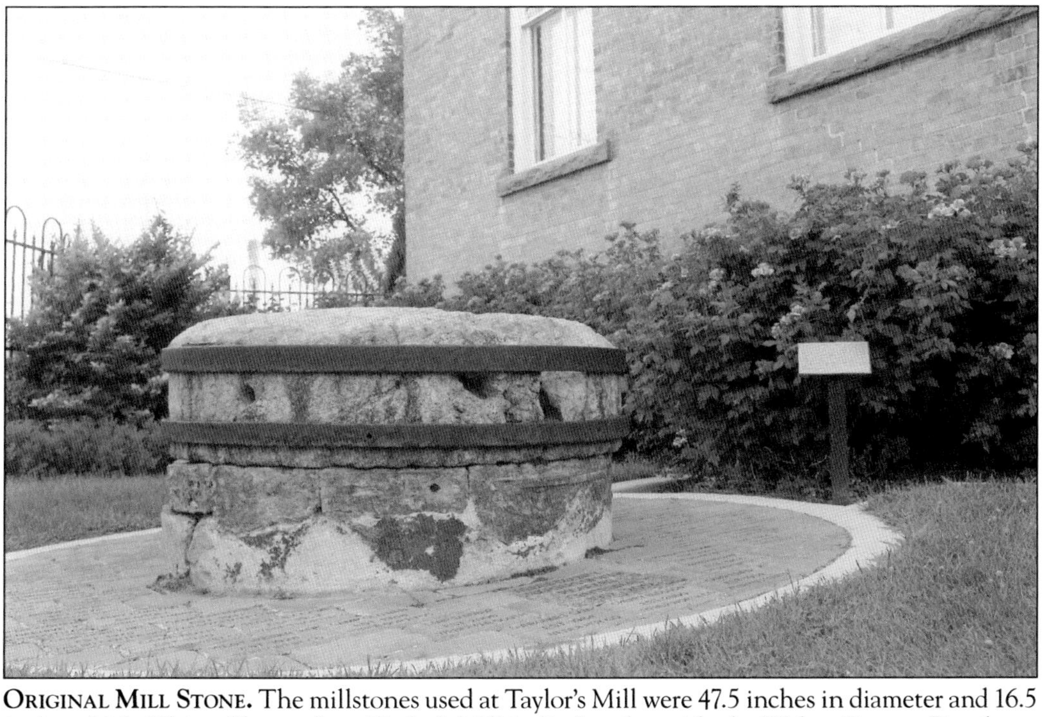

Original Mill Stone. The millstones used at Taylor's Mill were 47.5 inches in diameter and 16.5 inches thick. This millstone from Taylor's Mill is displayed outside the Weber County Daughters of Utah Pioneers Museum, located at 2104 Lincoln Avenue in Ogden. (Author's collection.)

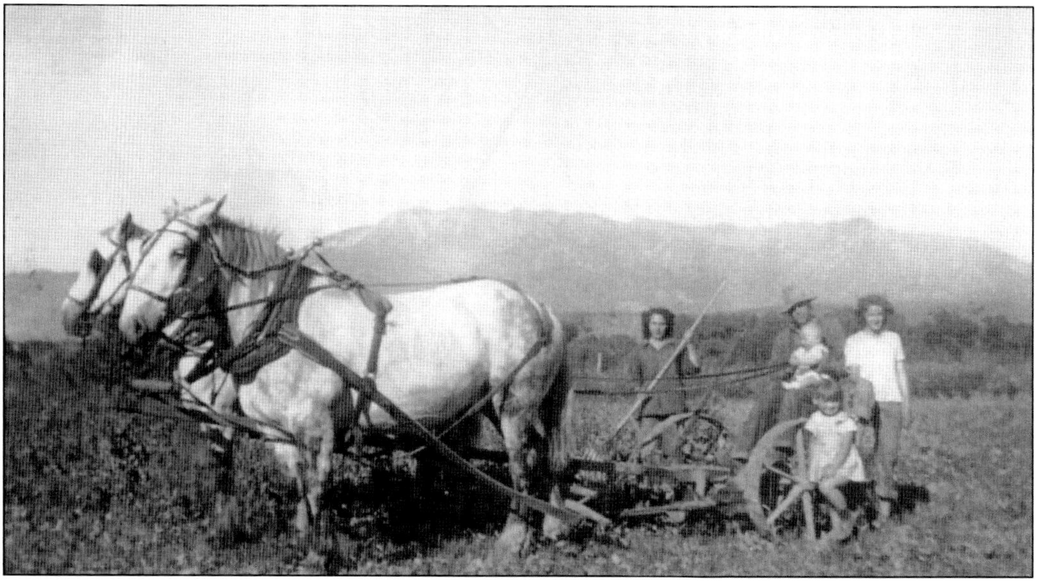

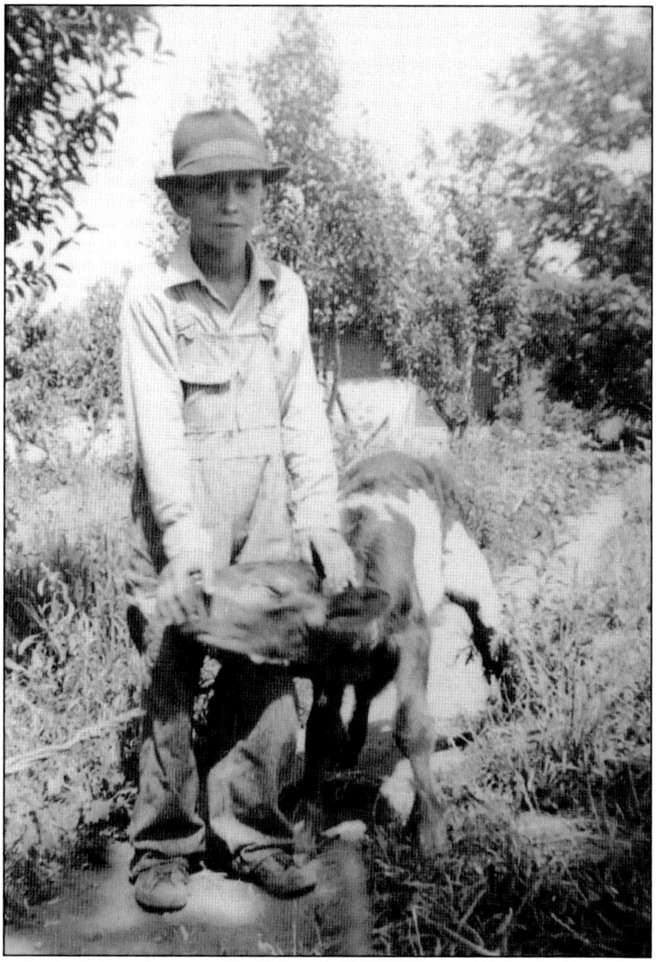

Adam Patterson and Children. As an agricultural community in its early days, life in Riverdale revolved around caring for crops, fields, orchards, and livestock. These workhorses were used to mow the pea crop in Riverdale before combines came into use. A pea vinery was located at the southwest end of Riverdale Park to prepare pea crops for market. Adam Patterson is pictured with his children, from left to right, Donna, Adam (holding his infant son Robert), Kathryn, and Karon (near the wheel). His eldest son Earl was in the US Army and stationed in Germany at the time. (Courtesy of Riverdale City.)

Joseph Ray Patterson, 1938. Born in 1923 in Riverdale, Joseph loved to farm and garden. Young children in Riverdale often helped with farm duties and chores, including taking care of livestock. Some children went home during school lunch breaks to care for their cattle. (Courtesy of the Joseph R. Patterson family.)

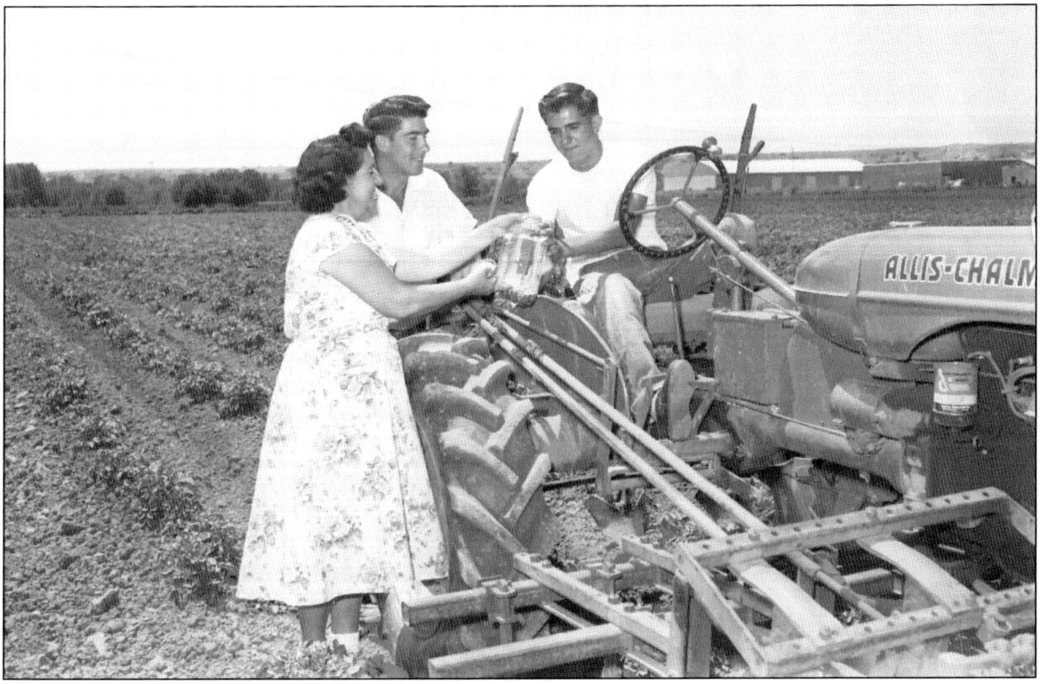

D'Agnillo Farm, 1964. The D'Agnillo family owned a 15-acre truck farm located where the Riverdale Town Square now sits. The family grew onions, peppers, tomatoes, dill weed, and cucumbers. The construction of Riverdale Road bisected the farm. Despite the road's four lanes, the family could easily cross the road by tractor or on foot. In the photograph, Mary D'Agnillo is giving a cold drink to her sons Joe (center) and John (on the tractor) as they cultivate a potato patch. (Courtesy of Weber State University Special Collections.)

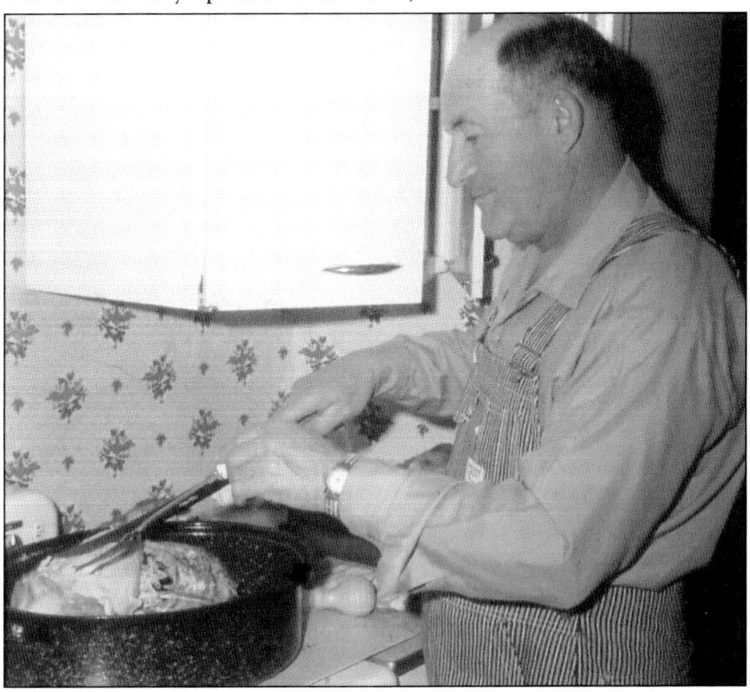

Carter's Farm. Lloyd Carter (pictured) and his wife, Minnie, took over a farm that had belonged to Minnie's father, Geert Boekweg. Boekweg, a Dutch farmer, sold his produce from Salt Lake City to Idaho. The Carter name is still found in the community with Carter Drive (3900 South) and the Carter's Farm subdivision built by Sanders Homes. (Courtesy of Gail and Doris Sanders.)

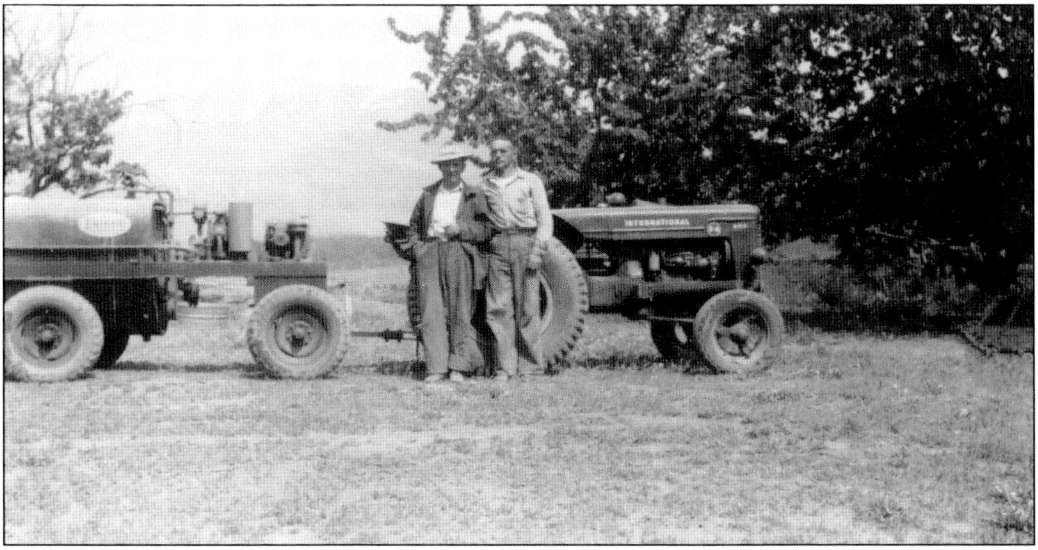

Pomona Orchard. Charles and Anna Marie Helland Taylor owned a 40-acre farm originally located on the west bench of Riverdale. The land that the orchard was on was later used for the Cinedome 70 theater, which was followed by today's Larry H. Miller dealership, Cherry Creek Apartments, and Golden Spike Park. Charles Taylor traveled to California to go to school to learn how to raise fruit trees. Upon his return to Riverdale, he named his farm Pomona Orchard, after Pomona the Greek goddess of fruit trees, gardens, and orchards. Pictured here are Charles Taylor (left) and his son-in-law Everett Johnson. (Courtesy of Sandra Judkins.)

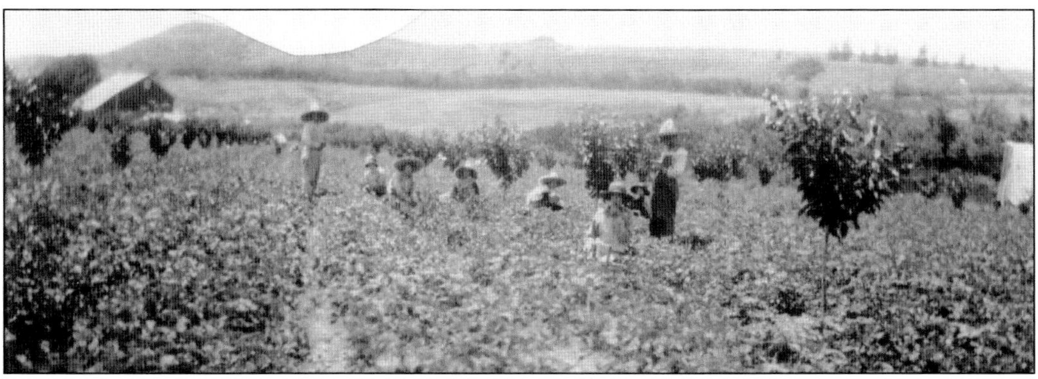

Strawberry Field. This view looking south shows the strawberry field at Pomona Orchard. Hired workers would come here to pick the produce. (Courtesy of Sandra Judkins.)

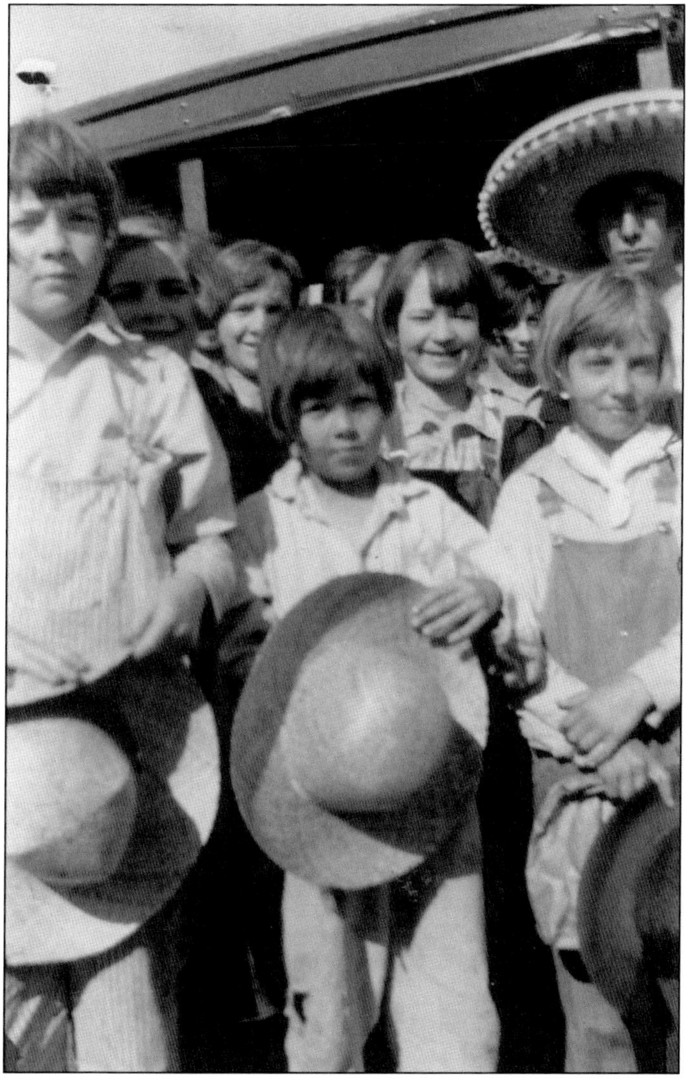

Strawberry Pickers. Charles Taylor's daughter Virginia Anderson was responsible for the strawberry pickers. About 40 to 50 girls from Ogden were picked up and taken to the fields each day, where they earned 12¢ per case of strawberries picked. Pomona Orchard was known for its well-topped cases of berries and quality produce. Virginia later married Ted Anderson, who served as the first mayor of Riverdale. (Courtesy of Sandra Judkins.)

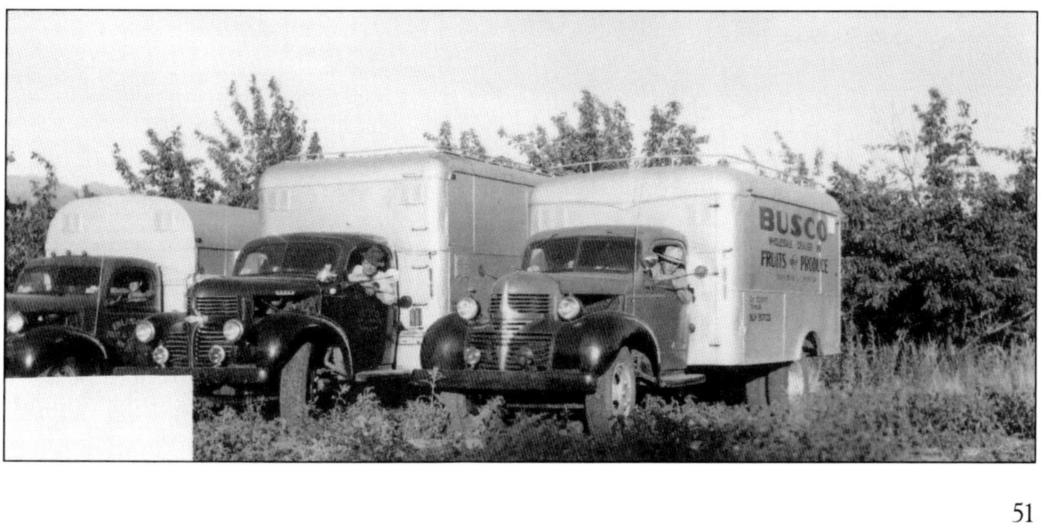

Busco Produce Trucks. Charles Taylor sold produce from his farm to Sylvester Busco. These trucks transported the produce from the farm to markets in Idaho and Montana. (Courtesy of Sandra Judkins.)

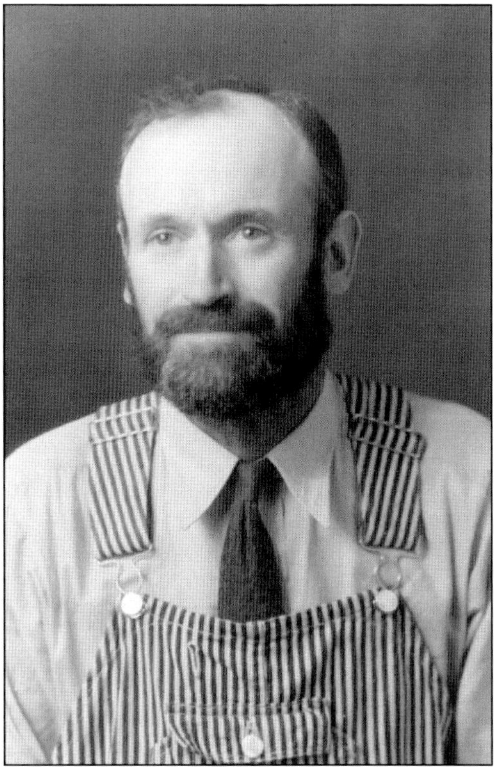

Alma Ellis. Born in Pleasant View, Utah, in 1889, Alma Ellis attended Utah State Agricultural College. In 1921, he moved to Riverdale to manage the Bigelow–Van Meter Orchard Company and spent most of his life as an orchardist. Since early in his life, he spent considerable time water witching with a peach twig, locating numerous wells throughout Utah. Ellis could determine the depth of a well and follow the course of underground streams. He served as a member of the first Riverdale Town Board. The Ellis home in Riverdale still stands, surrounded by apricot and cherry trees in an orchard that is now enjoyed by fifth-generation Ellis family members. (Courtesy of the Don and Ardis Ellis family.)

Alma and Mabel Ellis Family, c. 1944. Alma Ellis and his three sons, Don, Howard, and Glen, grew fruit in Riverdale and Pleasant View, Utah. From left to right are (first row) Leona Ellis Thompson, Alma Ellis, and Mabel Ellis; (second row) Don Ellis, Howard Ellis, and Glen Ellis. (Courtesy of the Don and Ardis Ellis family.)

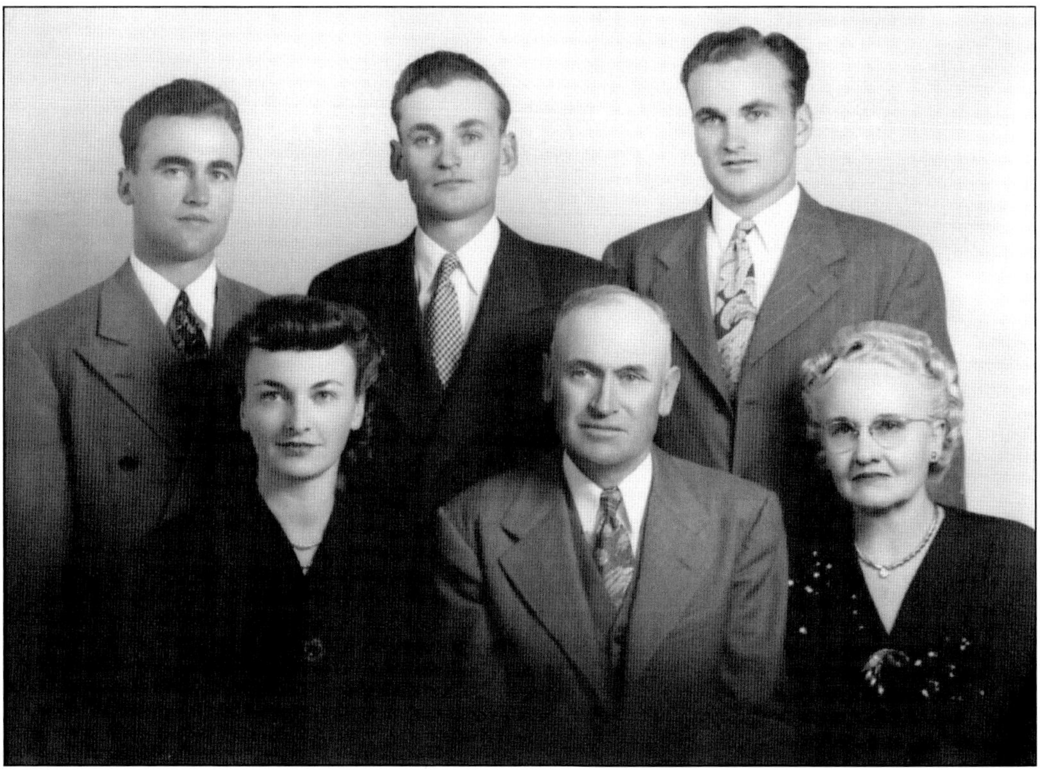

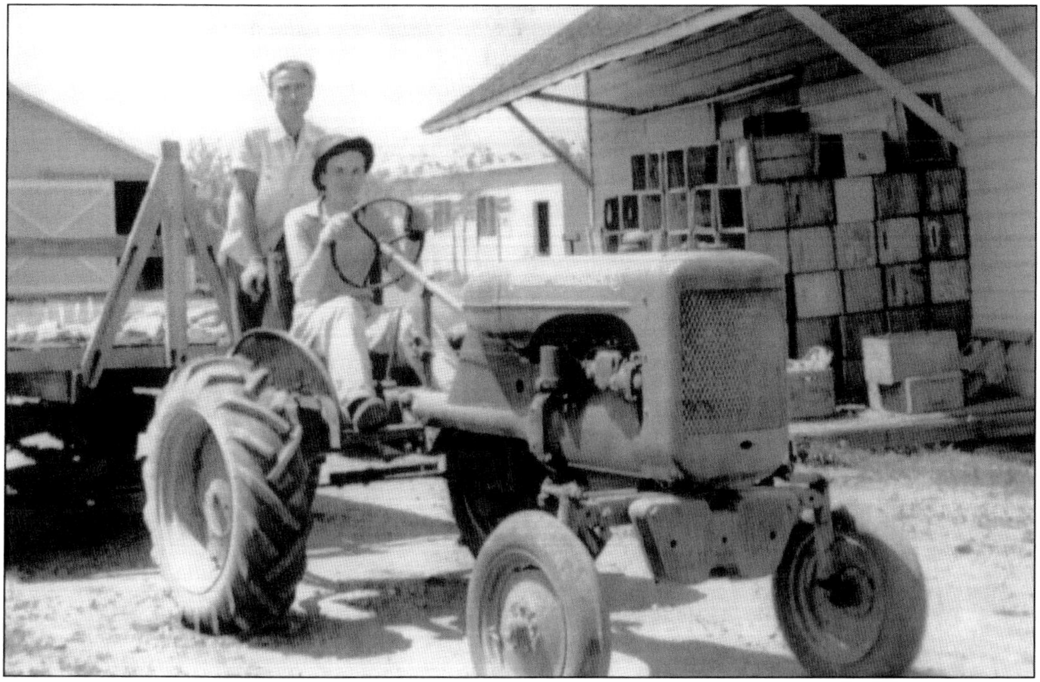

Farm Tractor and Packing Shed. On this tractor are Howard Ellis (driving) and his brother Don Ellis. The family employed seasonal workers to pick and harvest fruit and used a packing shed, seen in the background, to pack the fruit. The high quality of the fruit brought back many of the same buyers year after year. (Courtesy of the Don and Ardis Ellis family.)

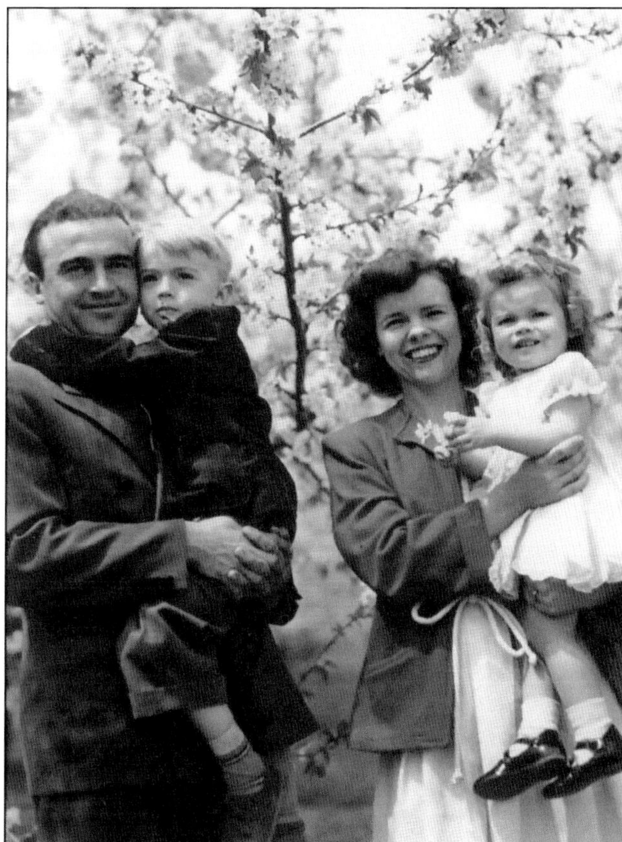

Don and Ardis Ellis Family, c. 1950. Each spring, cherry trees blossomed, brightening the farm. As a married couple, Don and Ardis Ellis were active in the Weber County Young Farmers Association. Pictured here with the blossoms in their orchard are, from left to right, Don Ellis, Brent Ellis, Ardis Hickenlooper Ellis, and Sherry Ellis. Jana Ellis (not pictured) was born later. (Courtesy of the Don and Ardis Ellis family.)

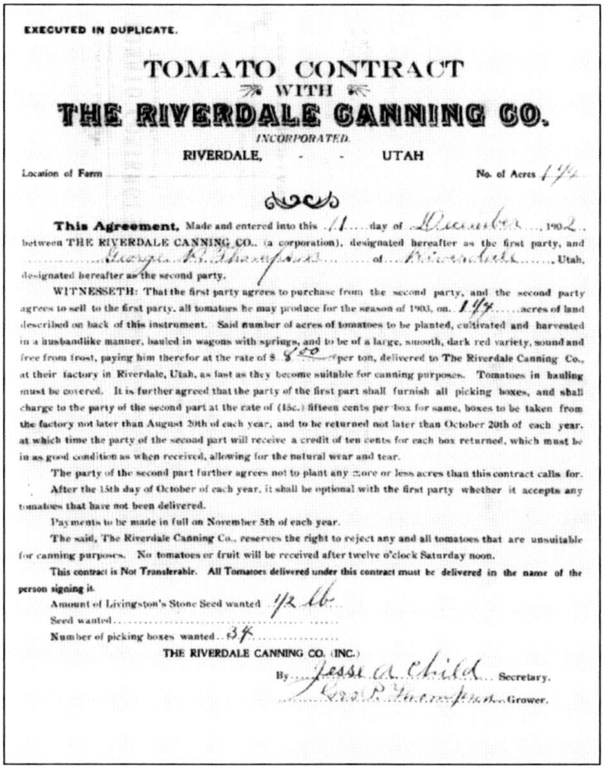

EXECUTED IN DUPLICATE.

TOMATO CONTRACT

WITH

THE RIVERDALE CANNING CO.

INCORPORATED.

RIVERDALE, - - UTAH

Location of Farm .... No. of Acres 1¼

This Agreement, Made and entered into this 11 day of December, 1902, between THE RIVERDALE CANNING CO., (a corporation), designated hereafter as the first party, and George P. Thompson of Riverdale, Utah, designated hereafter as the second party.

WITNESSETH: That the first party agrees to purchase from the second party, and the second party agrees to sell to the first party, all tomatoes he may produce for the season of 1903, on 1¼ acres of land described on back of this instrument. Said number of acres of tomatoes to be planted, cultivated and harvested in a husbandlike manner, hauled in wagons with springs, and to be of a large, smooth, dark red variety, sound and free from frost, paying him therefor at the rate of $ 8.00 per ton, delivered to The Riverdale Canning Co., at their factory in Riverdale, Utah, as fast as they become suitable for canning purposes. Tomatoes in hauling must be covered. It is further agreed that the party of the first part shall furnish all picking boxes, and shall charge to the party of the second part at the rate of (15c.) fifteen cents per box for same, boxes to be taken from the factory not later than August 20th of each year, and to be returned not later than October 20th of each year, at which time the party of the second part will receive a credit of ten cents for each box returned, which must be in as good condition as when received, allowing for the natural wear and tear.

The party of the second part further agrees not to plant any more or less acres than this contract calls for.

After the 15th day of October of each year, it shall be optional with the first party whether it accepts any tomatoes that have not been delivered.

Payments to be made in full on November 5th of each year.

The said, The Riverdale Canning Co., reserves the right to reject any and all tomatoes that are unsuitable for canning purposes. No tomatoes or fruit will be received after twelve o'clock Saturday noon.

This contract is Not Transferable. All Tomatoes delivered under this contract must be delivered in the name of the person signing it.

Amount of Livingston's Stone Seed wanted 1/2 lb.

Seed wanted ....

Number of picking boxes wanted 34

THE RIVERDALE CANNING CO. (INC.)

By Jesse A. Child Secretary.

Geo. P. Thompson Grower.

TOMATO CONTRACT, 1902. In the early 1900s, the Riverdale Canning Company stood on the east side of the railroad tracks, north of the viaduct. This 1902 tomato contract between George Peery Thompson and the cannery was typical for the time. Thompson agreed to deliver all the tomatoes he grew on 1.25 acres of land for $8 per ton. In 1910, William Jacob Parker, a local man prominent in the canning industry, purchased the Riverdale cannery. (Courtesy of Judy B. Anderson.)

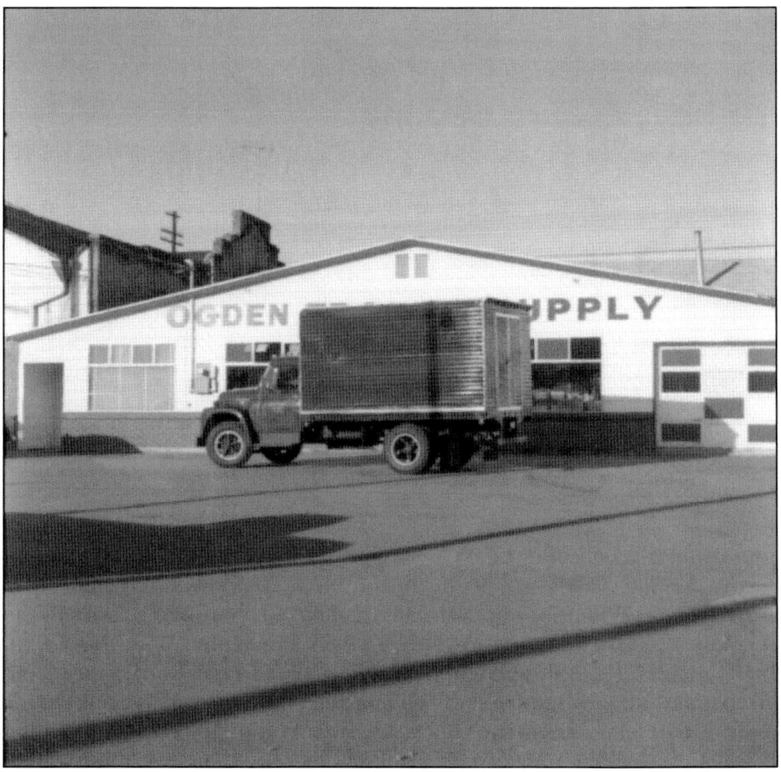

OGDEN TRAILER SUPPLY. After the Riverdale Canning Company closed, Ogden Trailer Supply occupied the building. The old cannery building is visible in the background to the left. A second cannery operated behind what was Heiko Boekweg's house at 1045 West 4400 South. (Courtesy of Mark and Phyllis Fackrell.)

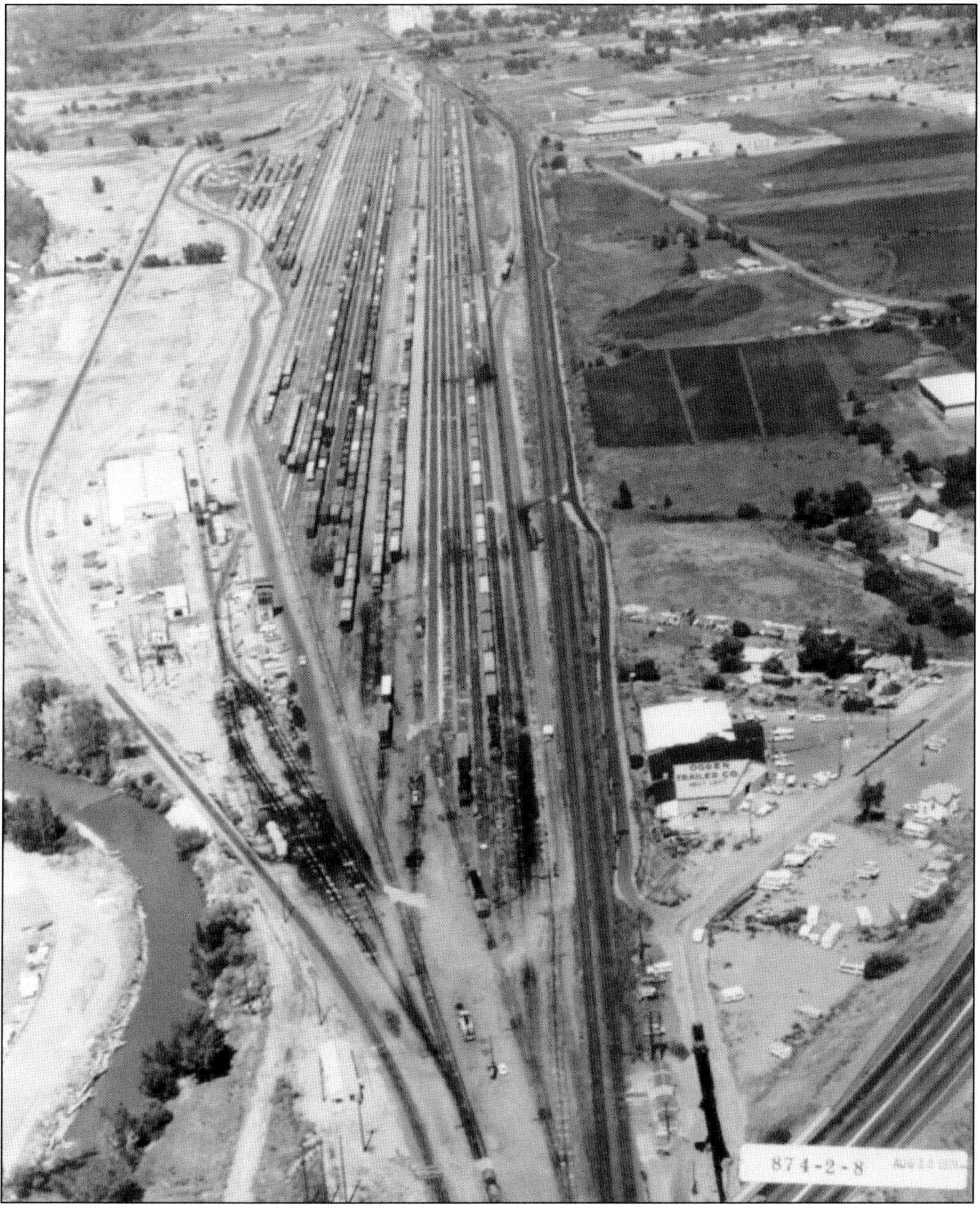

RIVERDALE RAIL YARD. This photograph shows the Riverdale rail yard between the Weber River to the west and farmland to the east. The old Riverdale Canning Company building and the All-O-Wheat mill are also visible in this north-facing view. (Courtesy of the Ogden Union Station Collection, 10249-4.)

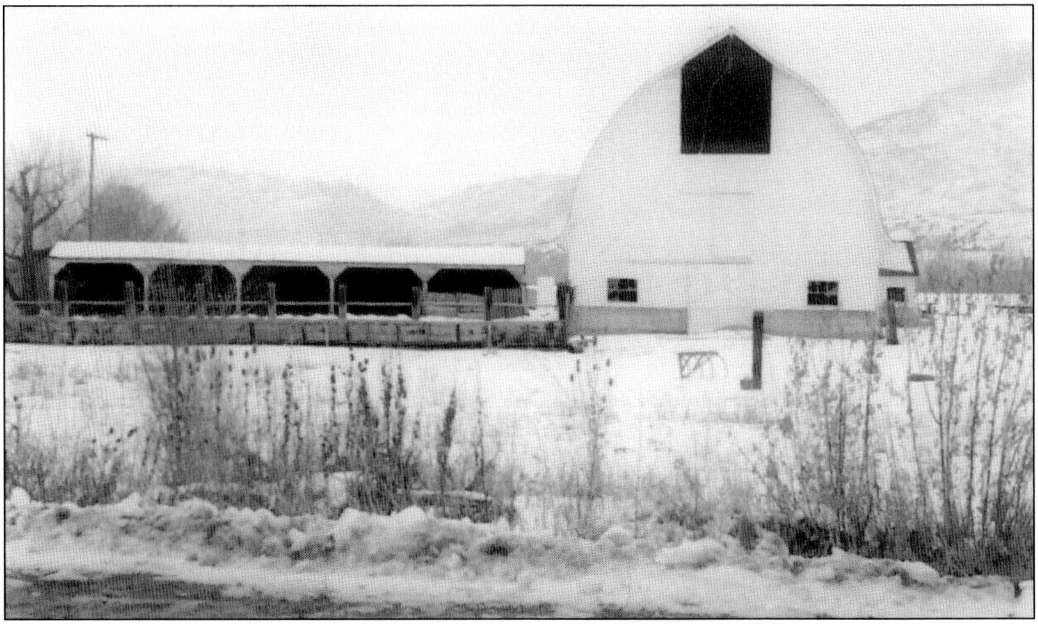

Ralph Ritter Dairy Barn, 1959. Schneiter's Riverside Golf Course, located at 5460 South Weber Drive, now occupies the former Ralph Ritter family homestead. Ritter, a dairyman and farmer, owned one of Utah's top Jersey cattle herds. Ralph and his wife, Ida, raised their family here. This photograph shows the Ritters' barn. Schneiter's Riverside Golf Course originally planned to use the barn as a clubhouse, but fire destroyed the building before renovation. (Courtesy of the Schneiter family.)

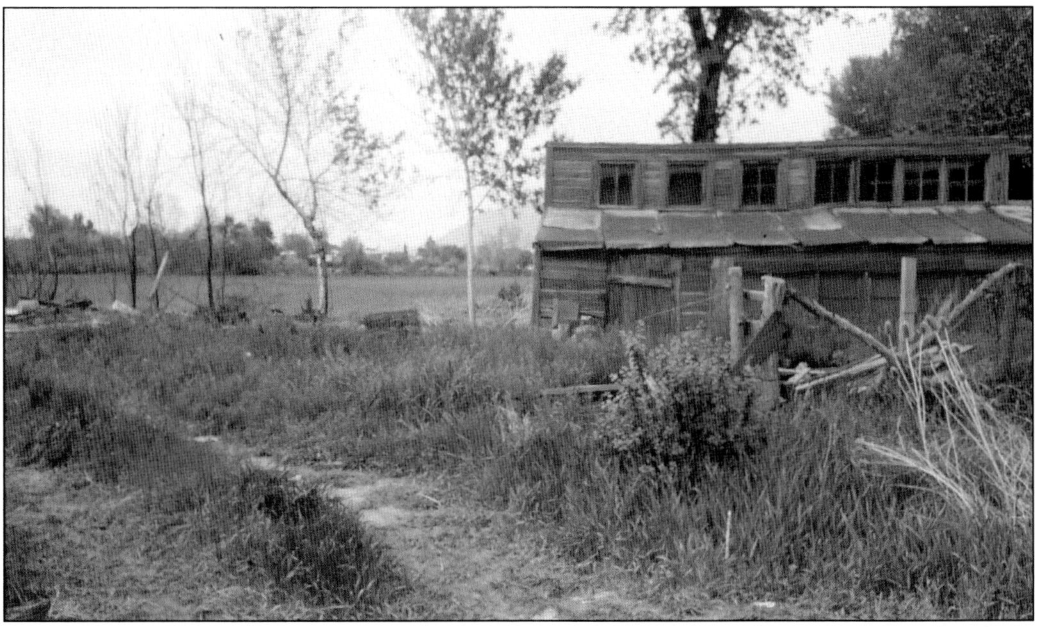

Chicken Coops. These chicken coops were once located on present-day Riverdale Road at about 1070 West. H.G. Vance owned the coops, a barn, and potato cellar. The Higgs family later owned the property and operated an automobile dealership and the Riverdale Barbershop at this location. (Courtesy of the Higgs family.)

Five

Transportation

Wagons and Bridges, Trains and Lanes

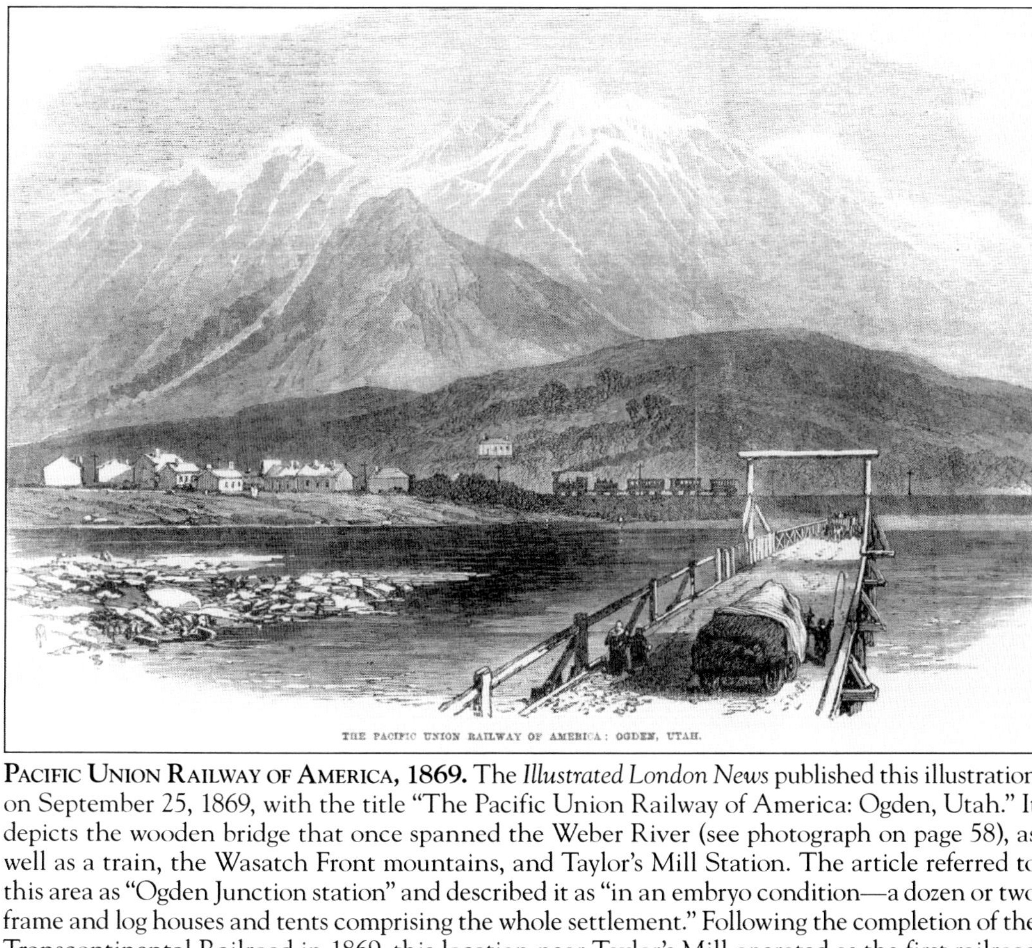

Pacific Union Railway of America, 1869. The *Illustrated London News* published this illustration on September 25, 1869, with the title "The Pacific Union Railway of America: Ogden, Utah." It depicts the wooden bridge that once spanned the Weber River (see photograph on page 58), as well as a train, the Wasatch Front mountains, and Taylor's Mill Station. The article referred to this area as "Ogden Junction station" and described it as "in an embryo condition—a dozen or two frame and log houses and tents comprising the whole settlement." Following the completion of the Transcontinental Railroad in 1869, this location near Taylor's Mill operated as the first railroad stop in the Ogden area. (Illustration by the *Illustrated London News*; author's collection.)

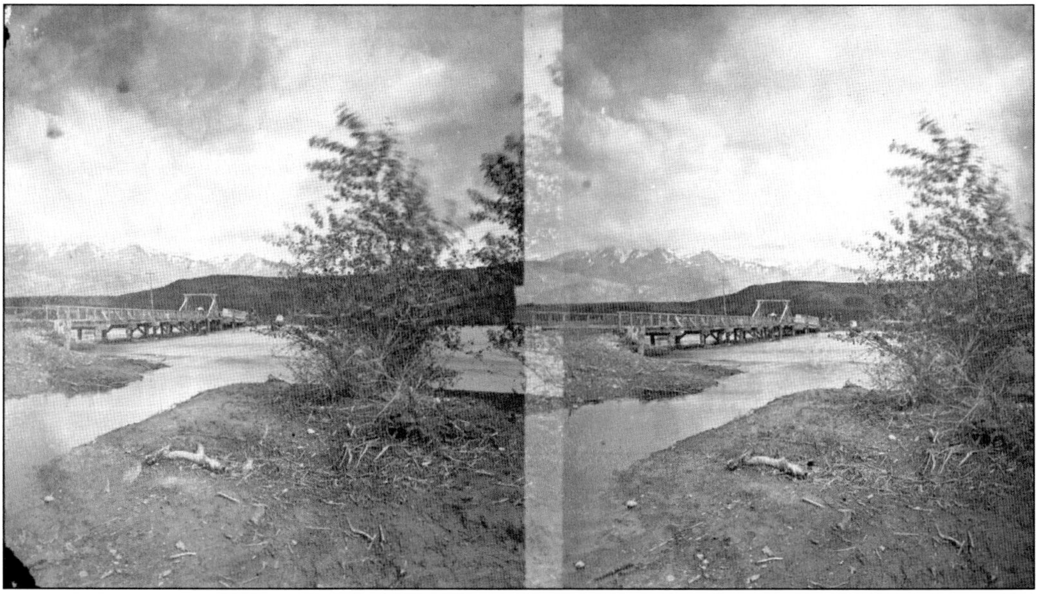

WEBER RIVER BRIDGE, 1869. The Weber River was an obstacle to transportation since the beginning of the settlement. This stereograph view by Andrew J. Russell shows one of the many wooden bridges built to cross over the river in Riverdale. W.H. Grow constructed a bridge in 1863, and David Moore and his son David M. Moore erected another one in 1881. Other bridges were built successively as the old bridges were destroyed or damaged. A steel bridge that was once in Riverdale was moved to Uintah in 1925. There have also been four viaducts built over the river and railroad tracks. (Photograph by Andrew J. Russell; courtesy of the Oakland Museum of California.)

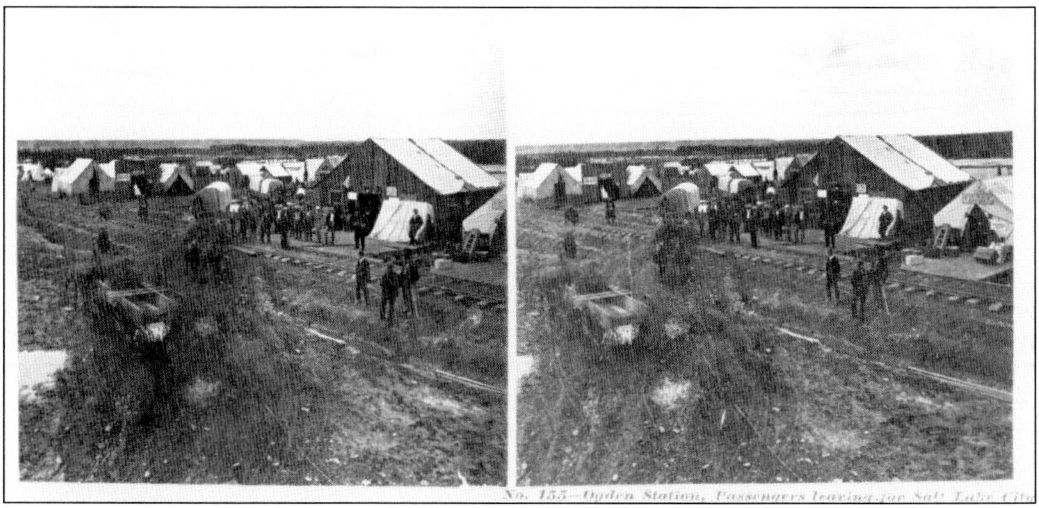

TAYLOR'S MILL STATION, 1869. This Andrew J. Russell stereoview shows Taylor's Mill Station in 1869. Wooden structures and tents are seen at the station, including ticket offices where passengers purchased tickets to Salt Lake City and Corinne, Utah. The covered wagons in the photograph would take arriving railway passengers to their destination. The wooden bridge in the background spanned the Weber River, connecting Taylor's Mill Station to the main road in Riverdale. (Photograph by Andrew J. Russell; courtesy of the Union Pacific Railroad Museum.)

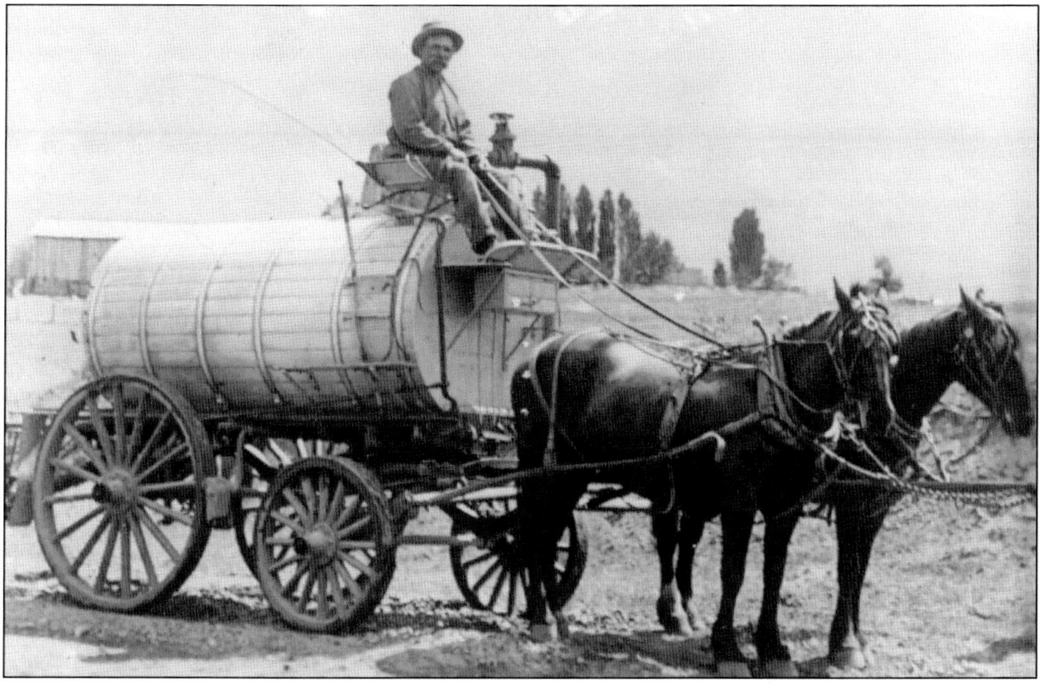

Water Wagon. William Stimpson Jr., the road supervisor, drove the first water wagon in Riverdale and nearby Burch Creek. The wagon sprinkled the dirt roads with water to decrease the amount of dust. (Courtesy of the Lucille Child Judkins family.)

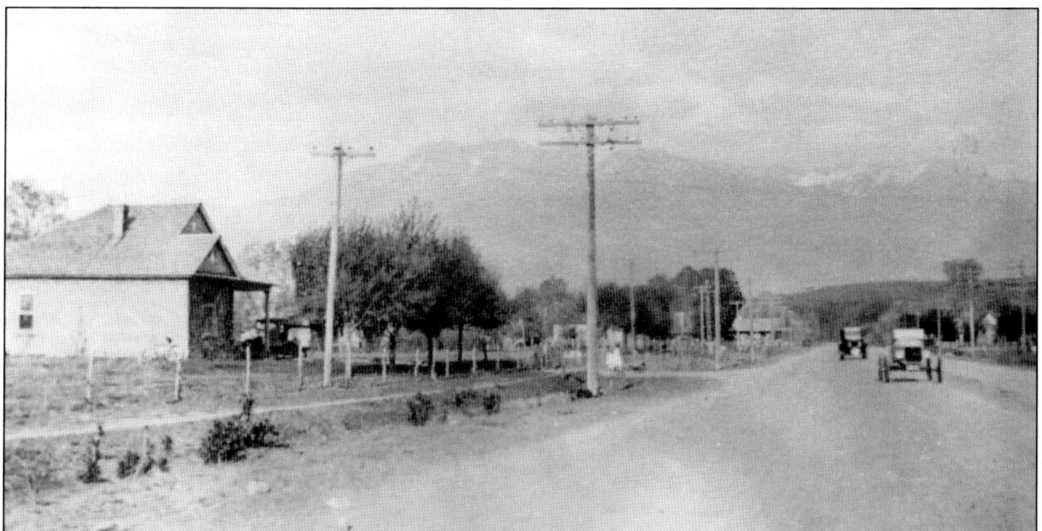

Old Riverdale Road, Early 1900s. Before the multilane Riverdale Road existed, the territorial road (present-day 4400 South) was the main road in Riverdale. The road proved difficult to travel with heavy loads due to the deep, sandy clay, and numerous natural springs in the area. State prisoners paved the road with concrete in 1916. This view looking east shows what the road looked like in the early 1900s. A section of this road, as well as other roads in Riverdale, were part of the historic Lincoln Highway, an early transcontinental highway. (Courtesy of the Lucille Child Judkins family.)

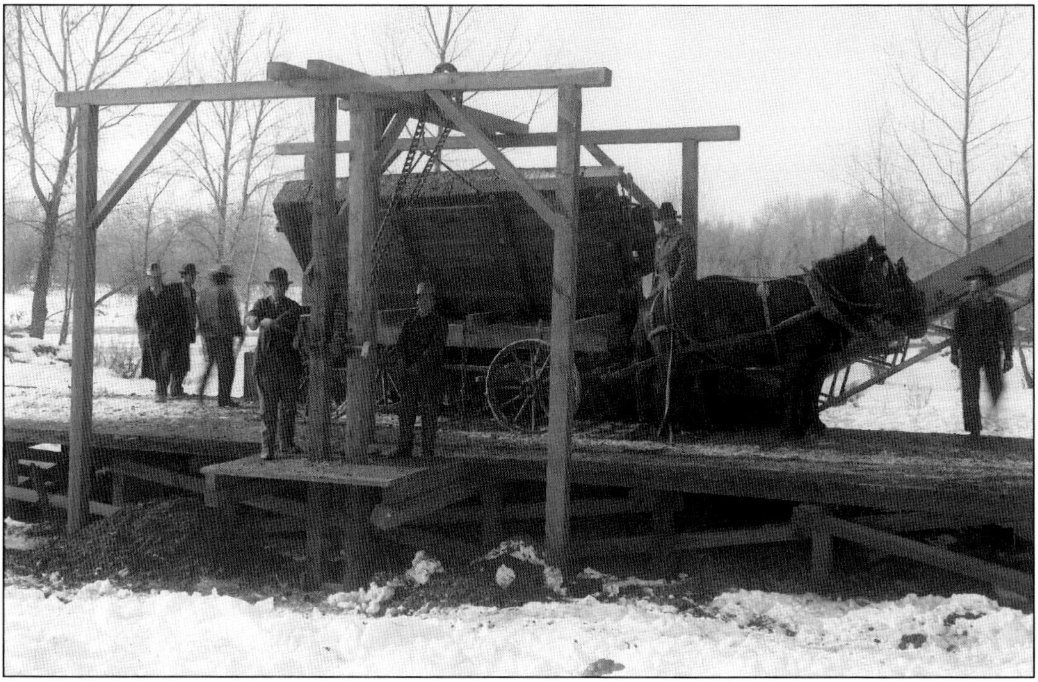

SUGAR BEETS ON SCALE, 1917. The close proximity of the railroad simplified the shipping of produce from the area. This photograph shows a horse-drawn wagon filled with sugar beets being weighed on a scale on January 17, 1917. (Used by permission, Utah State Historical Society.)

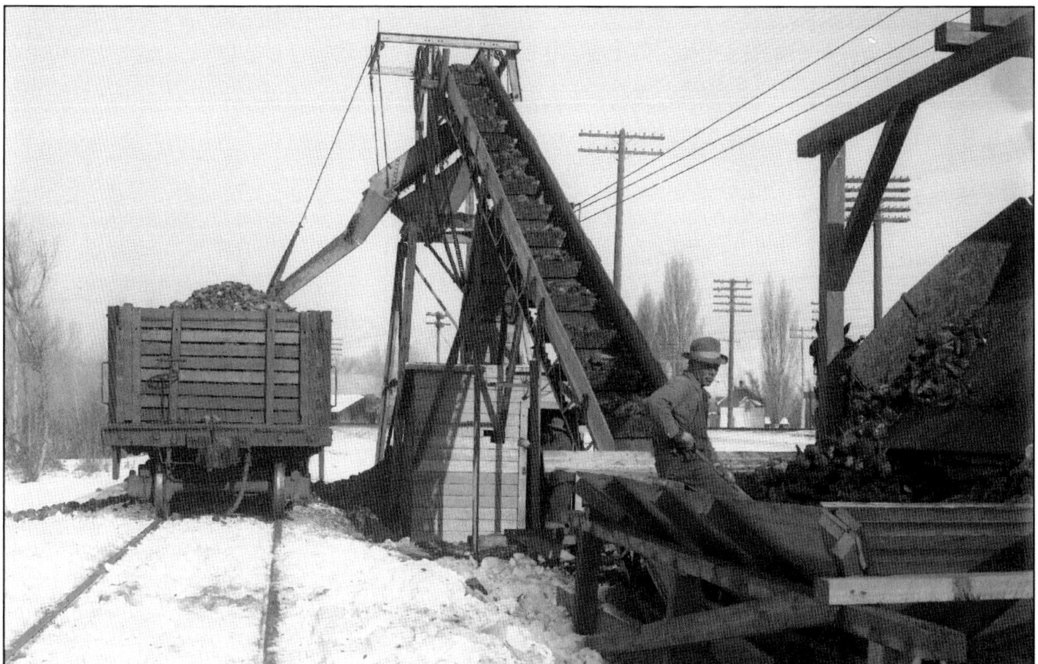

RIVERDALE BEET LOADER, 1917. The Riverdale beet loader was a Weller Manufacturing machine used to sort sugar beets. The beets went up the conveyer and dropped into a railroad car. (Used by permission, Utah State Historical Society.)

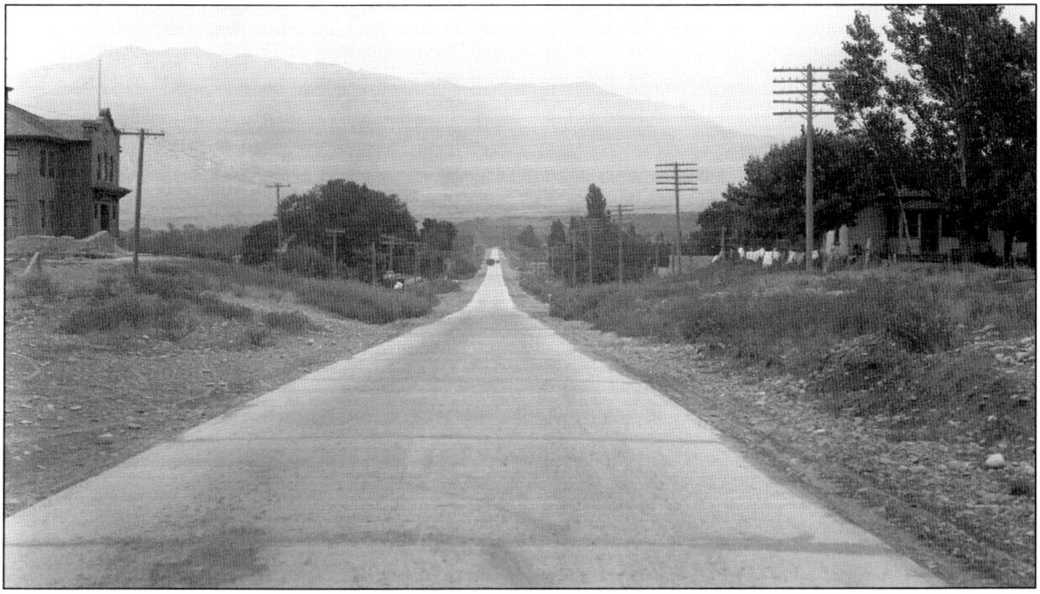

Old Riverdale Road, 1920. An east-looking view of the old Riverdale Road (modern-day 4400 South), this *Deseret News* photograph was titled "Approach to Ogden." Taken in 1920, it shows a narrow, paved road. Riverdale School is on the left, and an early home with laundry hung out to dry is on the right. Remains of the Riverdale Amusement Hall are to the left of the school. Founded by the Riverdale Amusement Company, the building was used for dances and socials from about 1904 until it was razed in 1920. (Used by permission, Utah State Historical Society.)

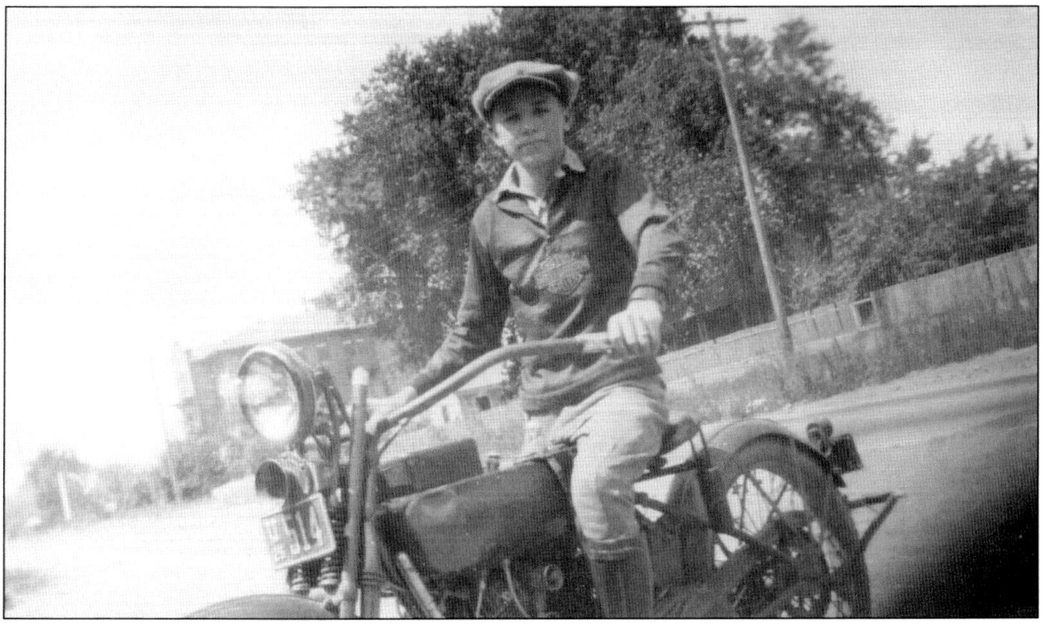

Leland Bingham, c. 1927. Born in Riverdale on March 31, 1909, to Adam Aranthon and Annie Stratton Bingham, Leland Joseph Bingham was elected class president of Riverdale Junior High School and delivered the *Deseret News* throughout town on horseback. By saving his earnings from working at the A&W drive-in, Bingham bought this brand-new Harley Davidson 74 in 1927 for $400. (Courtesy of the Mike and Wilma Bingham family.)

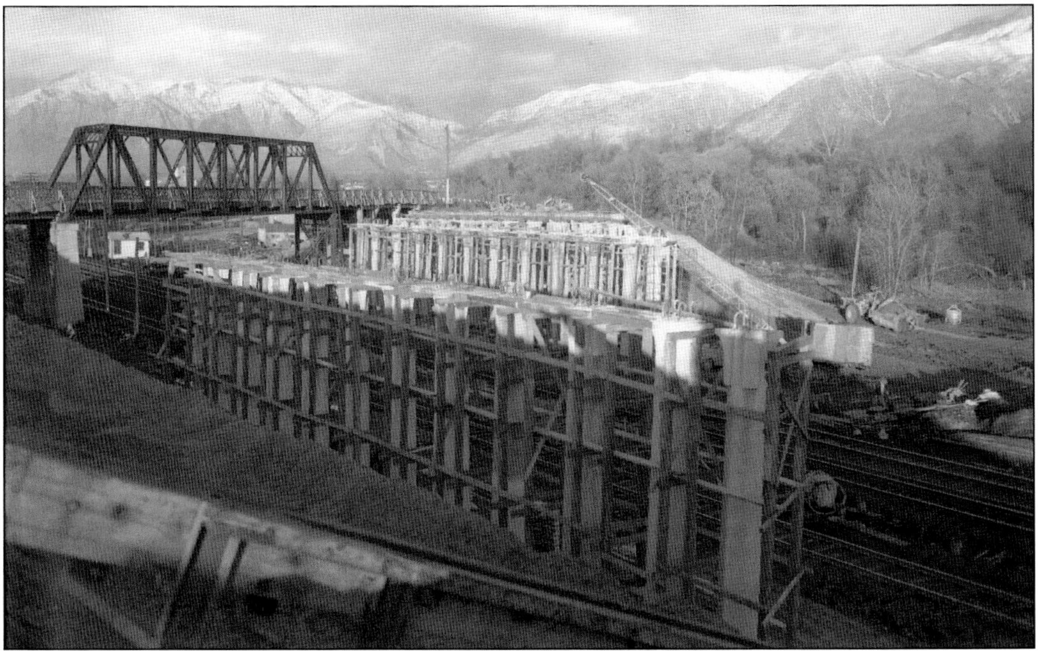

Viaduct Construction, 1946. On November 16, 1946, a headline in the *Ogden Standard-Examiner* read, "New Viaduct Represents Man's Triumph Over Nature." The $500,000, four-lane viaduct had two structures, one to cross the river and the other to cross the railroad tracks. It replaced the old, curved, two-lane bridge. The area had become a dangerous bottleneck with the increase in traffic due to wartime efforts. A portion of the old viaduct is seen above, and the support structure of the new viaduct is in the foreground. The scale of the project is seen below. At far left are completed piers for the Weber River bridge with fill dirt between the two new structures. At center, 4400 South is seen with Riverdale School at the top of the hill along with the many farms that once existed here. (Courtesy of Weber State University Special Collections.)

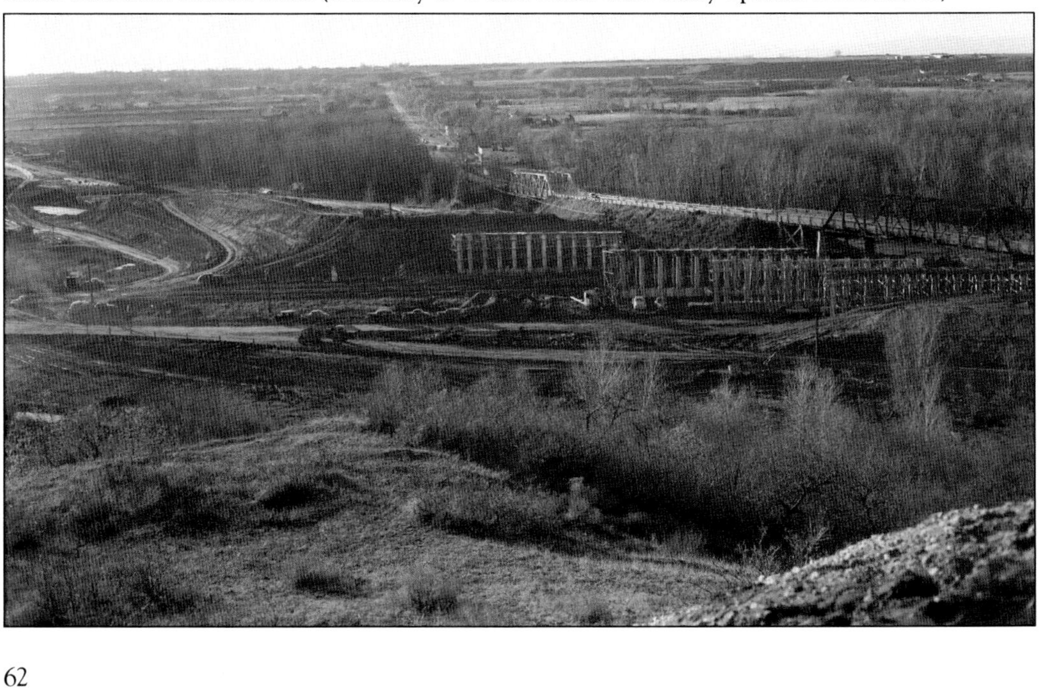

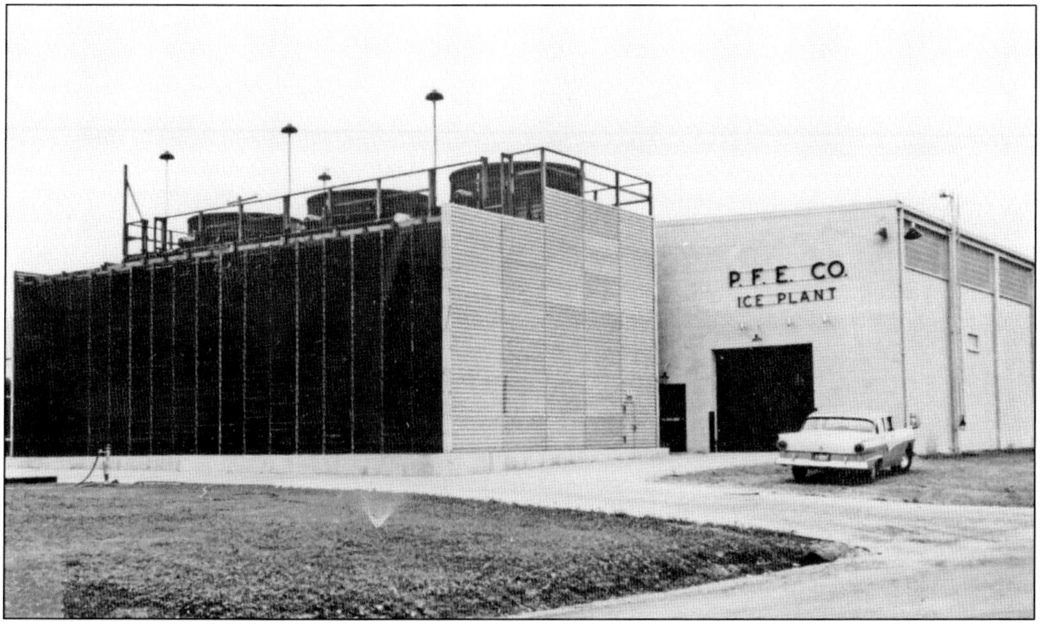

Pacific Fruit Express Company Ice Plant. In the first half of the 20th century, farmers utilized the railroad to ship locally harvested fruit to market. The Pacific Fruit Express Company operated an ice plant in Riverdale. Its machinery placed large ice blocks into the boxcars, which kept the produce cool until the railroad began using refrigerated boxcars in the 1950s and 1960s. (Courtesy of the Ogden Union Station Collection, 01665.)

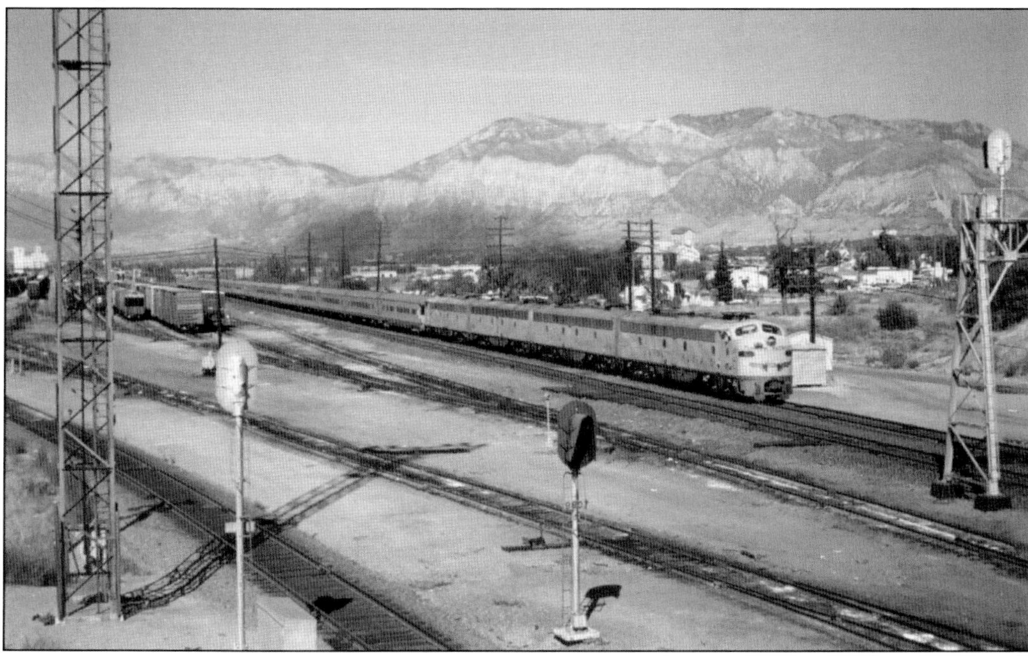

Riverdale Rail Yard. The railroad constructed this rail yard on 305 acres to alleviate congestion in the main rail yard in Ogden. The All-O-Wheat mill is seen near center. To this day, the Riverdale rail yard maintains a steady flow of rail traffic. (Courtesy of the Ogden Union Station Collection, 08837.)

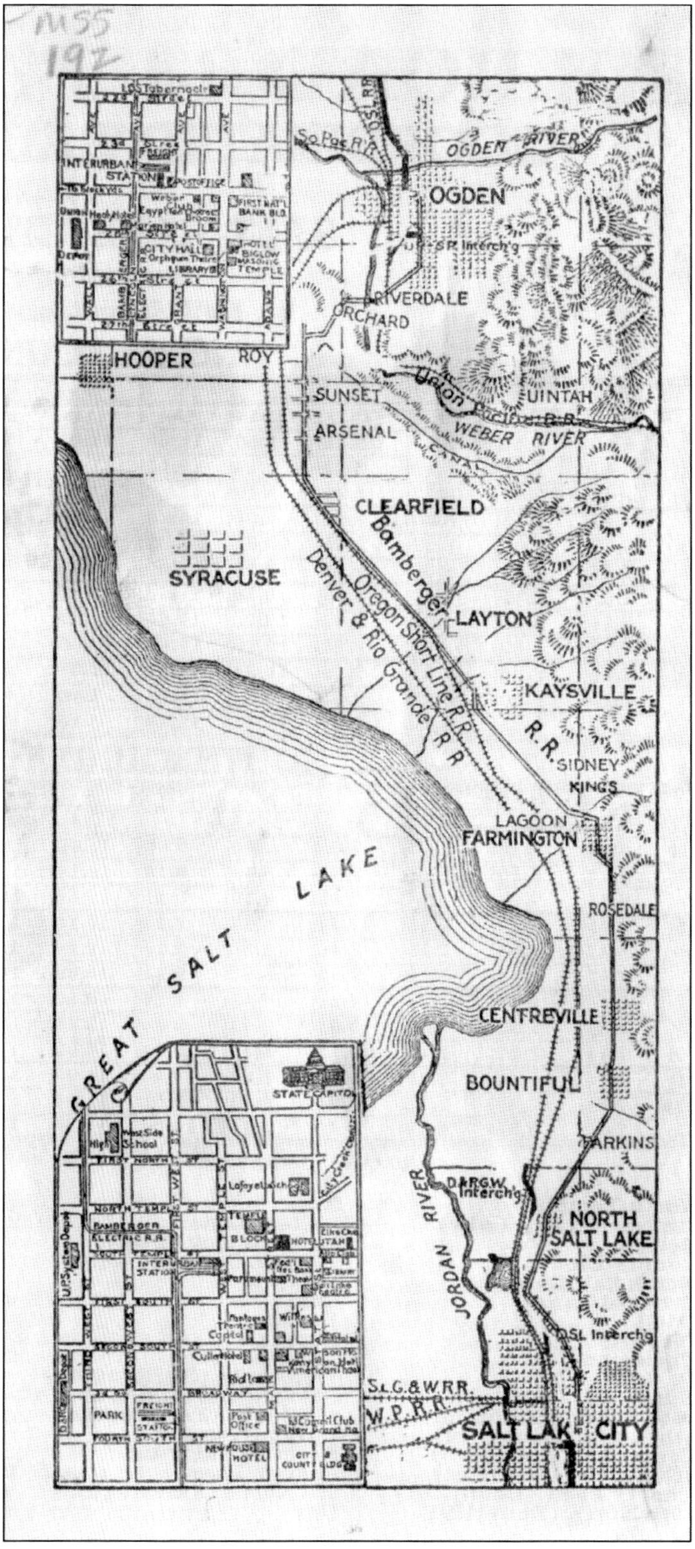

Bamberger Railroad Map, 1950. Many Riverdale residents traveled to Salt Lake City or Ogden on the Bamberger, an interurban railroad. The line served two stops in Riverdale: Orchard, just south of the Ogden Airport, and farther south at Cozy Dale, 100 yards north of the current Roy Eagles building at 5130 South 1700 West. Born in Germany in 1845, the owner Simon Bamberger also opened Lagoon and served as the fourth governor of Utah. (Courtesy of Weber State University Special Collections.)

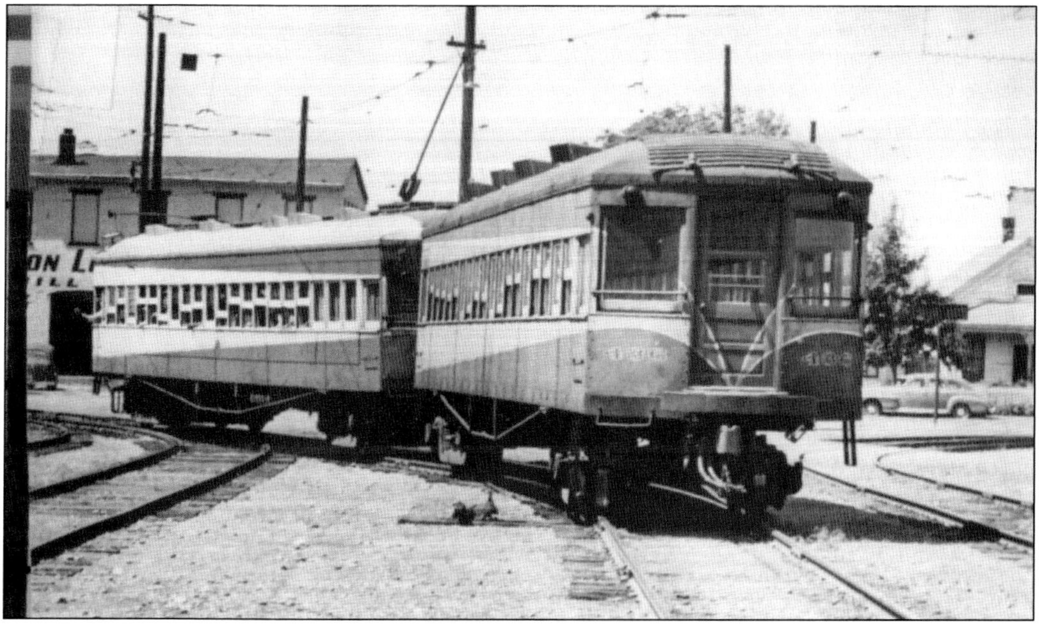

Bamberger Railcar. This Bamberger railcar is leaving the Ogden depot on Lincoln Avenue, heading south to Riverdale. In 1950, a one-way ticket from Ogden to Farmington cost 56¢, and 95¢ to Salt Lake City. Remnants of the Bamberger rail line still exist today. (Courtesy of the Ogden Union Station Collection, 00154.)

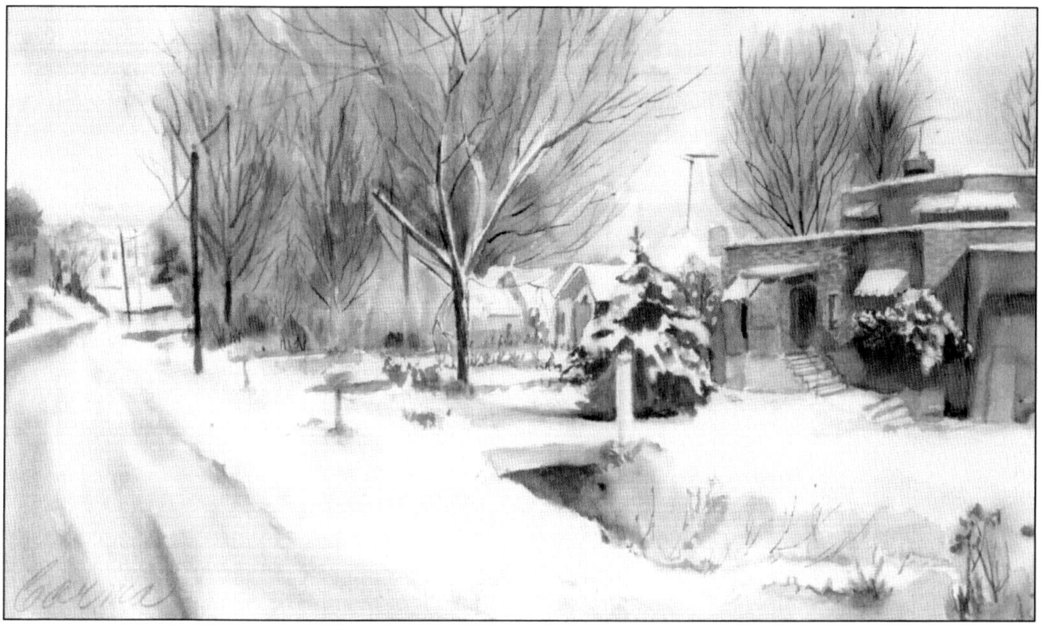

Kid Lane. South of Riverdale Elementary School is 1150 West, which once had so many children living on it and playing there that the residents affectionately called it "Kid Lane." This 1963 painting by Carma Hull Hendryx shows the Hull family home, built in 1943. Hendryx captured the agricultural landscape showing a canal ditch—a typical element on the Utah landscape—in front of the home at 4560 South 1150 West. Kid Lane is on the left, with the old Riverdale School in the background. (Courtesy of the Hull family.)

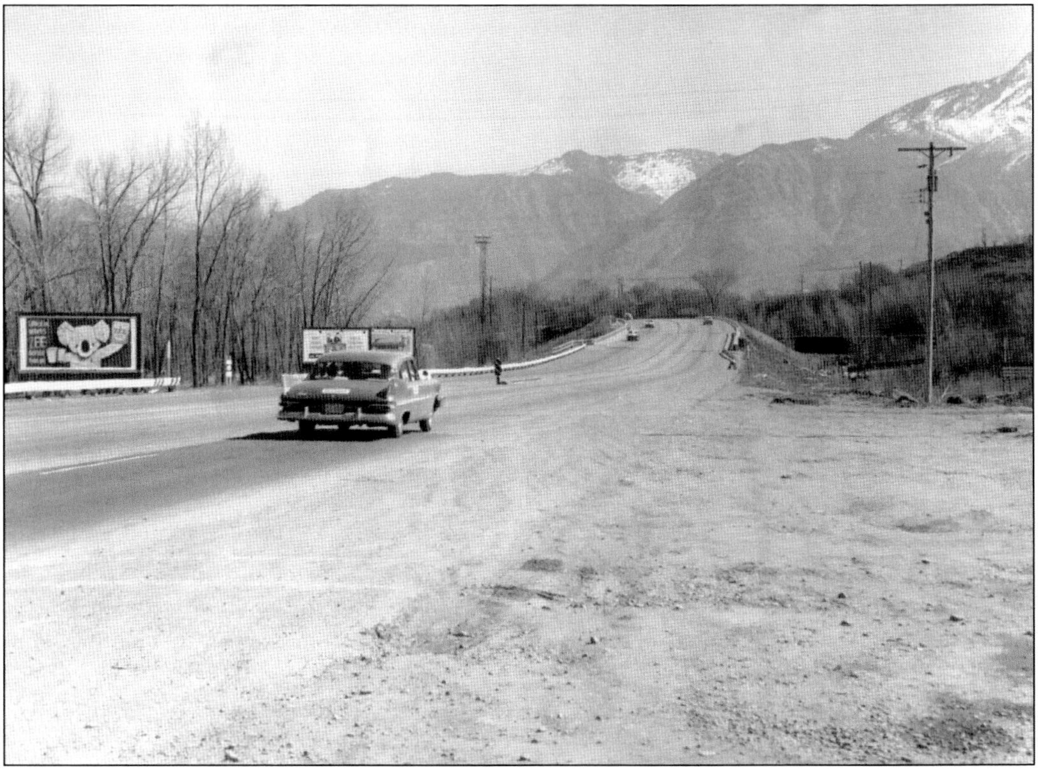

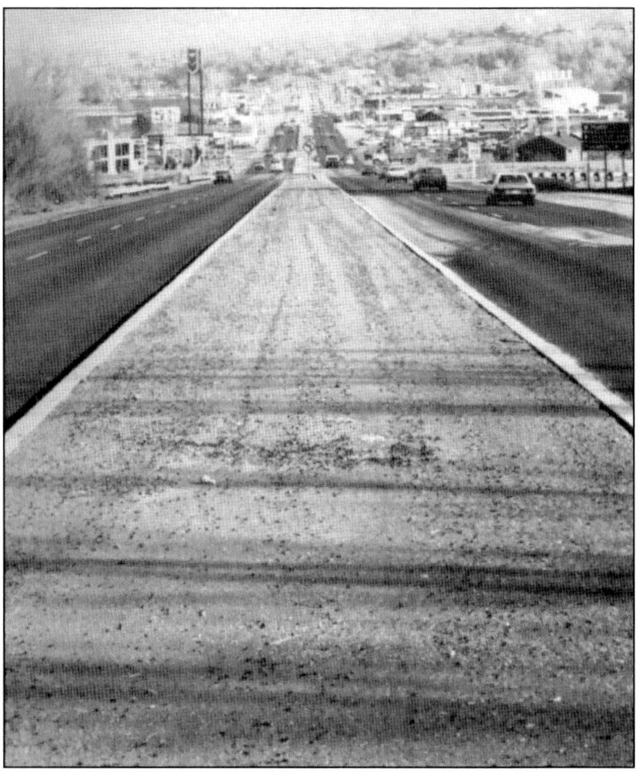

RIVERDALE ROAD VIADUCT, C. 1959. On its east side, Riverdale Road crosses the Weber River and the rail yard. In the early years of the settlement, several bridges were built to cross the river. Used for nearly 50 years, this viaduct had as many as 35,000 vehicles crossing it daily by 1996. Due to its age, the state constructed a new, wider viaduct in the late 1990s. (Courtesy of Riverdale City.)

RIVERDALE ROAD, 1977. This view looking east shows how Riverdale Road appeared in the 1970s. Businesses started filling in on both sides of the road, once divided by a median. (Courtesy of Riverdale City.)

Six

Civics

From Farm Town to Prosperous City

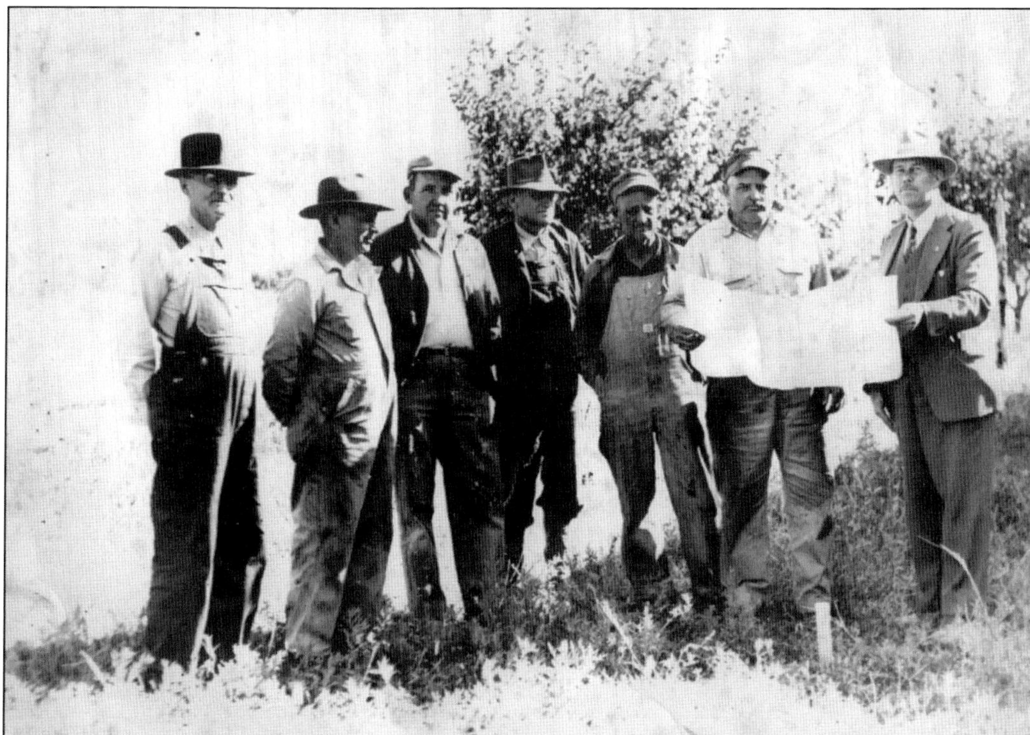

Riverdale Town Board, 1946. Riverdale was incorporated as a town on March 4, 1946. This photograph shows members of the first Riverdale Town Board on Ralph Ritter's property. The first central water system well for the town was located here. The well's site, indicated by the stake in the ground, was determined by Alma Ellis, who located the water by means of water divining. Ellis held a forked peach twig in his hands, and the actions of the branch indicated the location of a good water supply. From left to right are Luther K. Bailey, J. Edward Child, Frank Warner Jr., Alma L. Ellis, Ralph Ritter (treasurer), Alexander Carlsen (town president), and an unidentified engineer/contractor. (Courtesy of Riverdale City.)

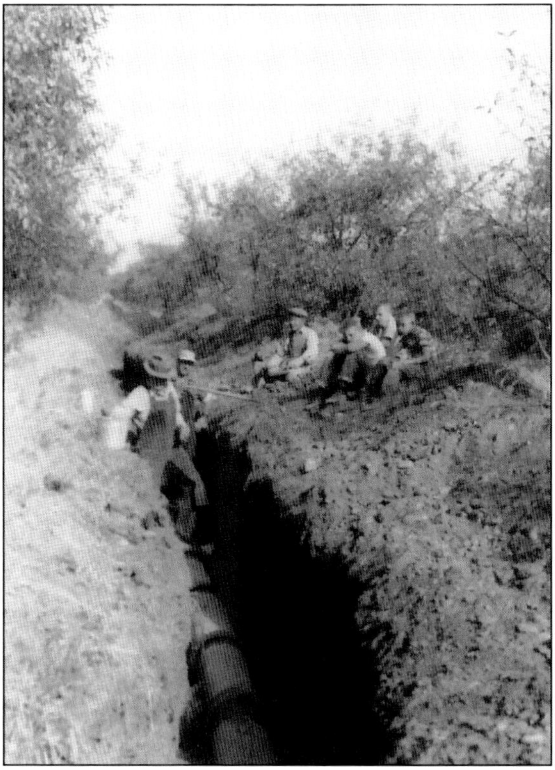

Digging Irrigation Lines. In 1945, Riverdale residents held a meeting in the Riverdale Ward meetinghouse. Those in attendance elected Mondell Bennett (president), Luther K. Bailey, Alma L. Ellis, Alexander Carlsen, and J. Edward Child as members of a temporary town board, with Chauncey W. Burton as treasurer and Helen L. Adams as town clerk. Water is essential to any community. According to town minutes, if they pursued incorporation, "the procurement of suitable culinary water and [the] establishment of a satisfactory sewage disposal system were of equal primary importance and would both receive first attention." These photographs show Alma Ellis digging irrigation water lines. At left, standing on the pipes are Alma Ellis (front) and his son Don Ellis. Below are, from left to right, unidentified, Don Ellis, Alma Ellis, and unidentified. (Courtesy of the Don and Ardis Ellis family.)

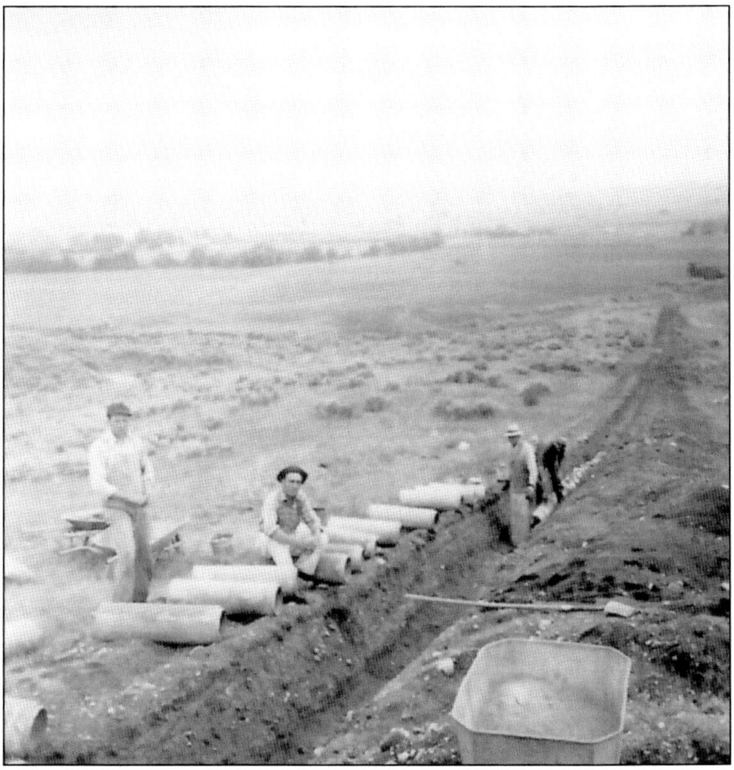

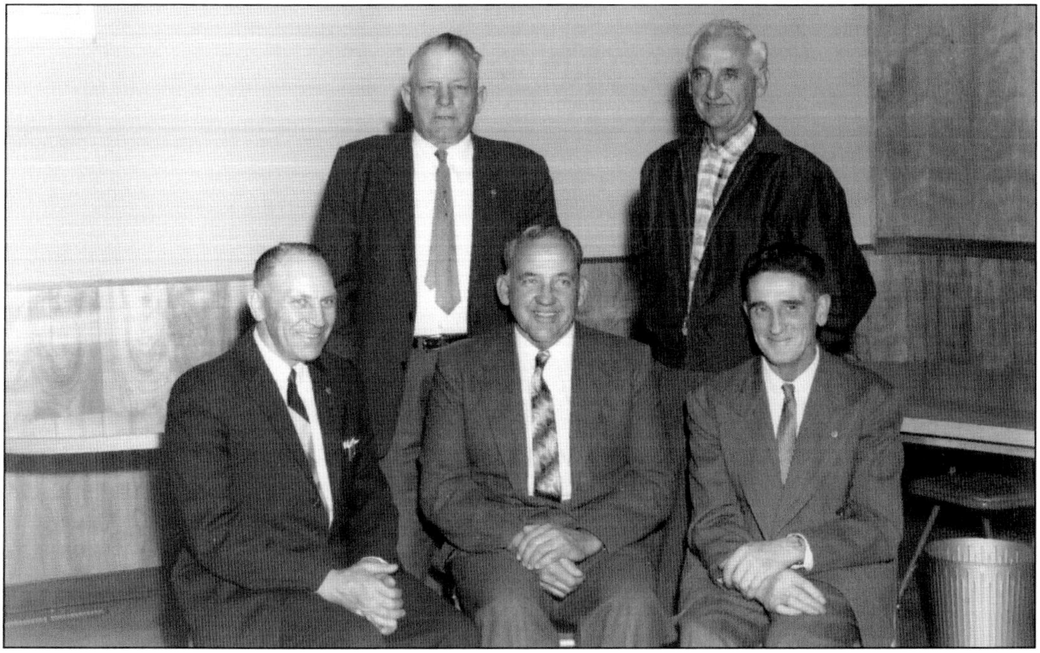

SECOND TOWN BOARD. This photograph shows members of the second Riverdale Town Board. From left to right are (first row) Herman Fiet (board member), Frank Warner (president), and Elmer Call (board member); (second row) Alexander Carlsen (board member) and Jim Warner (water system). George Deem was not present. (Courtesy of the Lucille Child Judkins family.)

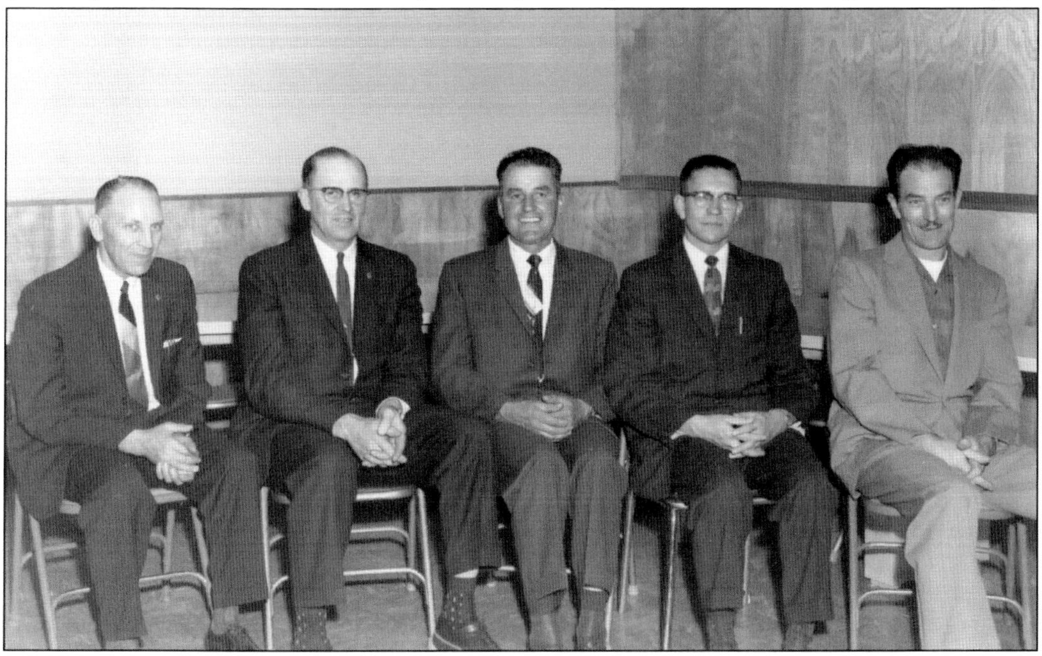

THIRD TOWN BOARD. From left to right are Herman Fiet (board member), Ted Anderson (president), Delbert Stimpson (board member), Wallace Knight (board member), and Lyle Farrer (board member). On March 22, 2006, Mayor Bruce Burrows honored Knight in a resolution for his years of service and dedication to the city of Riverdale. (Courtesy of the Lucille Child Judkins family.)

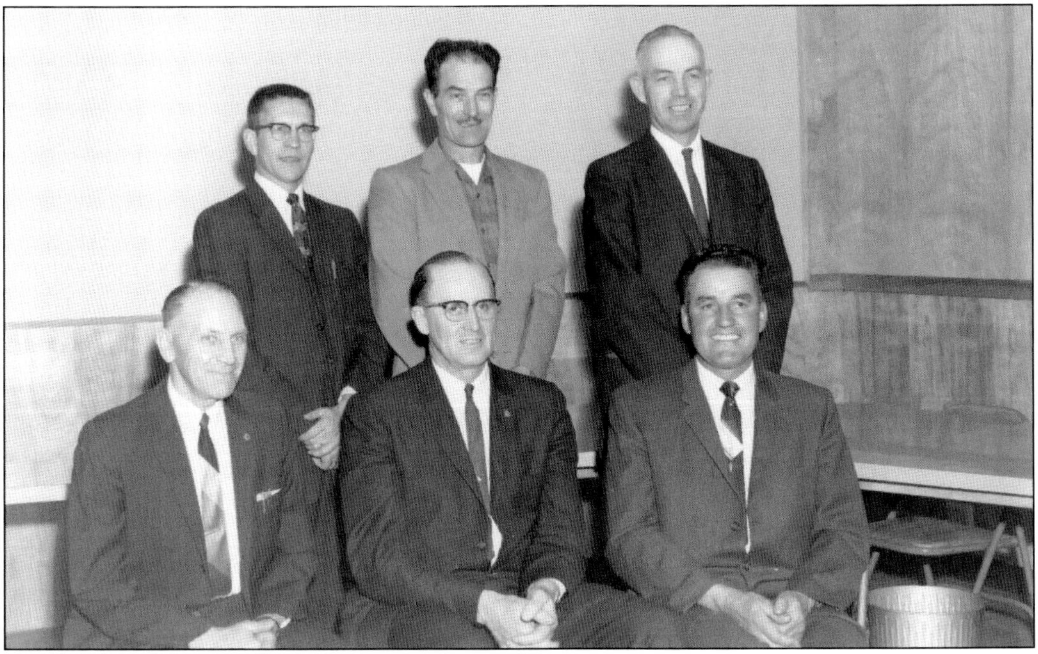

First Mayor and City Council, 1956. Riverdale became a third-class city on July 9, 1956. From left to right are (first row) Herman Fiet (city councilman), Ted Anderson (mayor), and Delbert Thompson (city councilman); (second row) Wallace Knight (city councilman), Lyle Farrer (city councilman), and E. Grant Gibby (city councilman). Anderson served as mayor from 1956 to 1966. Other mayors have included Gail Sanders (1966–1974), Keith Oram (1974–1978), Leon Poulsen (1978–1994), Ben Jones (1994–2001), Howard Coleman (2001–2002), Bruce Burrows (2002–2014), and Norm Searle (2014 to present). (Courtesy of the Lucille Child Judkins family.)

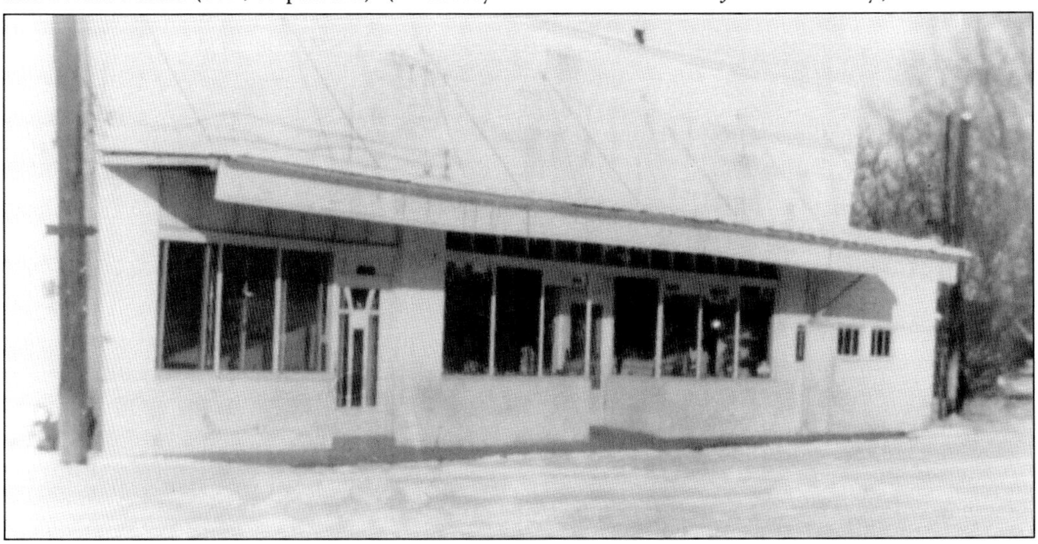

Riverdale City Office in W.J. Greaser Store. Civic leaders held town meetings in people's homes until Frank Warner asked Walter and Ruth Greaser for permission to use a room in their W.J. Greaser store. The Greasers agreed and emptied the hardware section of their store. The front-left corner of the store became the first city office until the city constructed a civic center. (Courtesy of the Lucille Child Judkins family.)

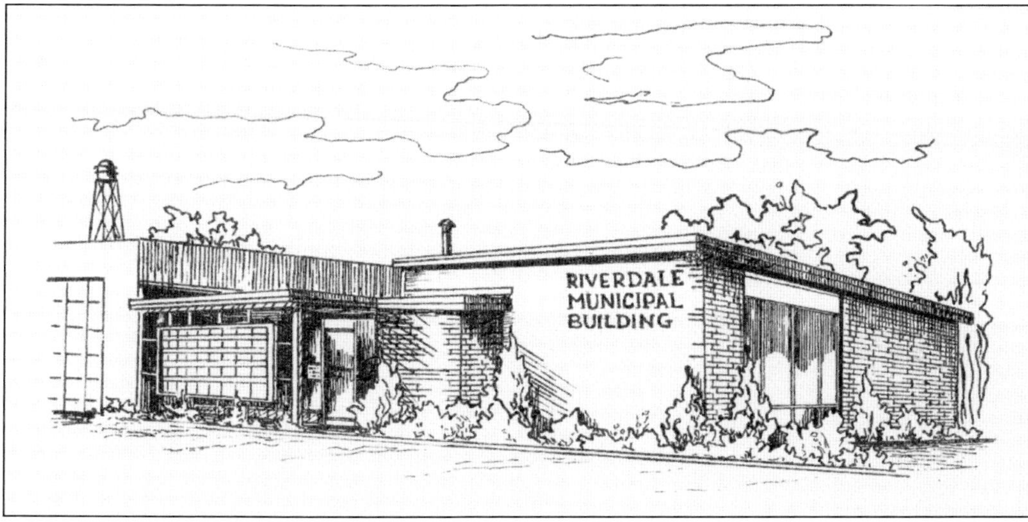

RIVERDALE MUNICIPAL BUILDING. Built in 1959, the first civic center was located at 4459 South 700 West. It housed a city council room, business office, police and justice of the peace offices, a vault, a garage for two firetrucks, and a locker room. In 1985, the city offices moved to a new civic center at 4600 South Weber River Drive. (Courtesy of the Riverdale Lions Club.)

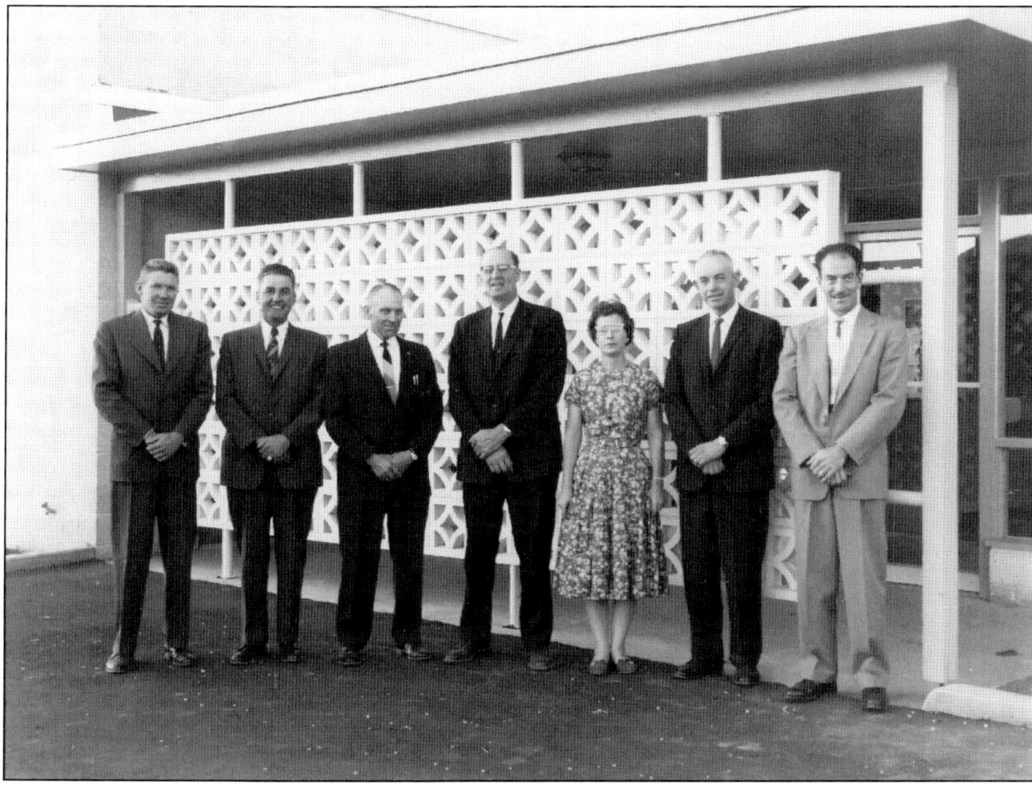

RIVERDALE CITY GOVERNMENT. City officials are seen standing on the east side of the Riverdale Municipal Building. From left to right are Norris Bingham, Delbert Stimpson, Herman Fiet, Ted Anderson (mayor), Martha Davis (clerk), E. Grant Gibby, and Lyle Farrer. (Courtesy of the Lucille Child Judkins family.)

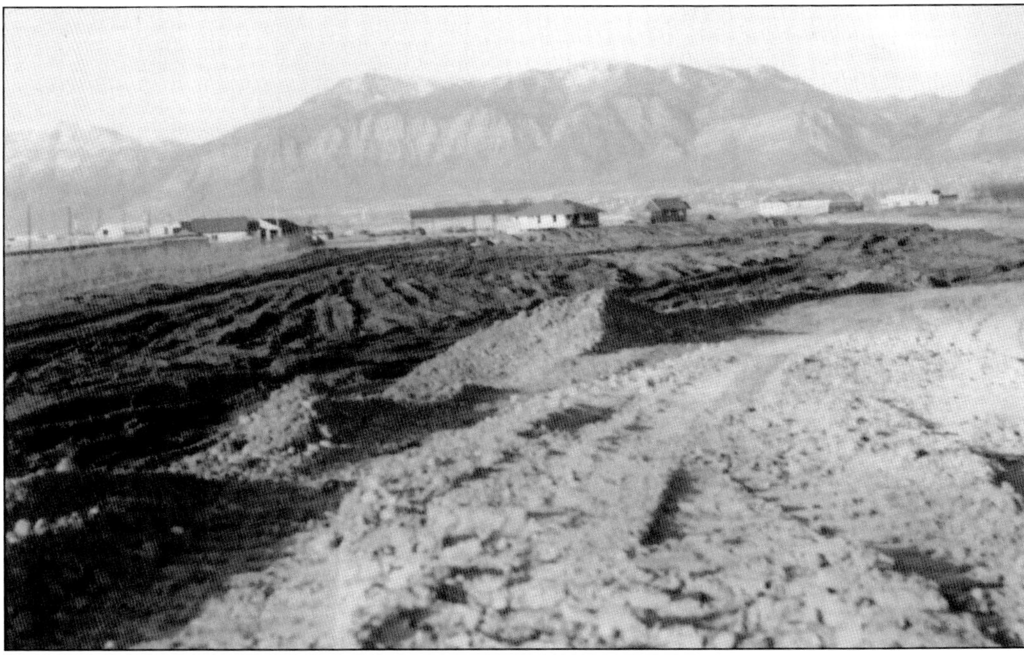

Interstate 15 Construction, 1963. This photograph was taken on the west bench, near the border of Riverdale and Roy. It shows the area before Interstate 15 was built. Prior to this, the land was pristine and filled with cottonwood trees and sego lilies. (Courtesy of Brent Ellis.)

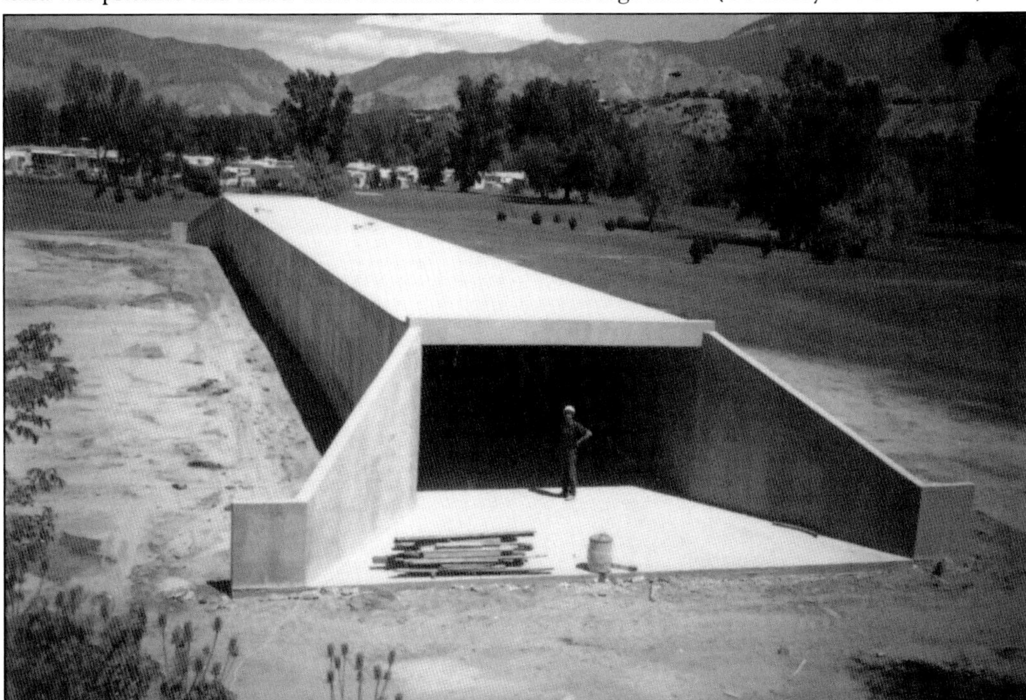

Interstate 84 Construction, 1972. Taken on June 20, 1972, at Schneiter's Riverside Golf Course, this photograph documents the construction of Interstate 84. The freeway bisected the golf course, requiring a tunnel to connect the two sides of the course. (Courtesy of the Schneiter family.)

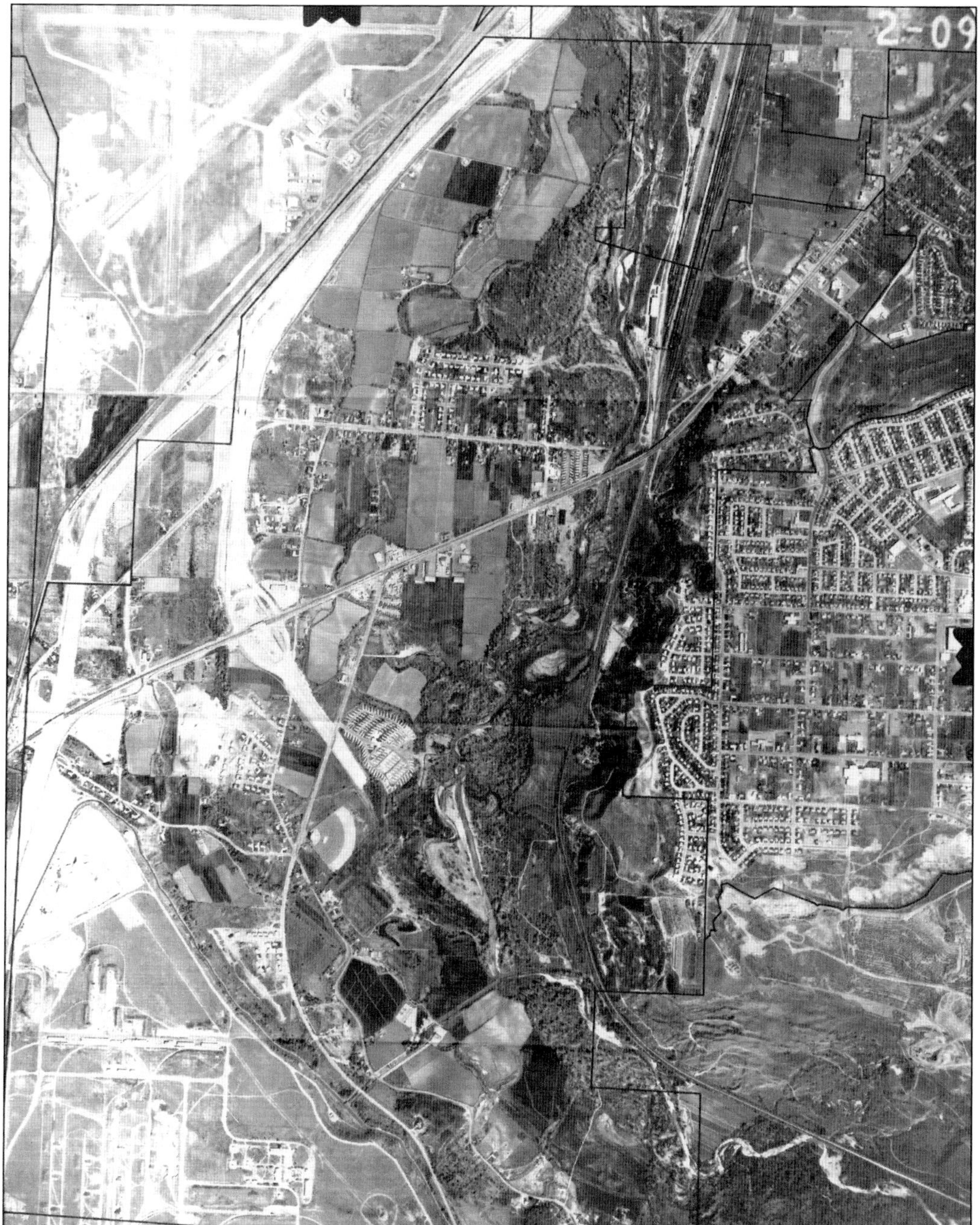

Riverdale City Aerial View, 1966. This aerial photograph was taken on April 30, 1966. It shows the effect that Interstate 15 and Interstate 84 construction had on the topography of the city. It also shows the farmlands, orchards, businesses, and homes that existed at the time. (Courtesy of Riverdale City.)

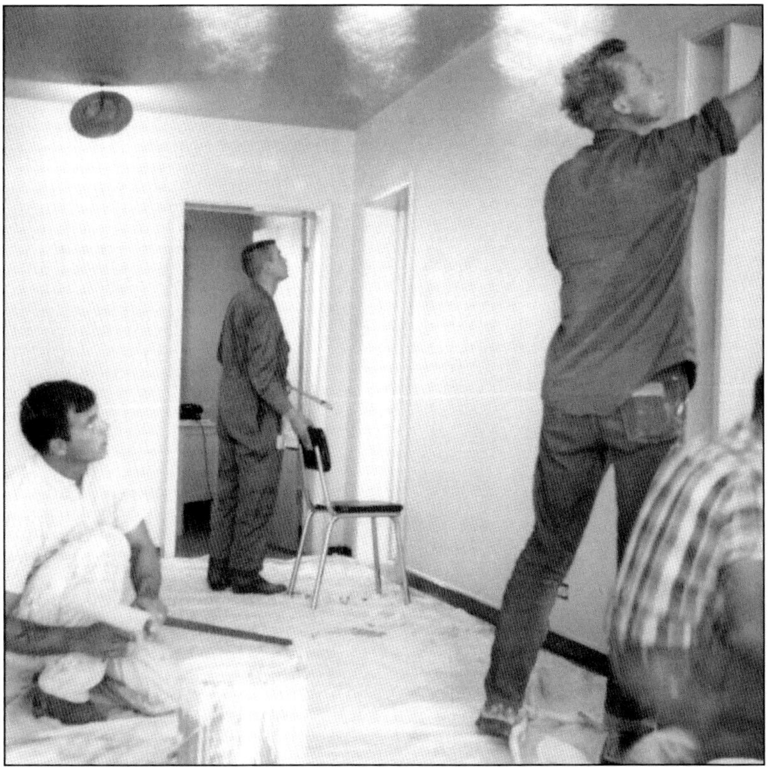

City Hall, 1966. Active in community projects, the Riverdale Jaycees painted city hall so that the city council members would have a nice place to meet. The Jaycees donated the funds they earned from the job to the little league program and to construct bus shelters following the 1966 fire that destroyed the Riverdale School built in 1911. (Courtesy of Norman W. Leishman.)

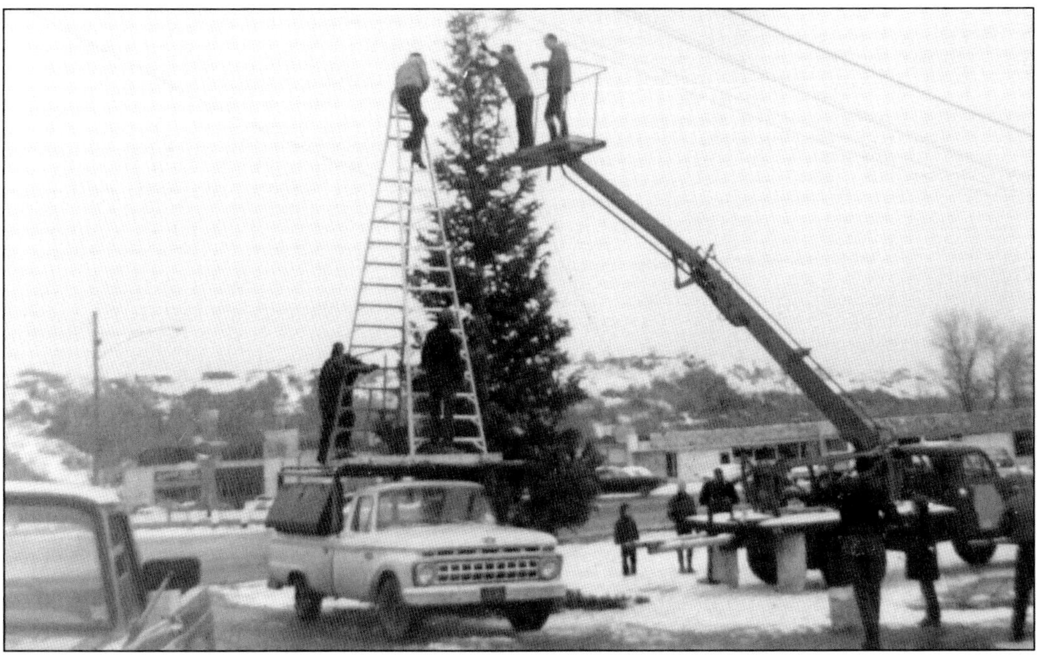

First Community Christmas Tree, 1966. The Riverdale Jaycees cut and hauled this 30-foot spruce tree from the mountains to serve as a community Christmas tree. The Jaycees' wives decorated the tree. A celebration commemorated the tree displayed in front of the municipal building. (Courtesy of Norman W. Leishman.)

Fly Your Flag Week, 1970. In 1970, Mayor Gail Sanders proclaimed May 4–8 as Riverdale City Fly Your Flag Week. The city encouraged businesses and citizens to fly flags to show patriotism and respect for the country. To kick off the week, Boy Scouts raised a flag made by World War II veteran William Otto Coder out of parachute fabric when he was a prisoner of war in Japan. The Jaycees placed the flagpole seen here. It was originally located at the Riverdale School until the devastating fire. (Courtesy of Riverdale City.)

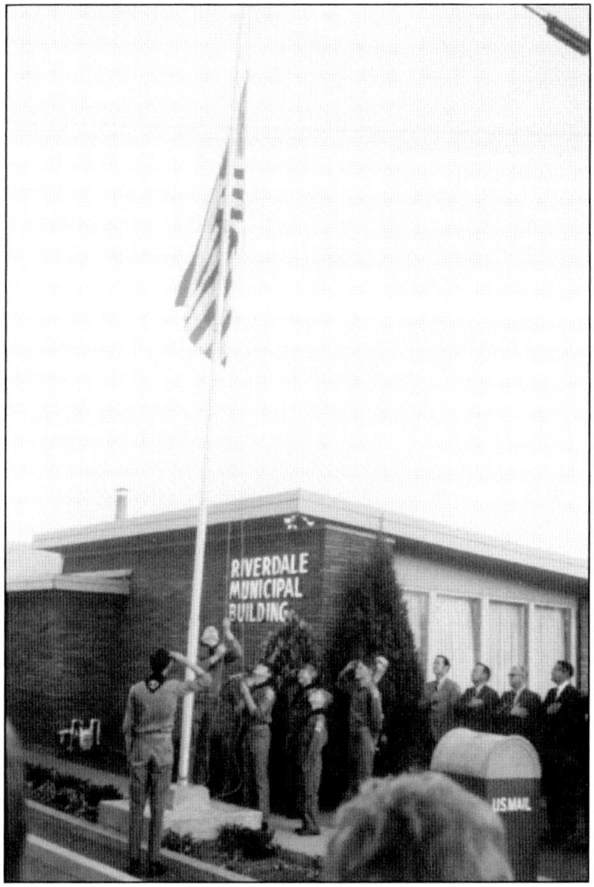

Former Riverdale Fire Station, 1998. After the city offices moved to the new civic center, the fire department continued to use the former offices through the 1990s. This photograph of the Riverdale Municipal Building shows a firetruck on the south side of the building. (Courtesy of Riverdale City.)

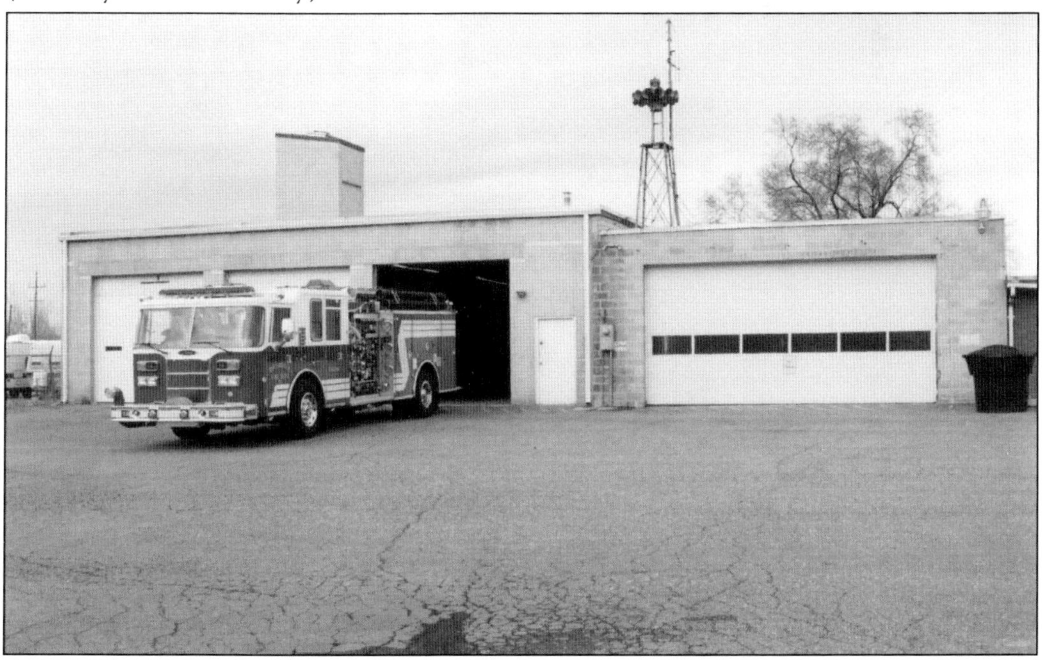

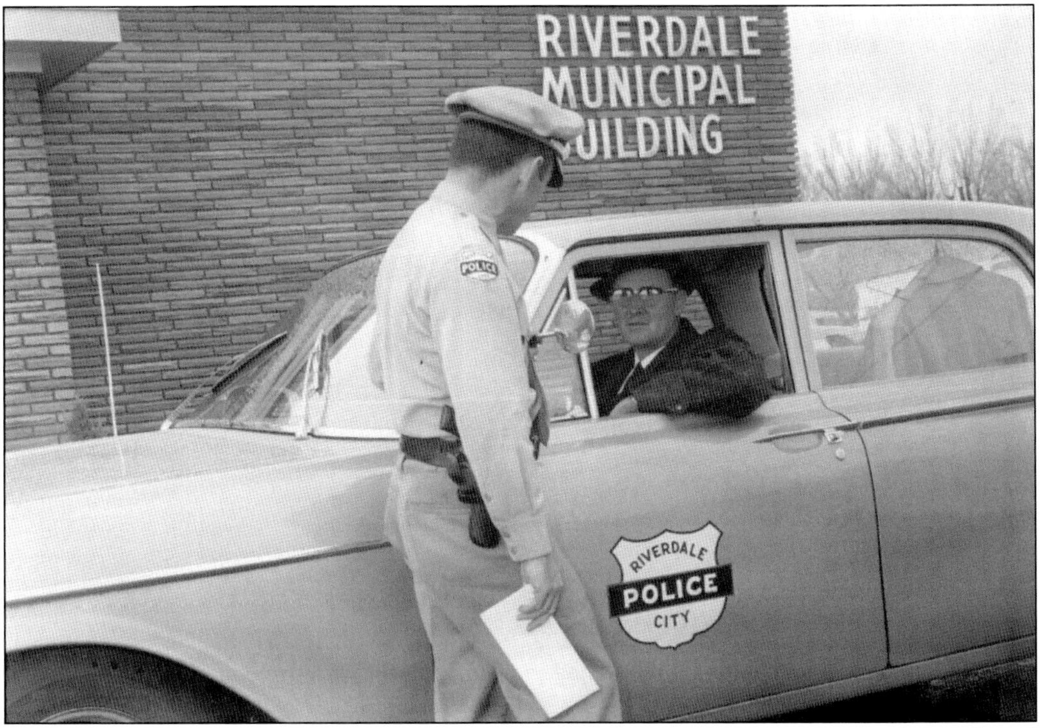

RIVERDALE POLICE PATROL CAR. Mayor Ted Anderson is shown sitting in a newly purchased police car and talking with Wes Woolsey. For years, Woolsey served as Riverdale's sole police officer. (Courtesy of Riverdale City.)

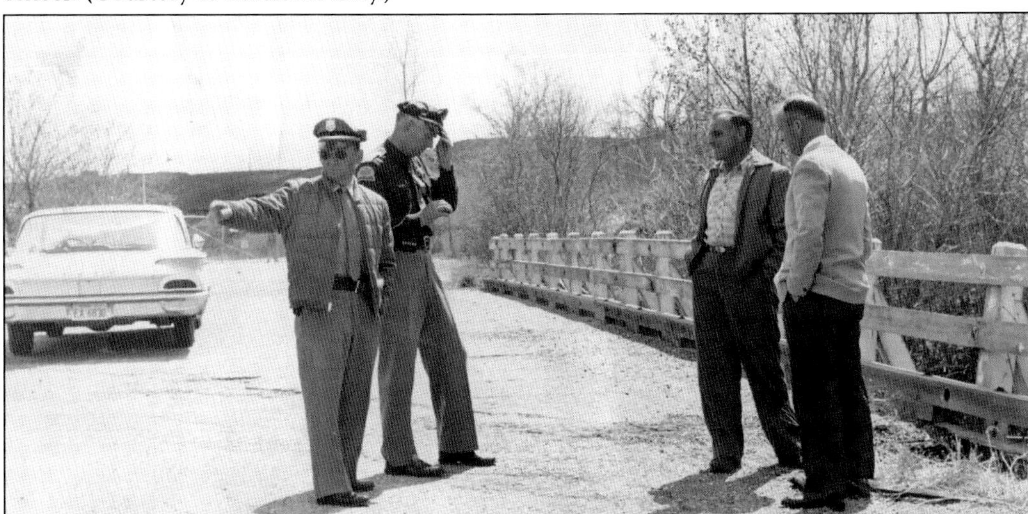

HILL AIR FORCE BASE GATE, 1961. This photograph was taken near the north gate of Hill Air Force Base. From left to right are Wes Woolsey (Riverdale police officer), Sgt. Eldridge Wood (Utah Highway Patrol), Roscoe E. Child (city councilman), and an unidentified state road representative. (Courtesy of Riverdale City.)

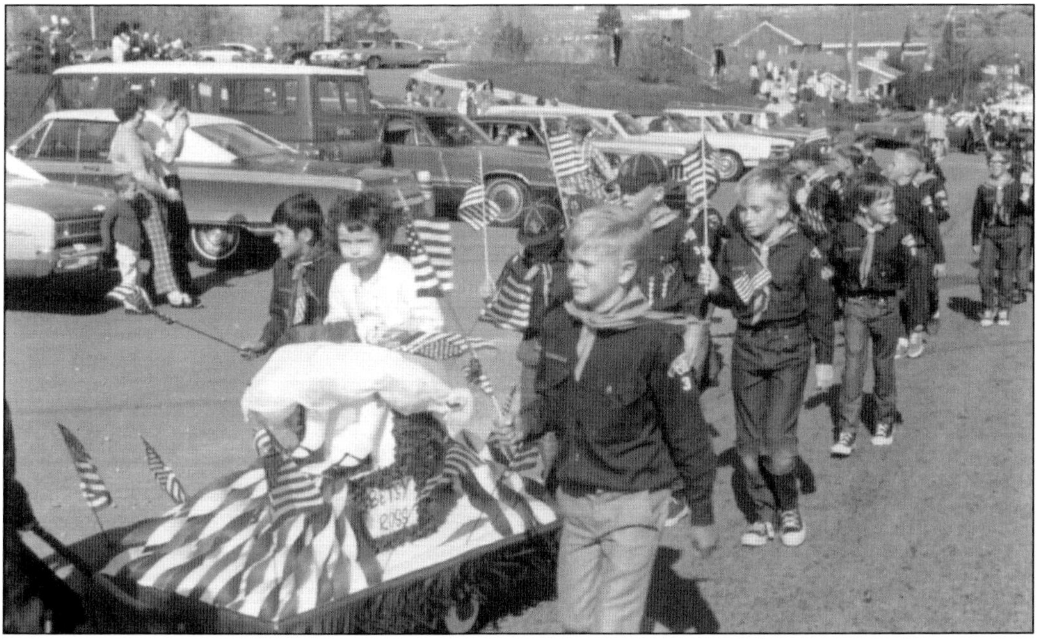

Fly Your Flag Week Parade, 1970. Fly Your Flag Week culminated with a parade on May 8, 1970. Bonneville High School's band, the Lakettes, and Miss Riverdale and her attendants participated. Dignitaries rode in antique cars, and Boy Scouts and children waved flags. The parade started at city hall and finished at Riverdale Park, followed by a short program where Utah governor Calvin L. Rampton gave remarks. (Courtesy of Riverdale City.)

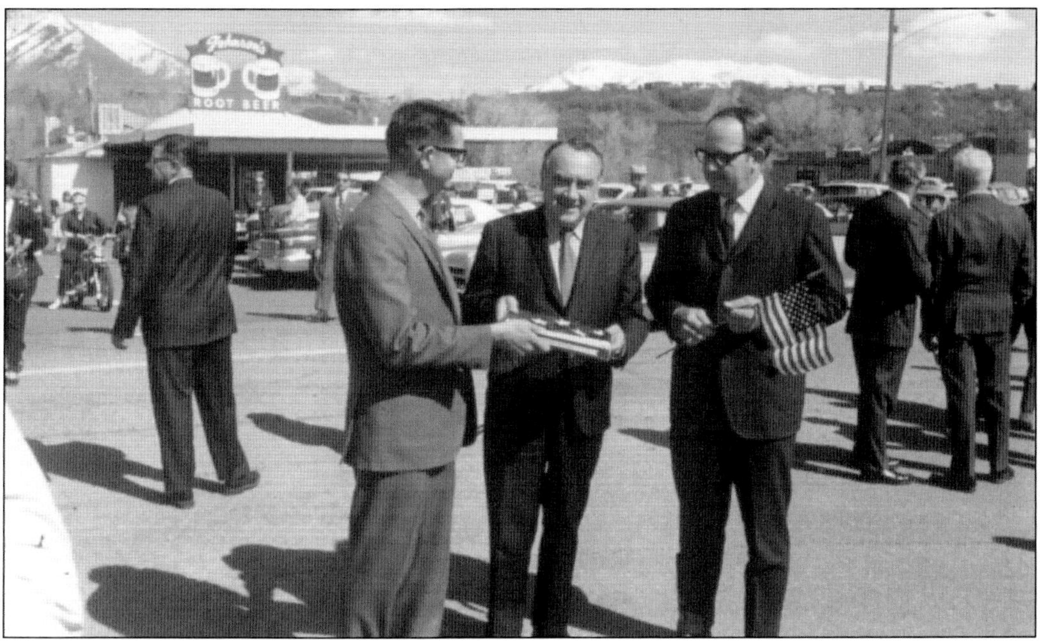

Flag Presentation to Governor Rampton, 1970. Mayor Gail Sanders presented a flag from Riverdale citizens to Gov. Calvin L. Rampton in appreciation for his service and interest in the city. In the background is Johnson's Root Beer stand, now the location of a Sinclair gas station. (Courtesy of Riverdale City.)

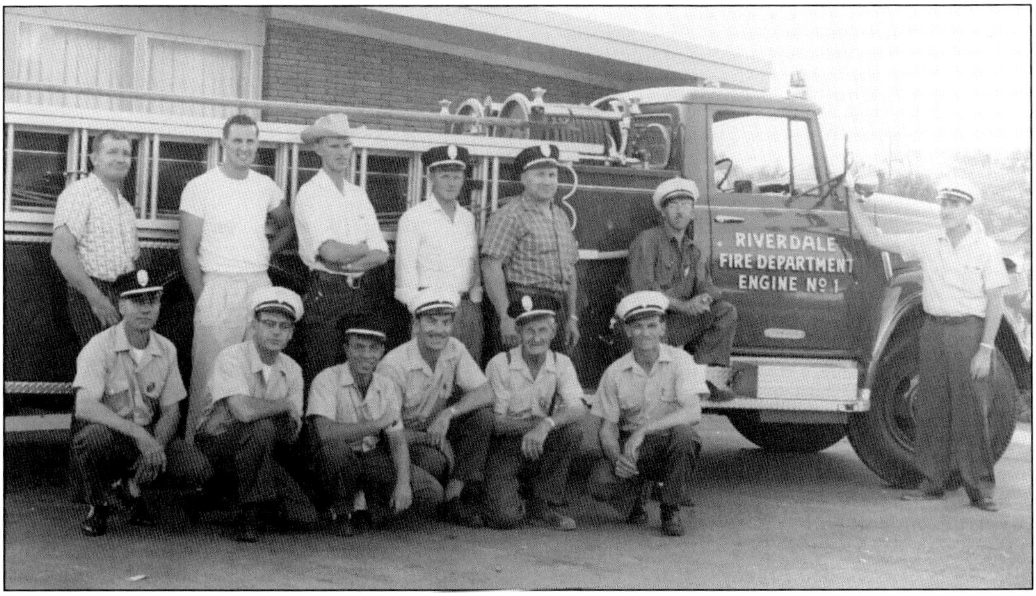

First Volunteer Fire Department, 1961. These men were the charter members of the fire department. From left to right are (first row) Irle Champneys (assistant secretary), Ken Herrick (assistant chief), Roland Child, Lyle Farrer (captain), Robert Swinton, and Parley Burrows (secretary and treasurer); (second row) Dick Carlsen (lieutenant), Leland Manning, Al Solum, David Taylor, Alex Carlsen Jr., Paul Flaig (lieutenant), and Everett Wells (chief). Not pictured are Sam Faddis (fire marshal) and John Martinez. (Courtesy of Riverdale City.)

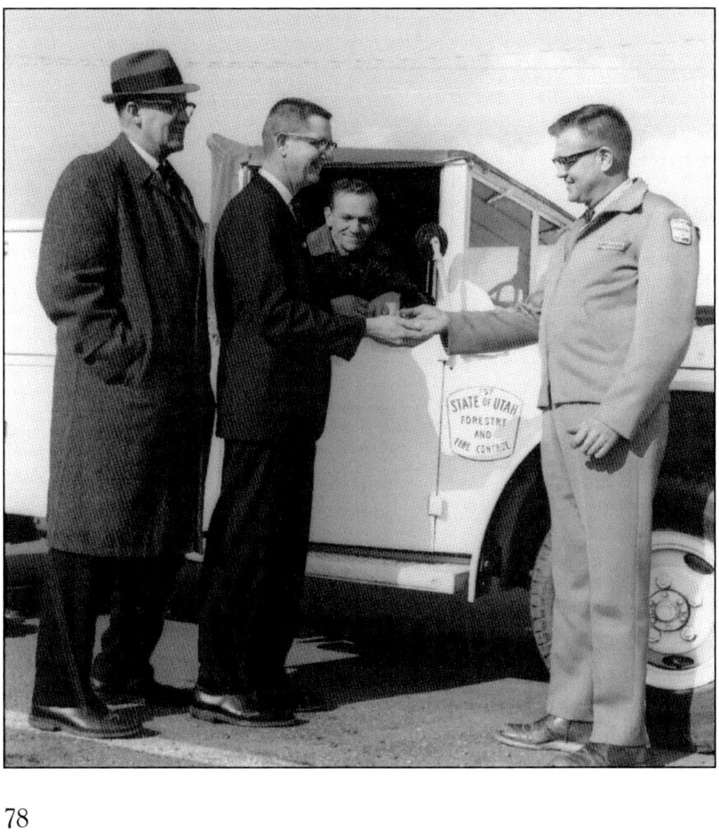

Fire Engine, 1965. Fire chief Parley Burrows (in the truck) watches the exchange of keys to a fire engine acquired from the state Department of Forestry and Fire Control. Also pictured are, from left to right, Mayor Ted Anderson, Gail Sanders, and an unidentified forest service worker. (Courtesy of the Lucille Child Judkins family.)

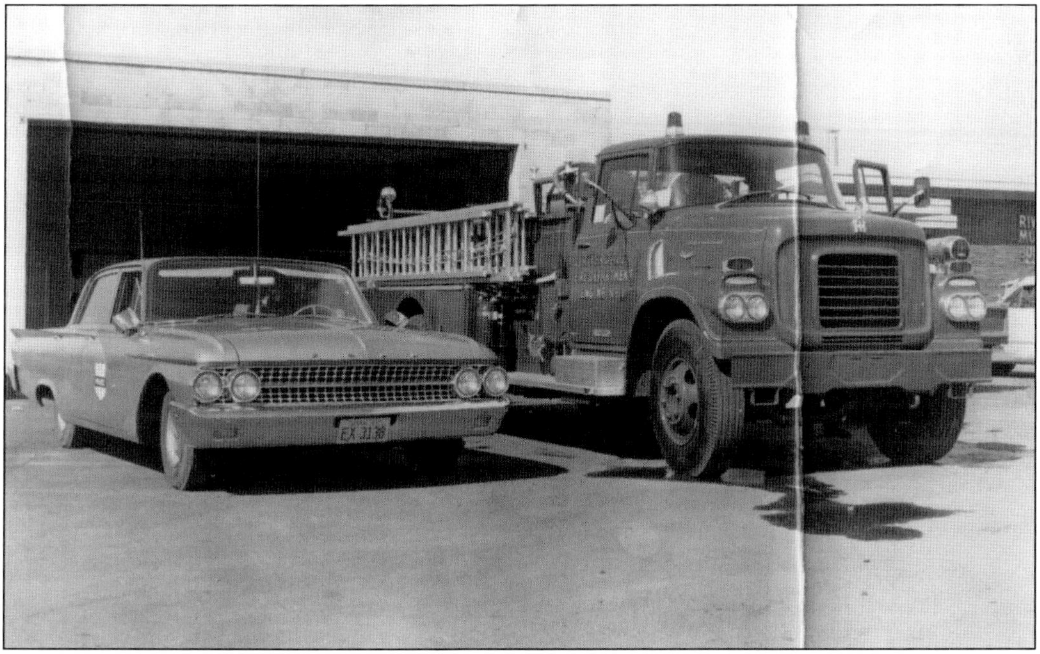

Patrol Car and Fire Engine. A Riverdale patrol car and fire engine No. 1 are parked in front of the Riverdale Municipal Building. It housed the city offices as well as the police and fire department facilities. (Courtesy of Riverdale City.)

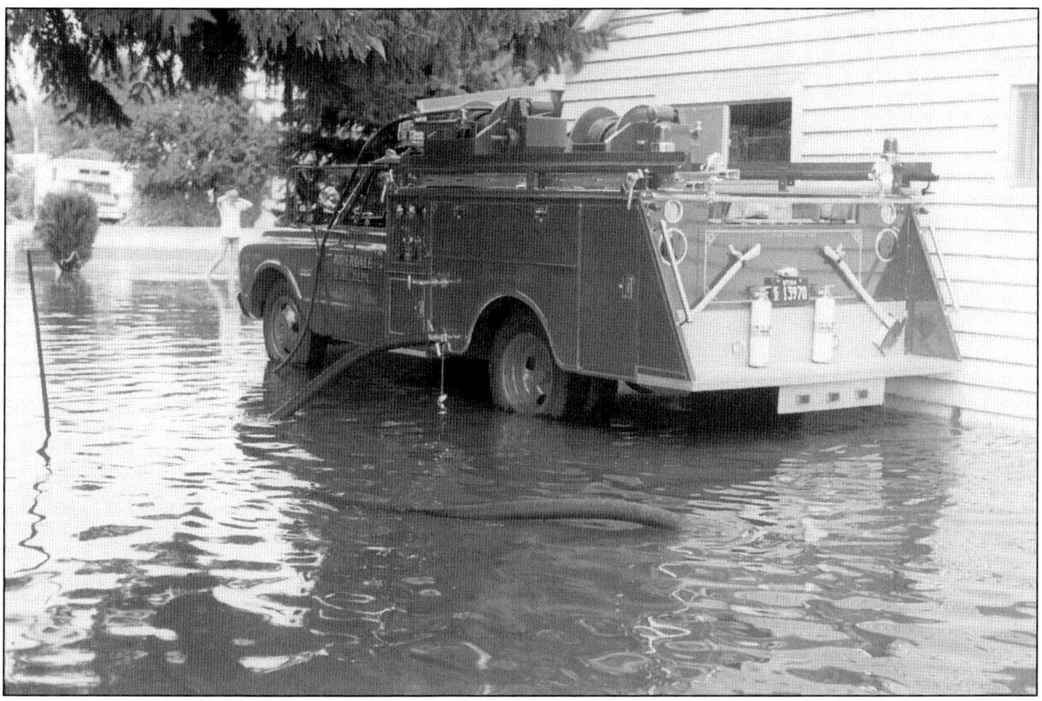

Flooding, Spring 1970. Heavy rains in the spring of 1970 caused flooding in the area. Don and Donna Child's home at 721 West 4400 South is seen here surrounded by floodwaters. The fire department assisted by pumping water from the flooded home. (Courtesy of Lee Child.)

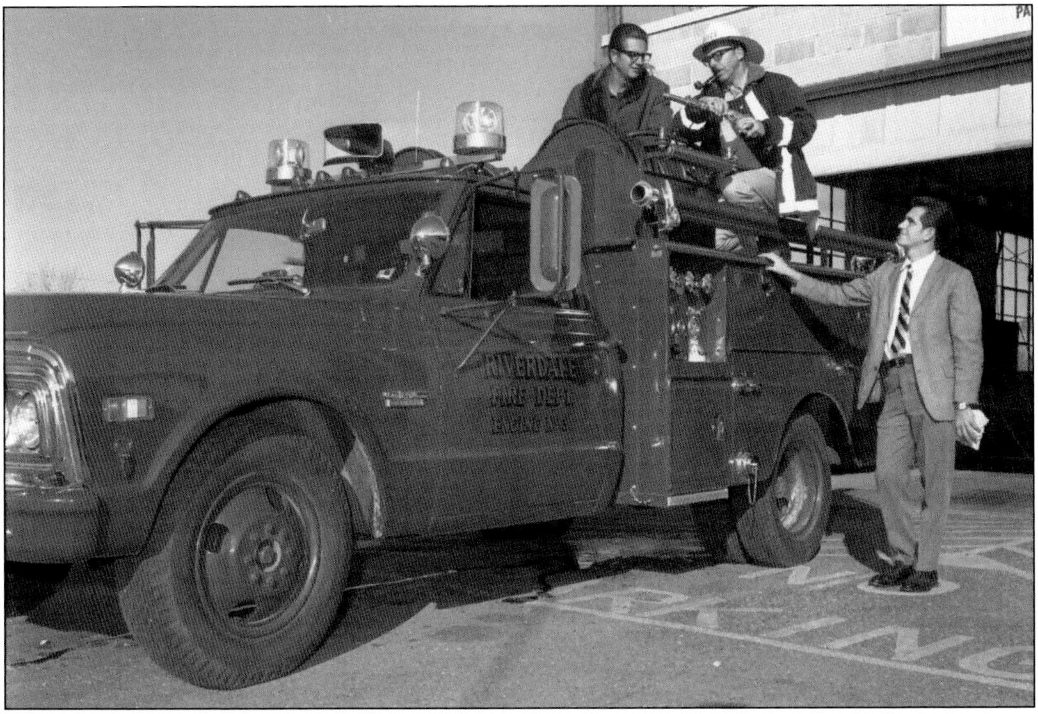

NEW FIRE ENGINE, 1970. Riverdale fire chief Paul L. Flaig (center) demonstrates the equipment on the city's new fire engine to Mayor Gail Sanders (left) and assistant fire chief John D'Agnillo. The truck could reach anywhere in Riverdale in less than five minutes. The 23-man volunteer fire department also utilized a large pumper truck and a four-wheel drive brush truck. (Courtesy of Weber State University Special Collections.)

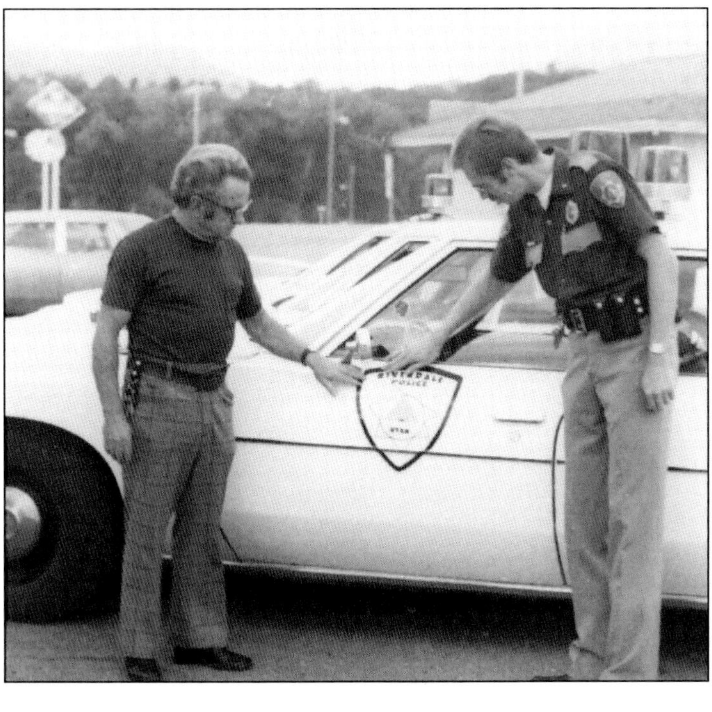

PATROL CAR. Police chief Wes Woolsey and patrolman Bob Vandenburg look over a new emblem that had just been placed on four of the city's patrol cars. For many years, the five-foot, four-inch but big-hearted Woolsey was Riverdale's only police officer. He served the city from 1958 to 1979. In 1991, city council honored Woolsey and his family for his service. (Courtesy of Riverdale City.)

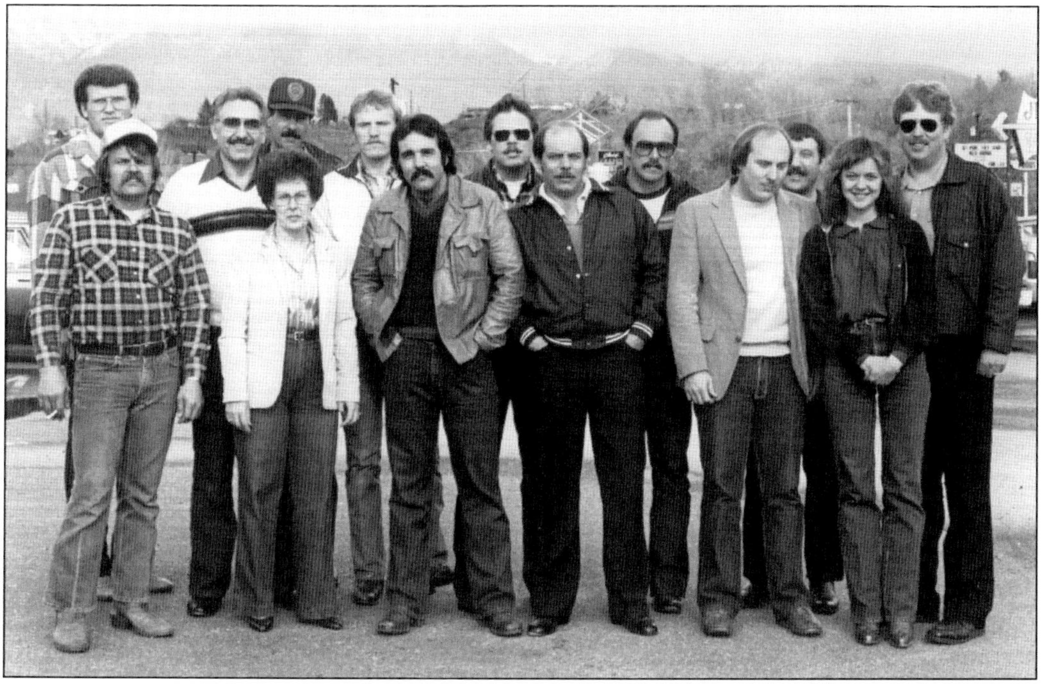

RIVERDALE POLICE DEPARTMENT, C. 1978. This photograph shows the staff of the Riverdale Police Department. From left to right are (first row) Bill Fuchs, Kay Vining (secretary), Pat Donehoo, Rod George, Brian Morgan, and Marianne Ross; (second row) Jim Young (city administrator), Glenn Clary (chief of police), Mike Daily, Skip Smith, Bruce Padelsky, Glen Peterson, Rich Dean, and Rex Cragun. (Courtesy of Riverdale City.)

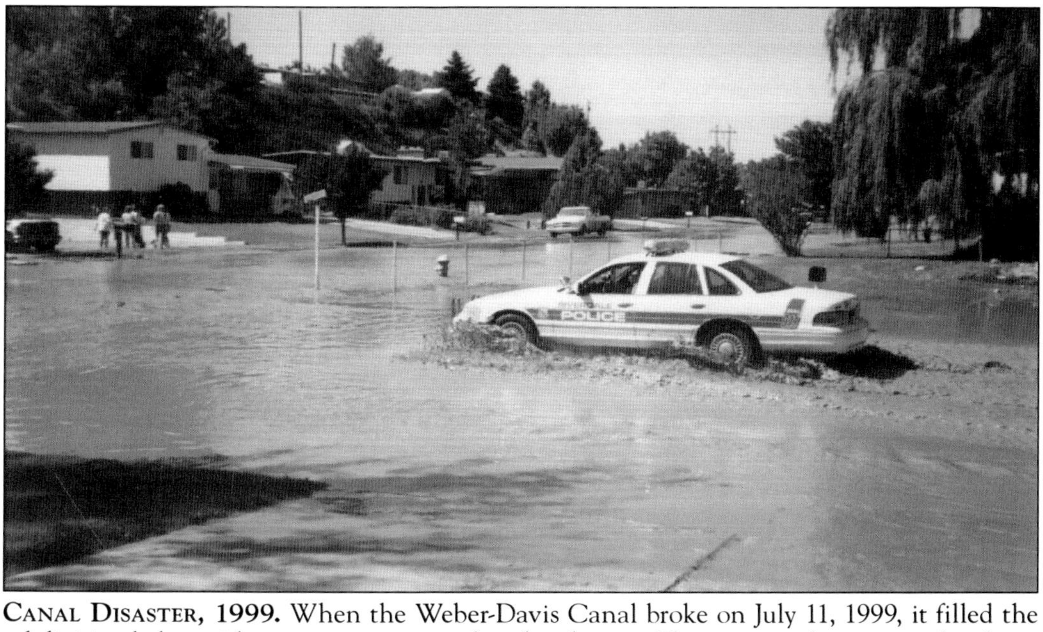

CANAL DISASTER, 1999. When the Weber-Davis Canal broke on July 11, 1999, it filled the subdivision below with a massive amount of mud and water. The water made its way to low-lying neighborhoods and Golden Spike Park. A Riverdale patrol car is seen here driving through floodwater at the corner of 5175 South and 1200 West. (Courtesy of Norman W. Leishman.)

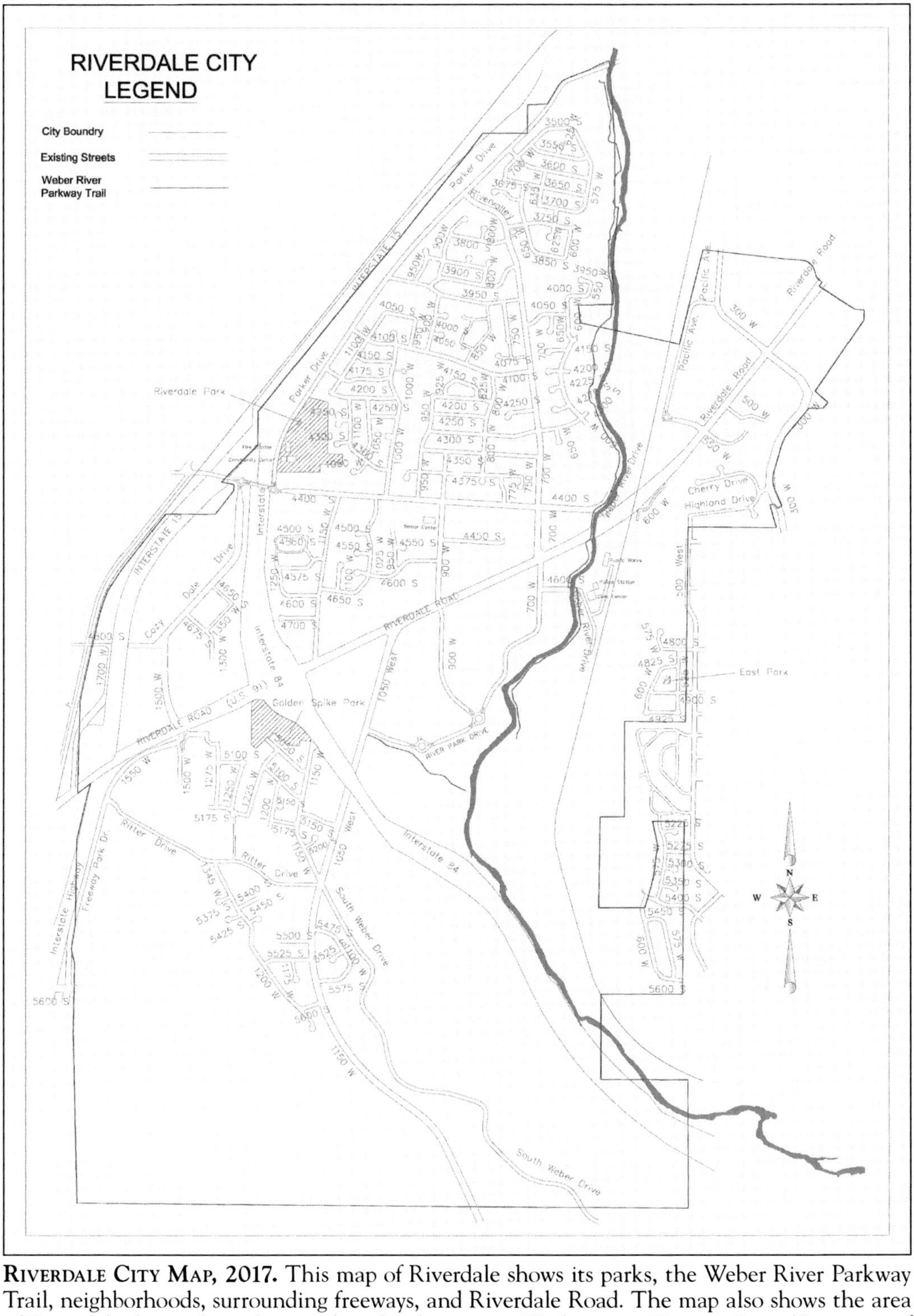

Riverdale City Map, 2017. This map of Riverdale shows its parks, the Weber River Parkway Trail, neighborhoods, surrounding freeways, and Riverdale Road. The map also shows the area of Riverdale, located on the east bench adjacent to Washington Terrace City. (Courtesy of Riverdale City.)

Seven

Businesses

Blacksmiths, Barbershops, and Brine Shrimp

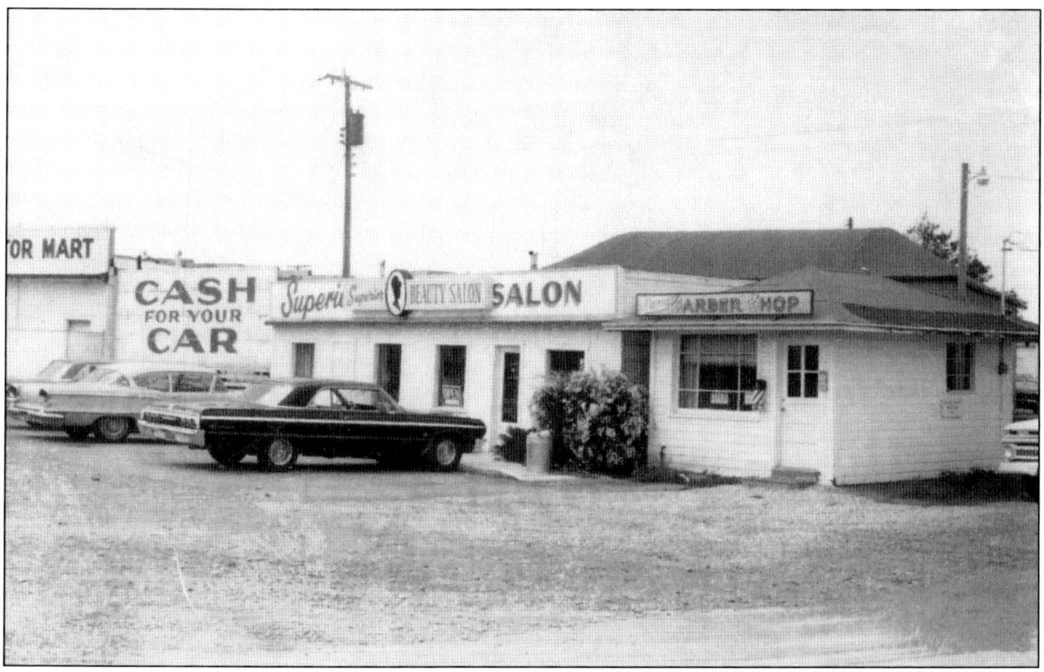

FAMILY BUSINESSES. Longtime residents recall spending time at Alan's Barbershop, owned by Alan C. Judkins. The businesses shown here were located on 700 West near Riverdale Road. Jesse Child owned land in this area, and the Child family operated several businesses, including the Riverdale Service station, Child's Signs, and Child Real Estate. (Courtesy of Weber State University Special Collections.)

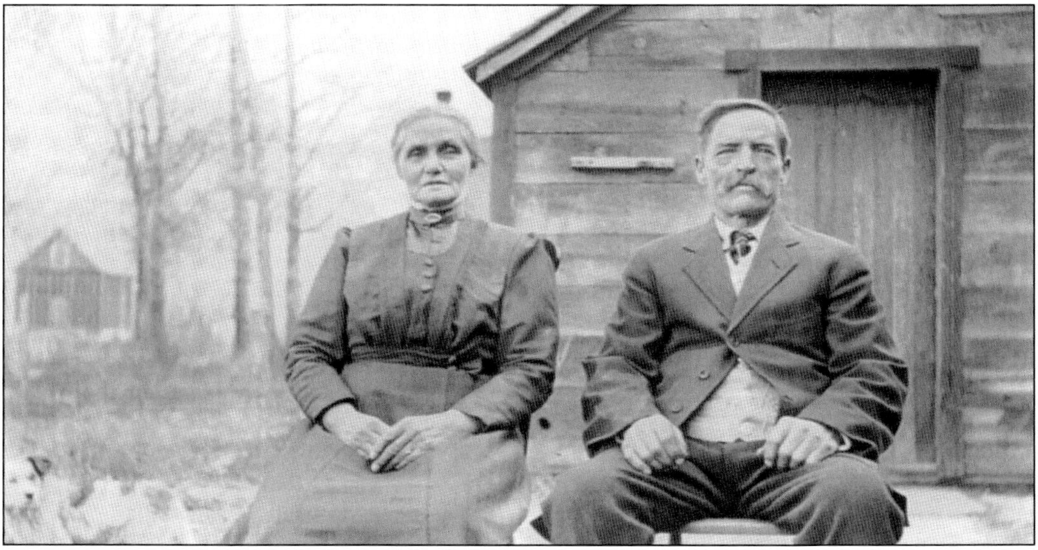

Mathilde and Even Carlsen. Even Carlsen and his wife, Mathilde Pernilla Torstendatter, were born and married in Norway where he worked as a blacksmith. They immigrated to the United States, living in Ogden and Eden, Utah, before they purchased nearly four acres of land, a home, and blacksmith shop in Riverdale in 1895. (Courtesy of Jennifer Carlsen Foote.)

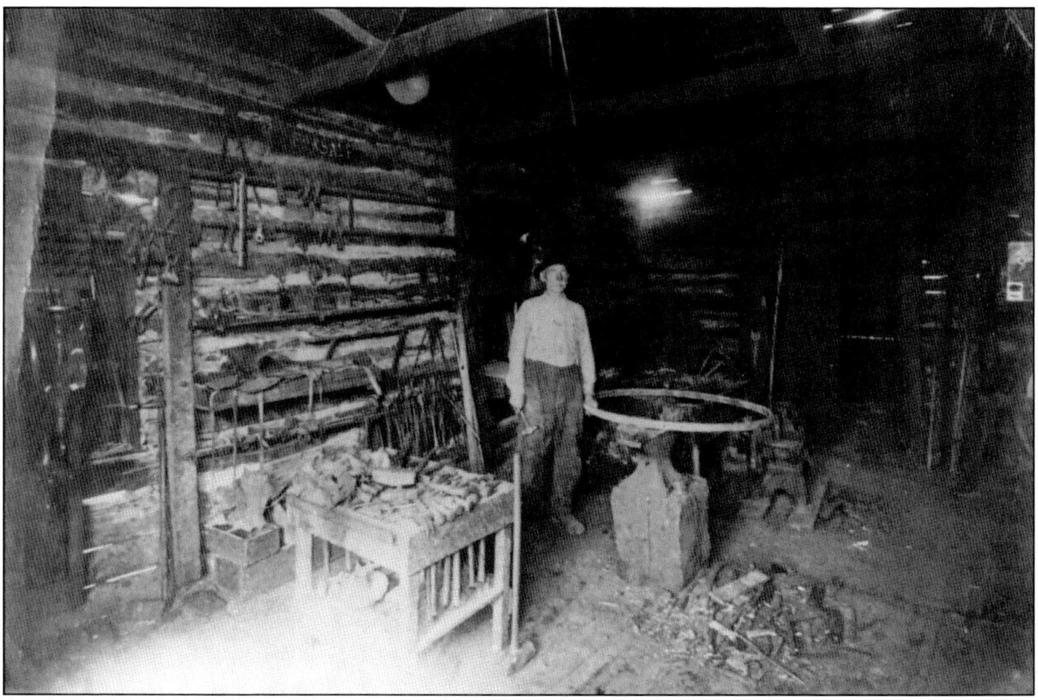

Blacksmith Even Carlsen, 1915. The Carlsens purchased the blacksmith shop from Anders Ahlander from Sweden. Ahlander's son John and two of Sanford Bingham's sons, Oscar and Tracy, drowned on December 26, 1893, after they fell through the ice while skating on the Weber River. Shortly following the tragedy, the Ahlanders moved to Provo. Even is seen here in his blacksmith shop originally located on the northwest corner of 4400 South and 700 West and built in 1860. (Courtesy of the Lucille Child Judkins family.)

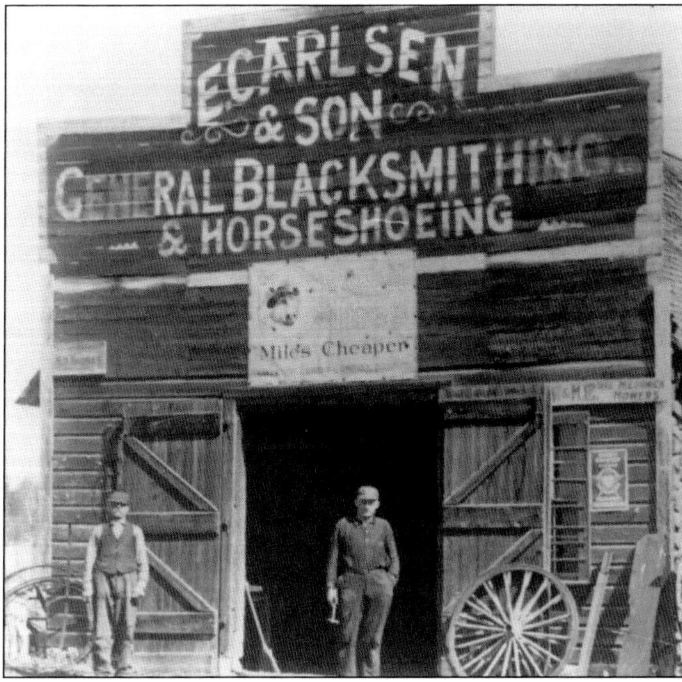

E. CARLSEN AND SON, c. 1915. Even Carlsen (left) and his son Alexander (right) worked as blacksmiths. When the mining boom came to Park City, Utah, large ore wagons passed through town and stopped at the Carlsen shop to have their iron wheels reset. Even also sharpened plow shears, shod horses, and repaired farm implements. He made many of his own tools, including hammers and tongs. The shop had huge billows that were nearly four feet wide and eight feet long. He did blacksmithing for many people in Weber and Davis Counties. (Courtesy of the Lucille Child Judkins family.)

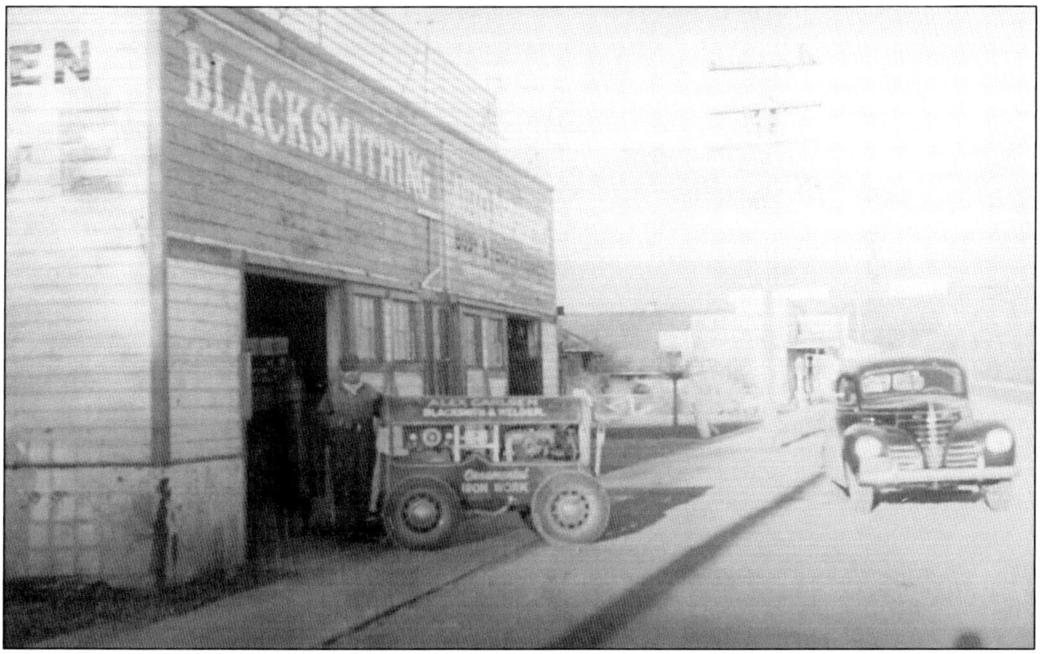

ALEX CARLSEN AND SONS, c. 1935. After Even passed away, Alexander bought his father's blacksmith shop. He razed the old building and built this new one—a combination blacksmith shop and auto repair garage—where he worked for 30 years. Other businesses later occupied the building, including Somers Industrial Service Company, Somer's Improvement Services Company, Somer's Market, a country music dance hall, Russ's Market, and Champion Meats. Alexander Carlsen also served as the first scoutmaster in Riverdale and as Riverdale's first town president. (Courtesy of Jennifer Carlsen Foote and Dean E. Carlsen.)

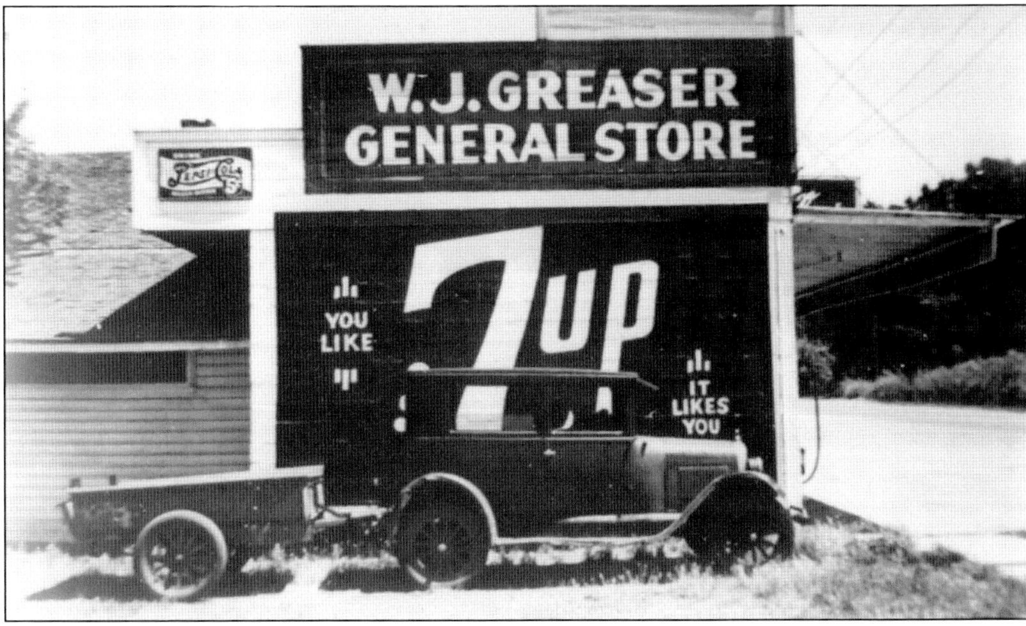

W.J. Greaser Store, c. 1936. Walter and Ruth Greaser's general store was located just west of their home at 690 West 4400 South. Customers could find general merchandise like rope, fabric, clothing, milk, butter, flour, bread, and sugar at the store. Locals enjoyed the soda fountain, ice cream sundaes, and penny candy. The store served as a gathering place for Riverdale residents and as the location of the Riverdale city office for a time. Shortly following the closure of the store on July 17, 1954, Ed Lesley purchased the building and converted it to a laundromat. (Courtesy of the Lucille Child Judkins family.)

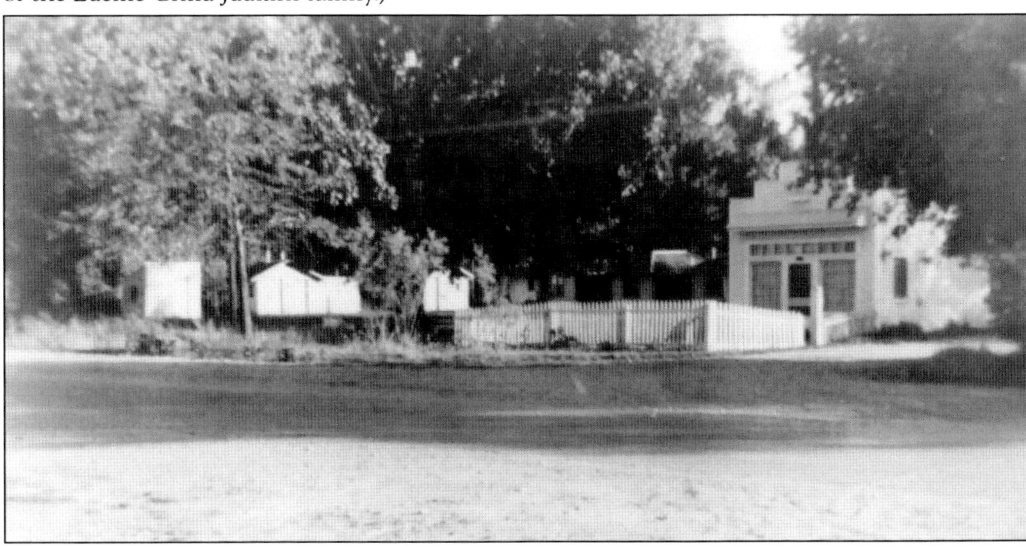

Tourist Cabins, c. 1934. A newspaper article from August 5, 1927, described this tourist camp as "one of the best and the only cottage auto camps between Ogden and Salt Lake City." Originally on the south side of 4400 South where Lesley's Trailer Park is located, the Greasers operated the camp. Riverdale residents often invited travelers into their homes for dinner. The site featured 15 neatly furnished cabins until it closed in January 1959. Migrant workers who harvested local crops also lived here for a time. (Courtesy of the Lucille Child Judkins family.)

Grocery Store, 1933. Originally located on 4400 South across from the Riverdale Ward meetinghouse, this store had hitching posts out front for horses. This photograph shows Avalyn Butler in her buggy and her brother Parley Narvin Butler standing next to her on the west side of the store. (Courtesy of Judy B. Anderson.)

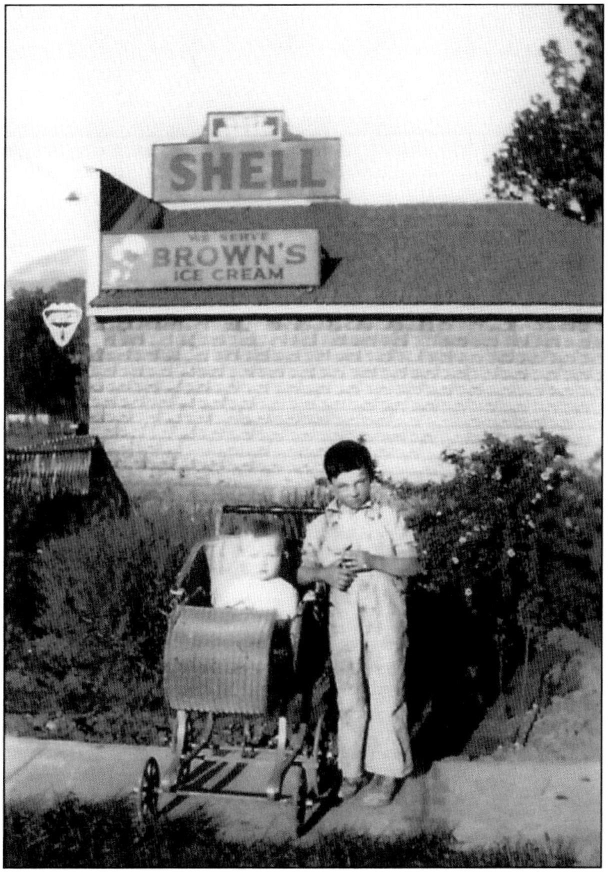

Farrer's A&W Root Beer, 1956. A favorite among residents, Lyle Farrer owned the A&W Root Beer stand. Customers could enjoy root beer in cold, frosted mugs for a nickel, big mugs for a dime, and kid's mugs for free. Hamburgers and hot dogs were a quarter and were served by carhops. The stand also had a candy counter and pinball machines. It later became Johnson's Root Beer stand and continued to sell delicious Mug Root Beer and hot scones with honey, fried chicken, and shrimp. The Sinclair station now occupies the site on the northeast corner of 700 West and Riverdale Road. (Courtesy of Joseph Sears.)

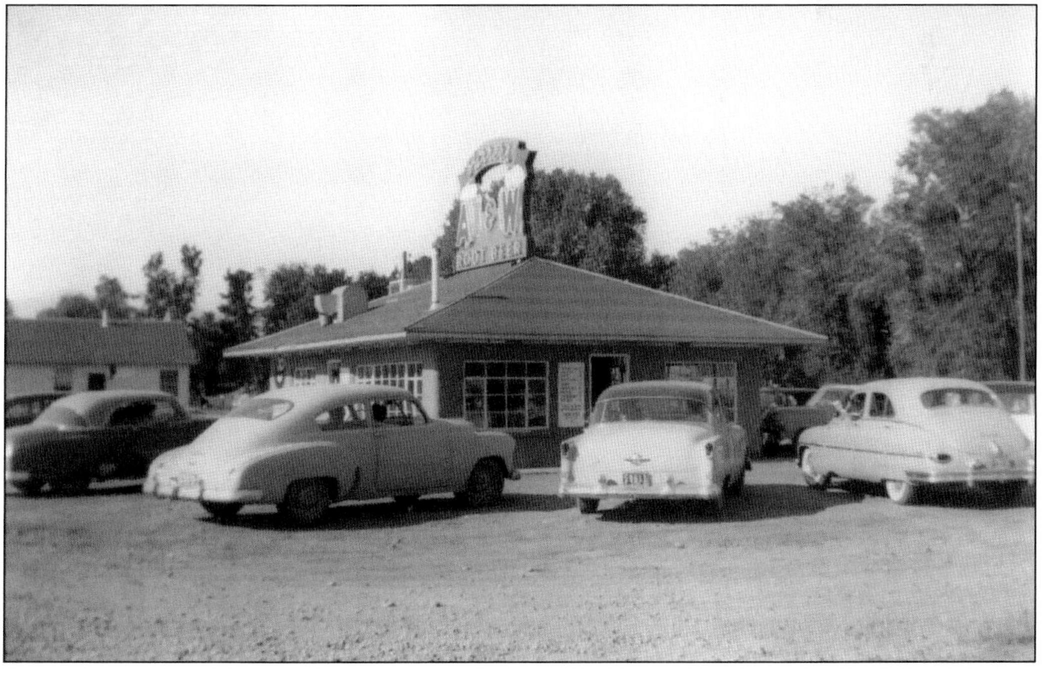

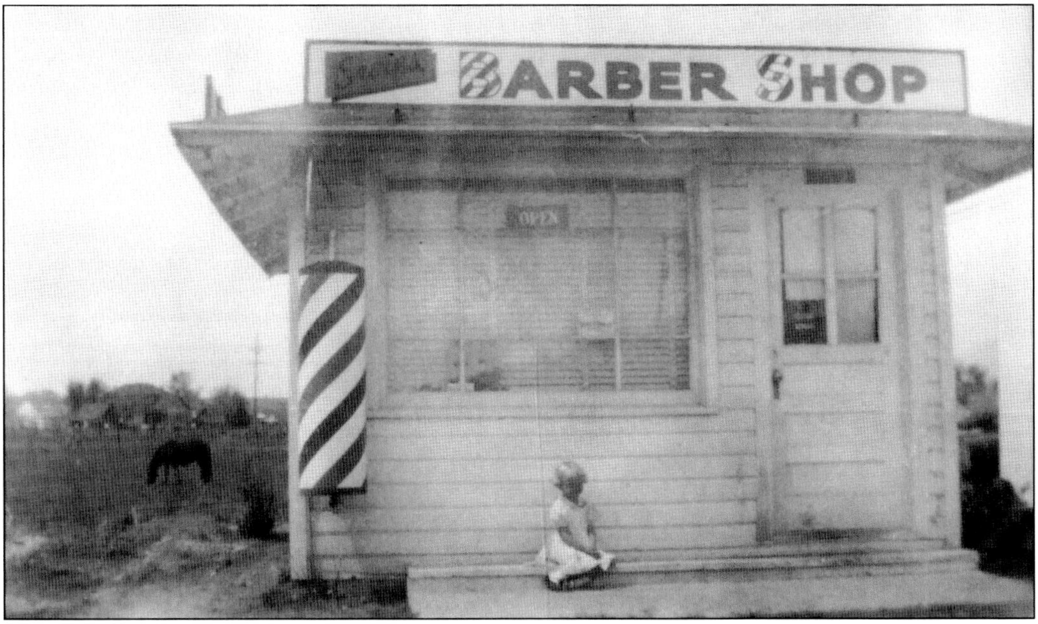

Ervin's Barbershop, c. 1953. Ervin Edward Judkins attended Moler's Barber College in Salt Lake City around 1940. He owned this barbershop at 712 West Riverdale Road. His daughter Lana Judkins (Seegmiller) is seen on the front step, and the Child family's pasture is in the background. (Courtesy of Ervin Garry Judkins.)

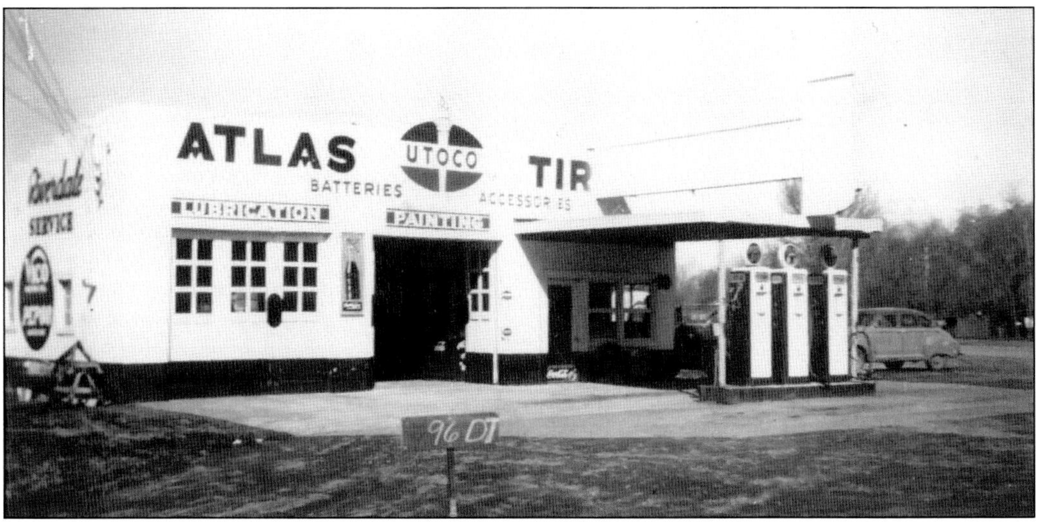

Child Garage/Riverdale Service. Jesse Edward Child and his son Roscoe opened the Child Garage and Filling Station in 1946. Jesse's son Donald helped with maintenance. The family had a chicken coop with about 300 chickens and a barn behind their home. Jesse's wife, Pearl Child, kept a basket of eggs in the garage and sold them to earn extra money. Child Garage later became Riverdale Service. (Courtesy of Weber State University Special Collections.)

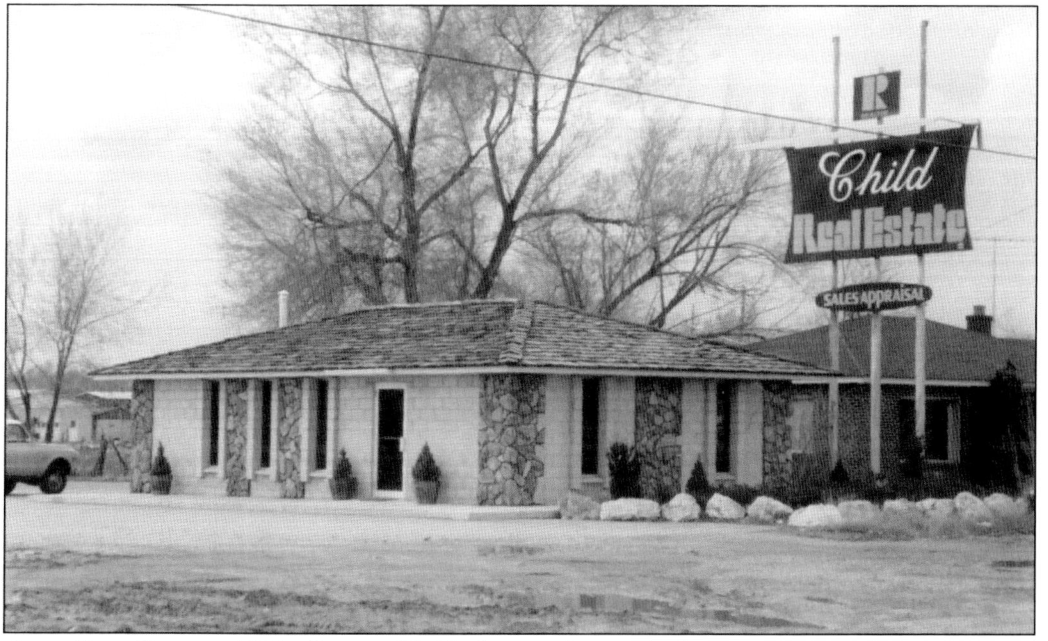

Child Real Estate, 1980s. Roscoe Child, also a real estate broker, operated a real estate business out of the service station. His daughter Marilyn Child (Savage) worked as his secretary. Later, he built Child Real Estate on 700 West, where his son Reid Child and son-in-law Larry Savage worked as realtors and another son Glenn Child kept the books. (Courtesy of Lee Child.)

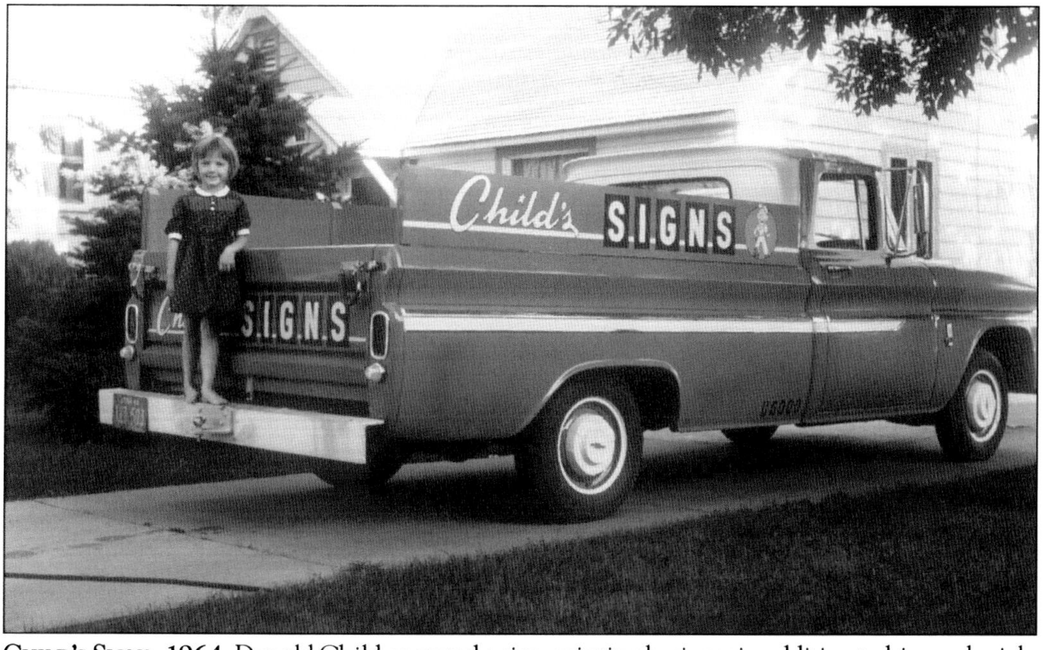

Child's Signs, 1964. Donald Child operated a sign-painting business in addition to his regular job. He had a large shop behind his house at 721 West 4400 South where he painted signs and vehicles for many local businesses. Pictured is his business truck with his daughter Ranae Child (Porter) standing on the bumper. The talented Donald Child also enjoyed photography and took photos at numerous events in Riverdale, some of which are in this book. (Courtesy of Lee Child.)

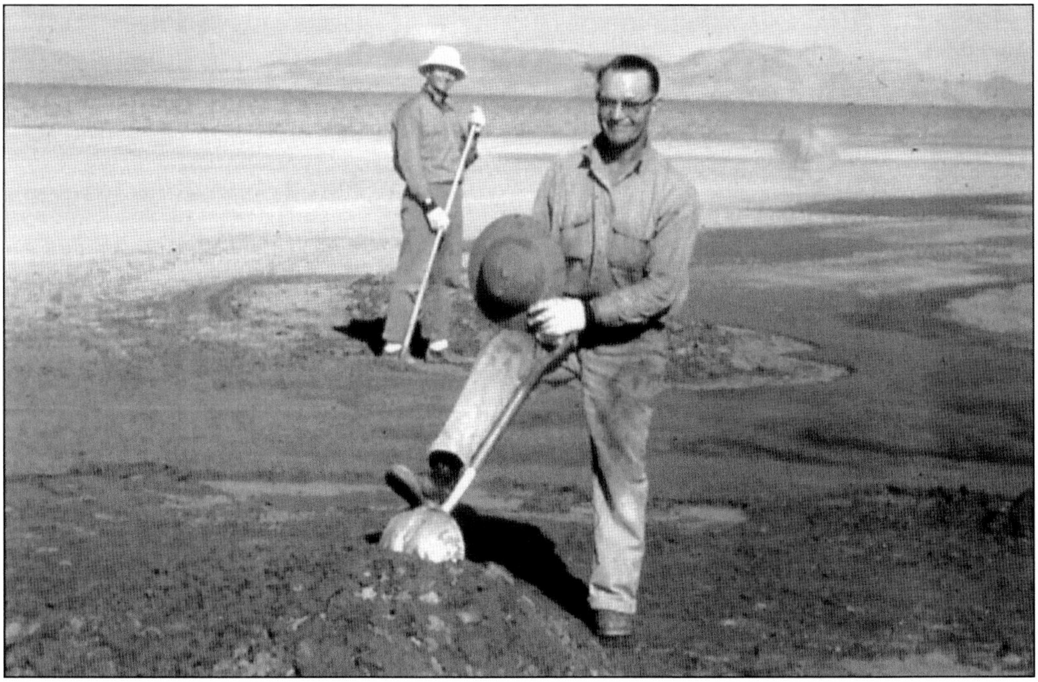

GREAT SALT LAKE BRINE SHRIMP. Cleon Sanders (front) is harvesting brine shrimp from the Great Salt Lake. Sanders owned the Berthana Ballroom and Roller-Skating Rink in Ogden. As a tropical fish hobbyist, he wanted good food for his fish. After hearing about brine shrimp in the Great Salt Lake, he gathered some for his fish, which went crazy for it. He and his son Gail wrote an article about it in a tropical fish hobby magazine and received many inquiries asking the Sanders to send brine shrimp. This marked the beginning of their family business with his sons Gail, Jerry, and Larry, and son-in-law Kenith Allen. (Courtesy of Gail Sanders and Kenith Allen.)

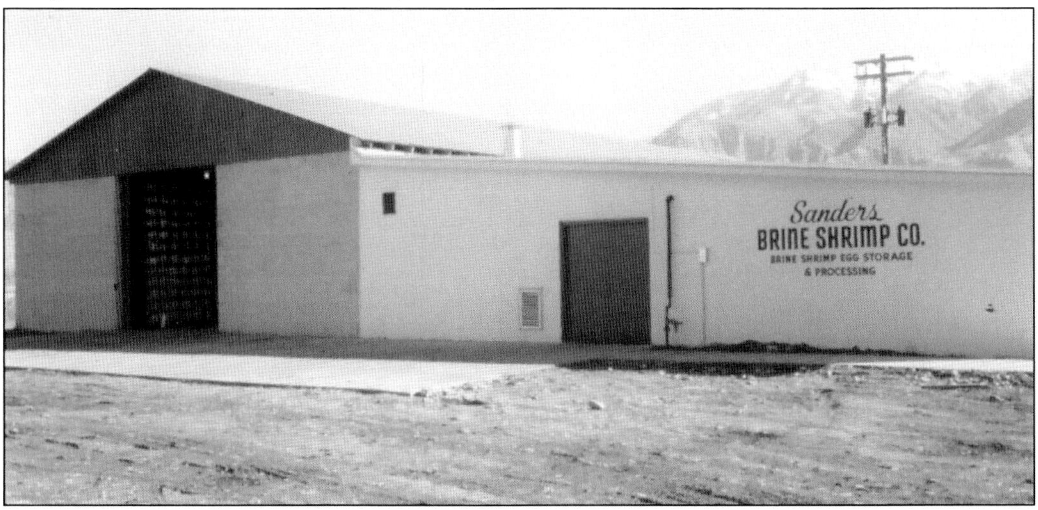

SANDERS BRINE SHRIMP CO. Cleon Sanders found that he could harvest brine shrimp eggs, then dry and can them, so they would be preserved for years. Customers could hatch the eggs in saltwater and have fresh baby shrimp for fish food. Gail Sanders purchased land from his father-in-law, Lloyd Carter, at 3850 South 600 West and built a processing plant. The site is still used today in the brine shrimp industry. (Courtesy of Gail Sanders and Kenith Allen.)

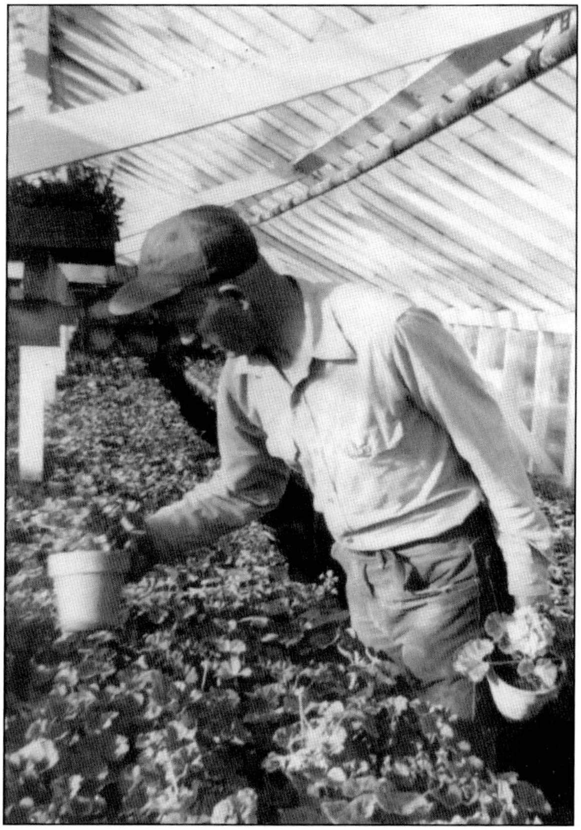

Grant Gibby in Greenhouse. Grant Gibby started his greenhouse business in Roy, Utah, in the 1930s before his marriage to Blanche. They later relocated to Riverdale in about 1954 and expanded the business. The Gibbys loved and served the community. Grant served on the city council, as a bishop, and as president of the Riverdale Utah Stake. He is seen here in his greenhouse. (Courtesy of Janet Gibby Cox.)

Gibby Floral. Since the 1930s, family-owned and -operated Gibby Floral has provided quality flowers and plants for local homes, gardens, workplaces, and special occasions. Located at 1450 West Riverdale Road, the land Gibby Floral sits on was once a campsite for Native Americans and wagon trains. A free-flowing spring called Blue Springs on the west side of the building once supplied water to travelers and their livestock. The numerous cottonwood trees at the site provided shade for weary travelers. (Courtesy of Janet Gibby Cox.)

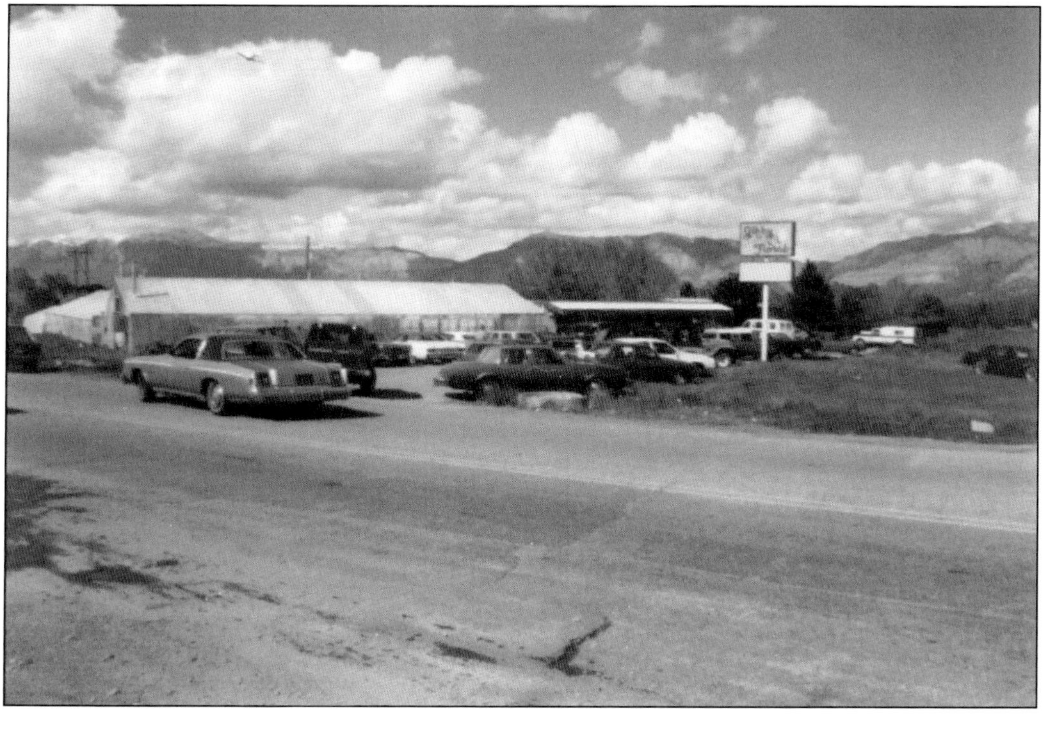

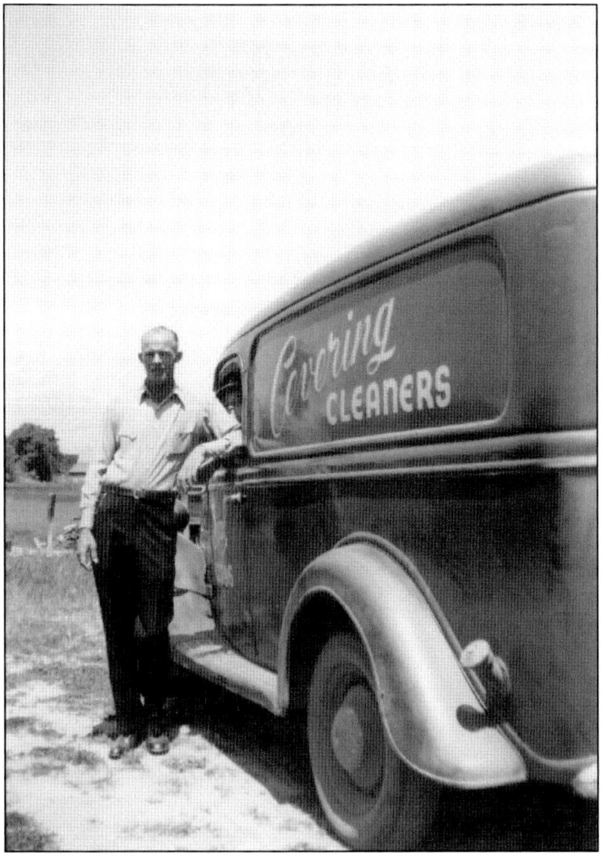

Afe Cevering. Afe Cevering was born in Ogden, Utah, in 1917. He owned and operated Cevering Cleaners. He married Phyllis Cevering and had three children, Jay, Ray, and Kathleen Cevering. He passed away in 1974. (Courtesy of Kathleen Cevering.)

Cevering Cleaners. Cevering Cleaners was located at 4286 Riverdale Road, near the present location of Ruby River, formerly Ebenezer's Restaurant, built in 1992. The owner was Afe Cevering. Behind the cleaners, the family operated Trailer Town. (Courtesy of Kathleen Cevering.)

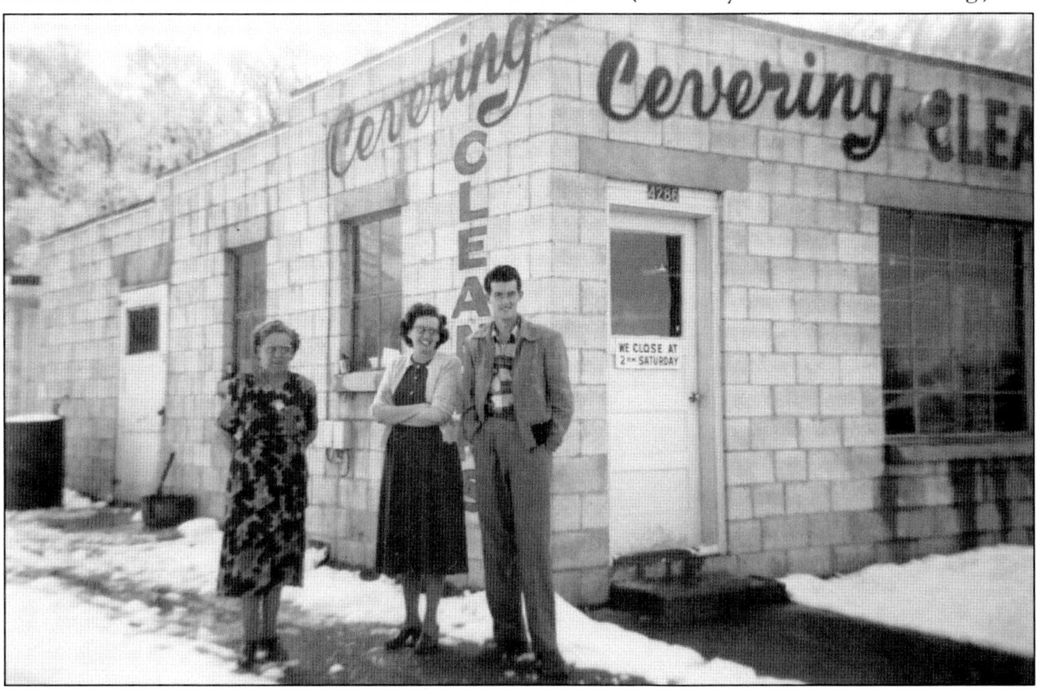

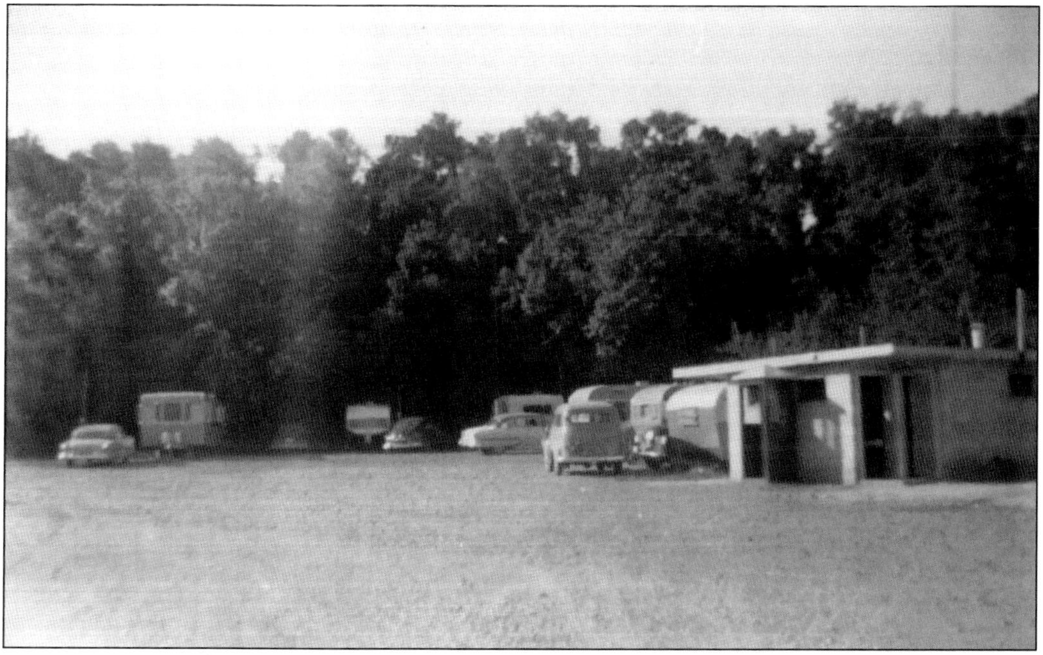

TRAILER TOWN. The Cevering family owned and operated Trailer Town. The building at right was used as a washhouse, which provided restrooms and laundry facilities for Trailer Town guests. (Courtesy of Kathleen Cevering.)

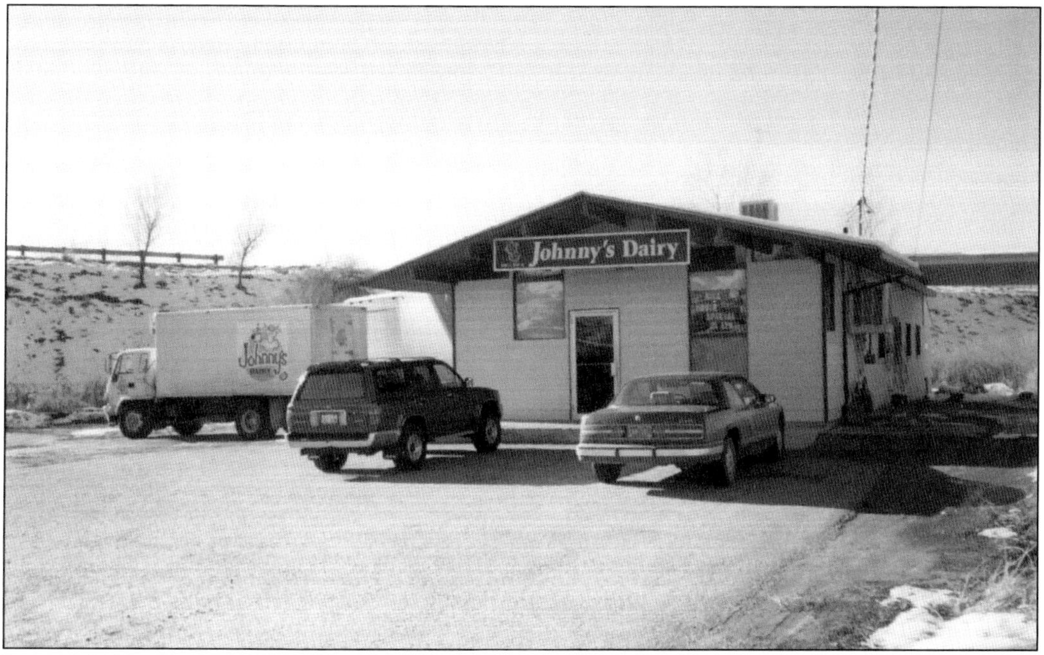

JOHNNY'S DAIRY, C. 1986. Johnny's Dairy produced and bottled its own milk starting around 1962. This was the original Johnny's Dairy located at 5091 South 1050 West. It previously had been Royal Dutch Dairy. Johnny's Dairy moved across the street to a new building at 5098 South 1050 West when Target was built in 1997. Johnny's Dairy closed in November 2017. (Courtesy of John and Gail Combe.)

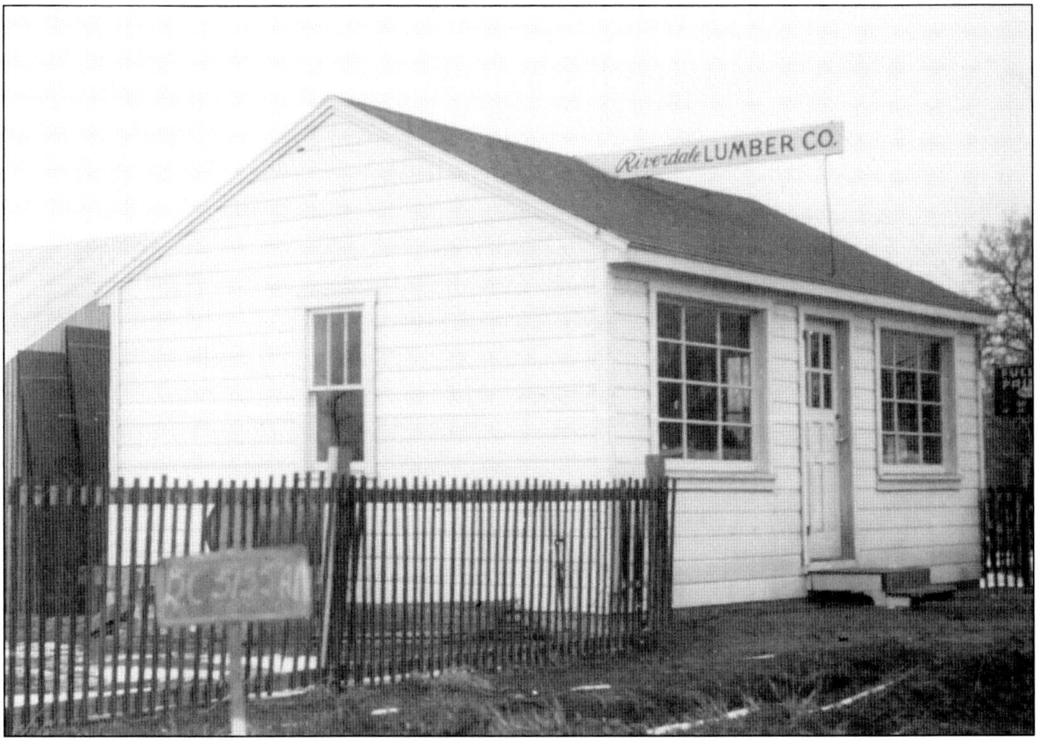

RIVERDALE LUMBER COMPANY. The lumber store was located at 4077 West Riverdale Road. Following the fire that destroyed the 1911 Riverdale School, the Riverdale Jaycees built bus shelters using materials donated by Riverdale Lumber. (Courtesy of Weber State University Special Collections.)

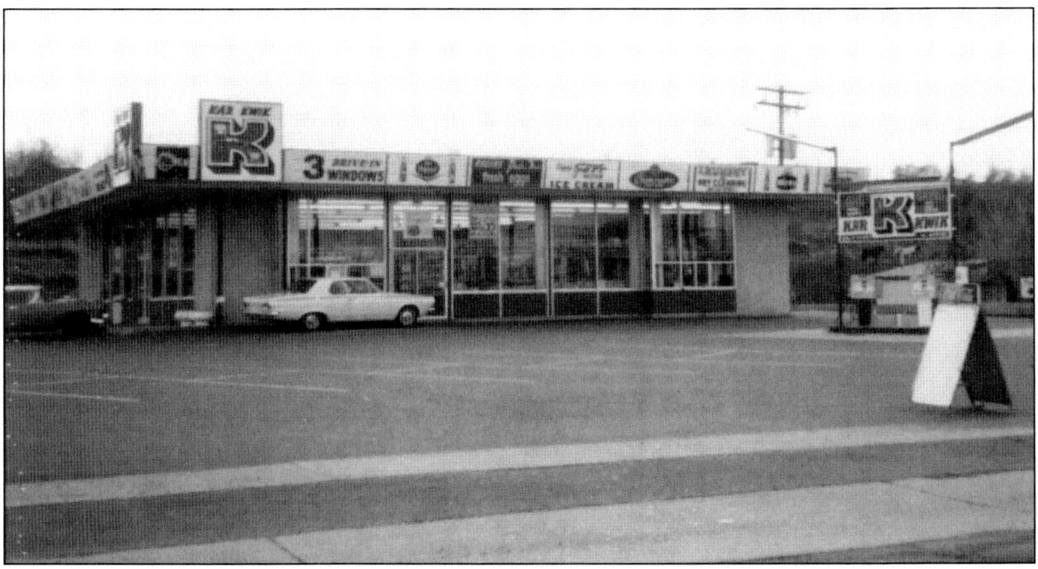

KAR KWIK. A gas station and convenience store, Kar Kwik had three drive-up windows, sold Roger's Fresh Eggs, Farr's Ice Cream, Cream O' Weber products, Hires Root Beer, and even offered dry-cleaning services. Located at 4104 Riverdale Road, the site is now a Chevron station. (Courtesy of Weber State University Special Collections.)

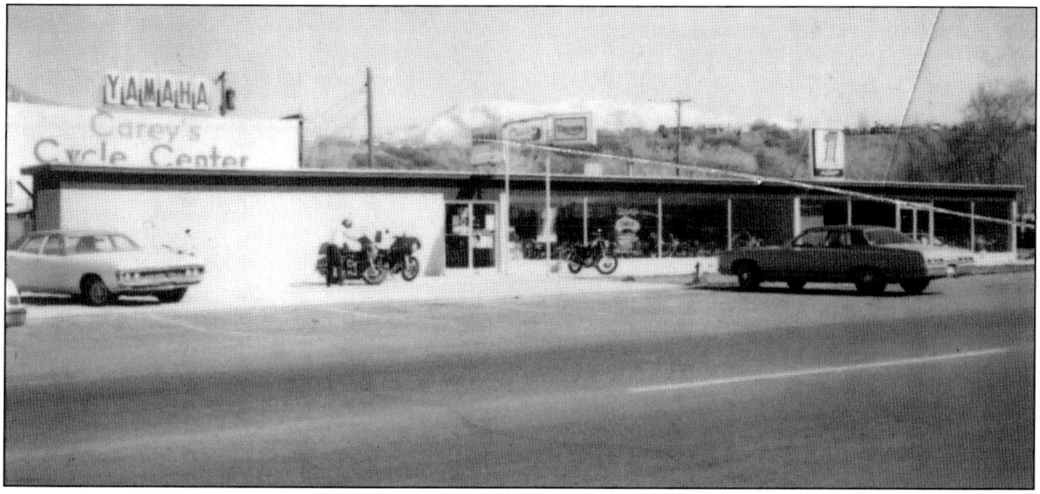

Carey's Cycle, 1980. In 1957, Paul Carey left his job at Hill Air Force Base and opened a motorcycle business with his wife, Joyce. The business started out selling three used motorcycles at 4099 Riverdale Road. As it grew, it moved to 3500 South Riverdale Road, and finally to 4450 South 700 West, where it is located today. It is operated by the Careys' daughter and son-in-law Caron and Brad Boswell. Carey's Cycle celebrated 60 years of business in Riverdale in 2017. (Courtesy of Paul and Joyce Carey.)

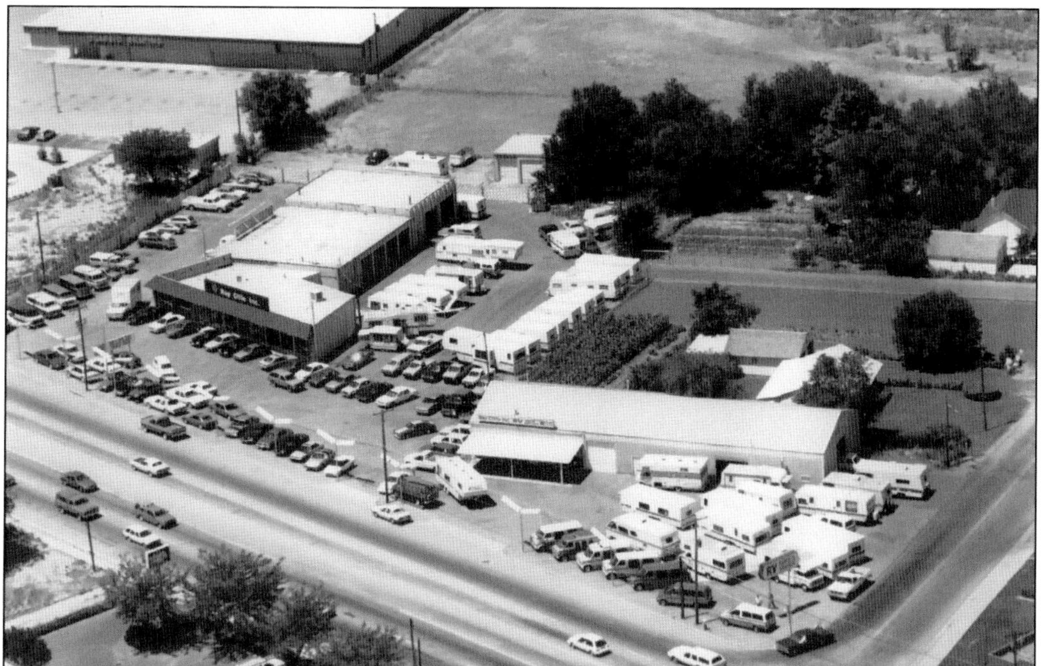

Ray Citte. Ray Citte started out as a used car dealership in 1964 at 4175 Riverdale Road. In 1969, it transitioned to an AMC-Renault, Peugeot, and Triumph dealership, and later started selling recreational vehicles. In 2000, Ray Citte moved to 1677 West Riverdale Road. It was managed by Ray Citte until his retirement in 1980, after which his son Neil Citte managed the family business. This aerial photograph shows the original location. At upper left is Classic Skating. (Courtesy of Neil Citte.)

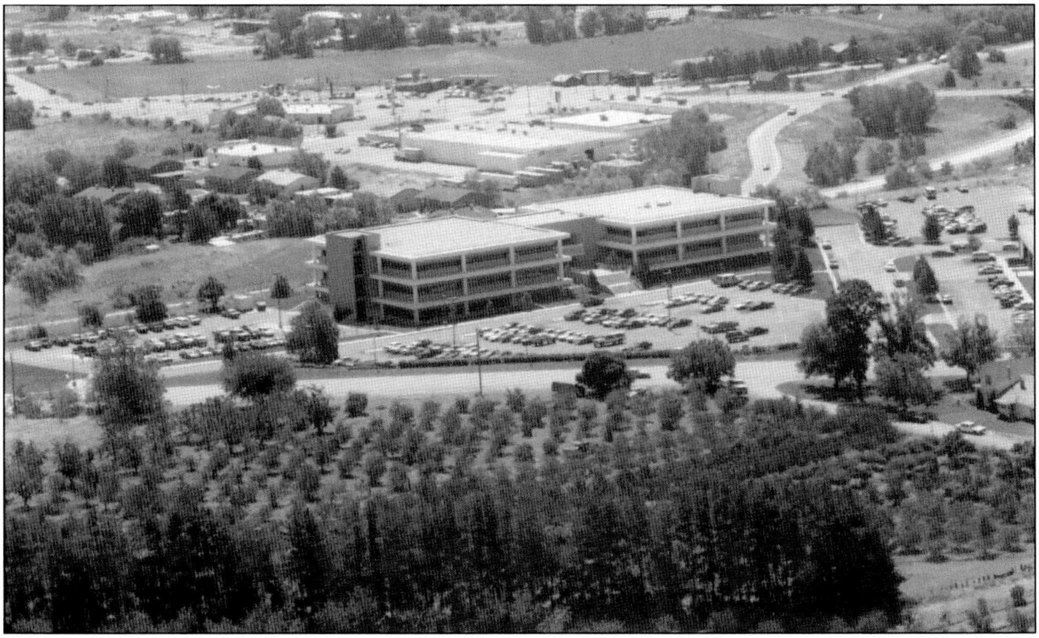

America First Credit Union, 1978. Originally founded on March 16, 1939, America First Credit Union has 123 branches, and its corporate offices are located in Riverdale at 1344 West 4675 South. The main building is seen here with Riverdale Road in the background and a portion of the Ellis family's orchard in the foreground. (Courtesy of America First Credit Union.)

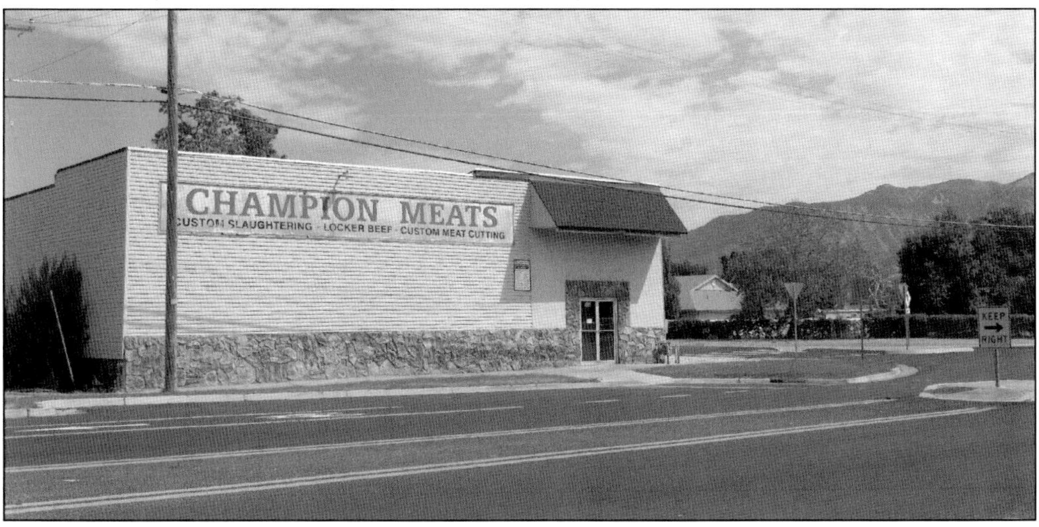

Champion Meats. A meat locker and butcher shop, Champion Meats is located at 704 West 4400 South. This corner has a long history in Riverdale. Said to have been owned initially by Brigham Young, he transferred the land to the railroad, which later sold it to a Mr. Bingham. He sold it to Anders Ahlander, a Swedish immigrant, who built a blacksmith shop around 1860. Even Carlsen, a Norwegian immigrant, later purchased the shop. His son Alexander Carlsen bought the shop, which he later tore down to build a new blacksmith shop and garage. He sold it to Robert Somers, who operated Somer's Improvement Services Company and Somer's Market. It then became Russ's Market, and finally Champion Meats. In the 1950s, it also served as a country-and-western dance hall, complete with live bands. (Author's collection.)

Eight

People

Coming Together through Clubs and Service

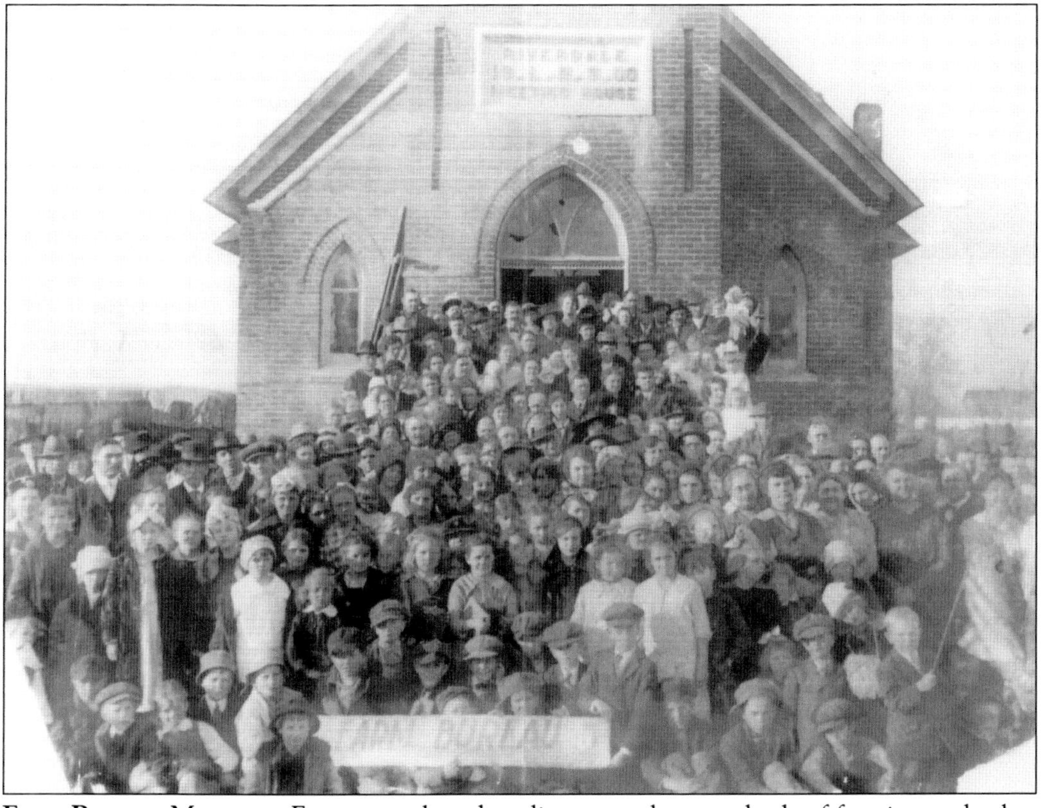

Farm Bureau Members. Farmers gathered to discuss modern methods of farming and other subjects of interest through the Riverdale Farm Bureau. This group posed for a Farm Bureau photograph in front of the Riverdale Ward meetinghouse, built in 1900. Riverdale has always had great community spirit, uniting in both good and trying times. (Courtesy of Riverdale City.)

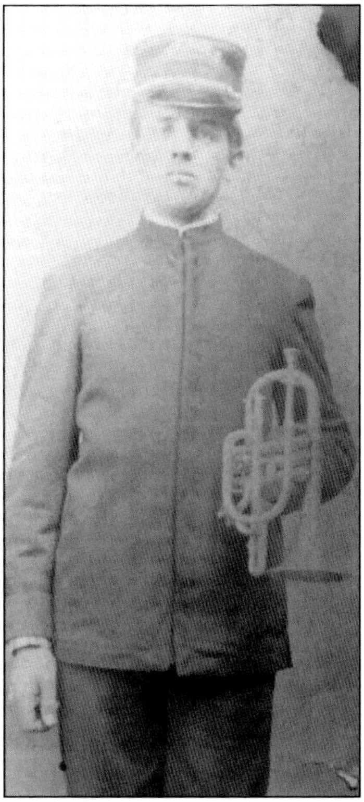

THURVAL CARLSEN, TOWN BAND LEADER. Around 1910, residents organized a town band with 12 to 14 pieces. Thurval Carlsen, son of Even Carlsen, was born in Norway in 1885 and led the band. The band played at Fourth of July celebrations, church functions, and other events. Carlsen worked as a blacksmith in Park City. (Courtesy of the Lucille Child Judkins family.)

BOY SCOUT TROOP 35. Twins Ray and Jay Cevering of Scout Troop 35, with the assistance of a cart pulled by their family horse named Pet, collect newspapers and rags to raise funds for their troop. The first scoutmaster in the Riverdale Ward was Alexander Carlsen, who later became the first town president. (Courtesy of Weber State University Special Collections.)

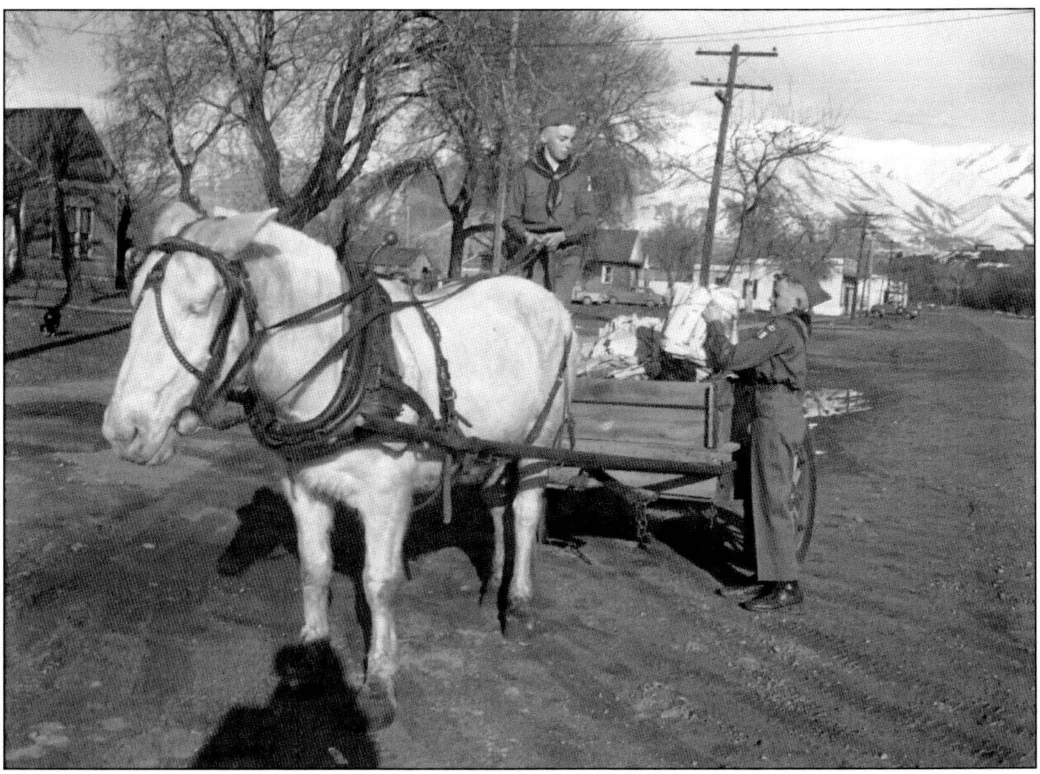

RIVERDALE RUN-AROUND. This wartime newspaper was distributed in town and to some 96 servicemen and servicewomen from Riverdale. Staff members included Ralph Dabb, Helen Adams, Evelyn Applonie, Yvonne Fabricus, Rose Thompson, Virgil B. Anderson, Beth Stephens, and Carol Adams. Reporters included Bette (Bingham) Doman, Jessie (Bingham) Moss, Dorothy McEntire, Luella Johnson, Joyce Pingree, Betty Boekweg, Nellie Boekweg, Betty Jean Bingham, Ethelyn Dickson, and Helen (Bingham) Clayburn. (Courtesy of Melanie Stone Hansen.)

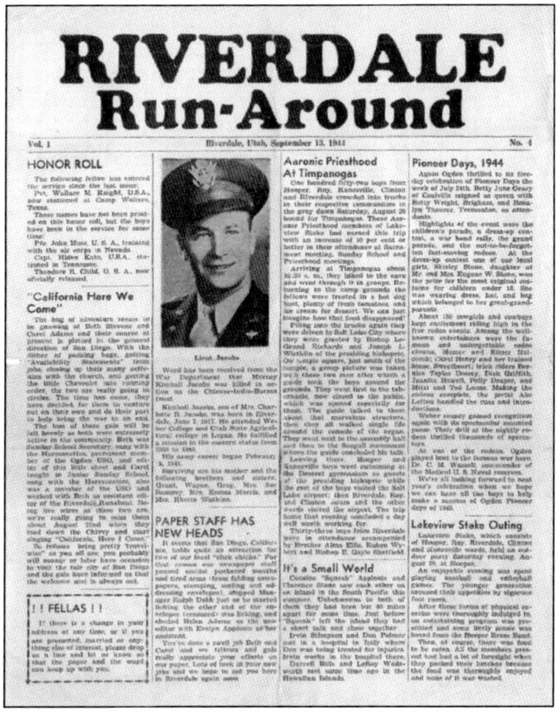

RIVERDALE
Run-Around

Vol. 1 — Riverdale, Utah, September 13, 1944 — No. 4

HONOR ROLL

"California Here We Come"

Lieut. Jacobs

Aaronic Priesthood At Timpanogas

PAPER STAFF HAS NEW HEADS

It's a Small World

Pioneer Days, 1944

Lakeview Stake Outing

!! FELLAS !!

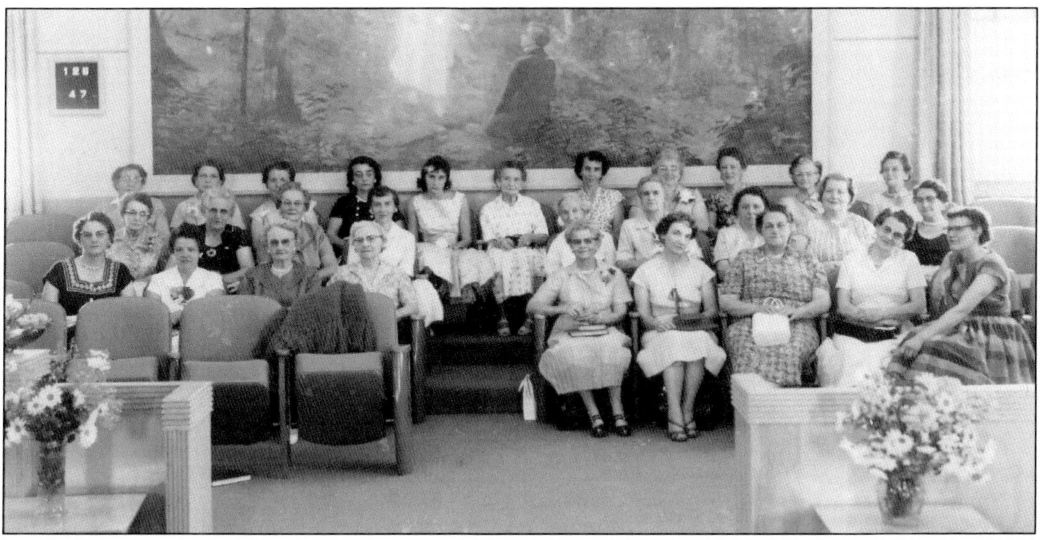

DAUGHTERS OF UTAH PIONEERS, 1958. The first Daughters of Utah Pioneers (DUP) camp in Riverdale was organized in 1914 as Camp P, with Martha Lewis Ritter as captain. The camp's name changed several times over the years to Camp K, Camp Martha, Camp No. 27, and Pearl Child Camp. Today, there are two DUP camps in Riverdale—the Pearl Child Camp and the Wild River Camp, both of the Weber West Company. Pictured on July 13, 1958, from left to right are (first row) Pernecia Fiet, Iola Dee, Mabel Ellis, Adelphia Bingham, Pearl Child, Afton Salisbury, Gladys Taylor, Ruby Stimpson, and Verla Hull; (second row) Ivy "Dolly" Child, Alta Patterson, Florence Fife, Bessie Boswell, Adele Fife, Amy Thompson, Lucille Judkins, Annie Taylor, and unidentified; (third row) Sophia Bingham, Lillian Kammeyer, Norma Tullis, Leila Bybee Mastin, Linda Ritter, Tillie Adams, unidentified, Leone Parker, and three unidentified. (Courtesy of the Lucille Child Judkins family.)

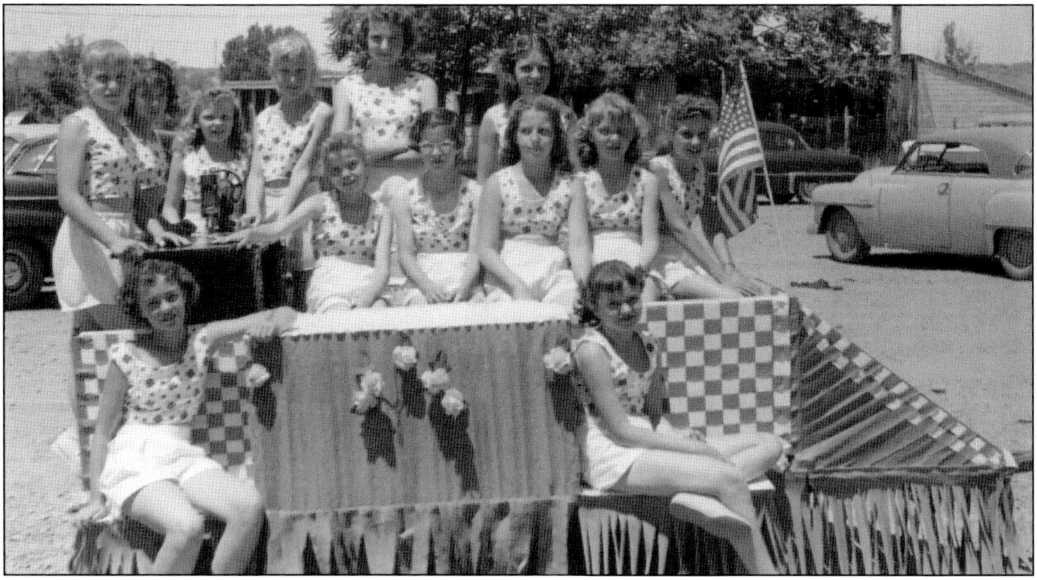

4-H Girls Club, 1950s. These 4-H Girls Club members are ready for a parade. The leader of the group was Margaret Zito Fuller. She taught the girls how to sew, and they did a sewing project each summer. From left to right are (first row) Ludonna Woodbury and Joyce Ritter; (second row, seated) Janet Gibby, Ethel Goff, Bonnie Somers, Cheryl Johnson, and Connie Fuller; (third row) Barbara Zito, Jean Henderson, Julie Boswell, GeNeal Myers, Karen Henderson, and Judy Miller. (Courtesy of Connie Fuller.)

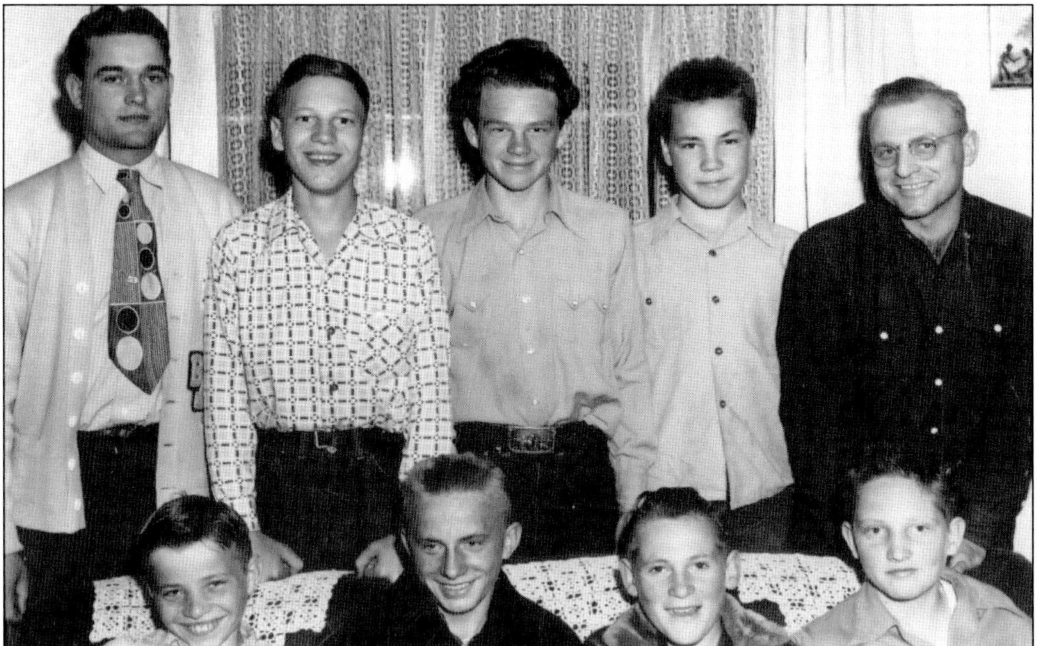

4-H Boys Club, c. 1949. The 4-H Boys Club met about once a month at the home of their leader, Roscoe Child, to discuss farming topics. From left to right are (first row) Roland Child, Ervin Garry Judkins, Danny Joe Seeds, and Harold Jay Stephens; (second row) unidentified, Vaughn Deem, Rowland "Junior" Bingham, Lewis Price, and Roscoe Child. (Courtesy of Ervin Garry Judkins.)

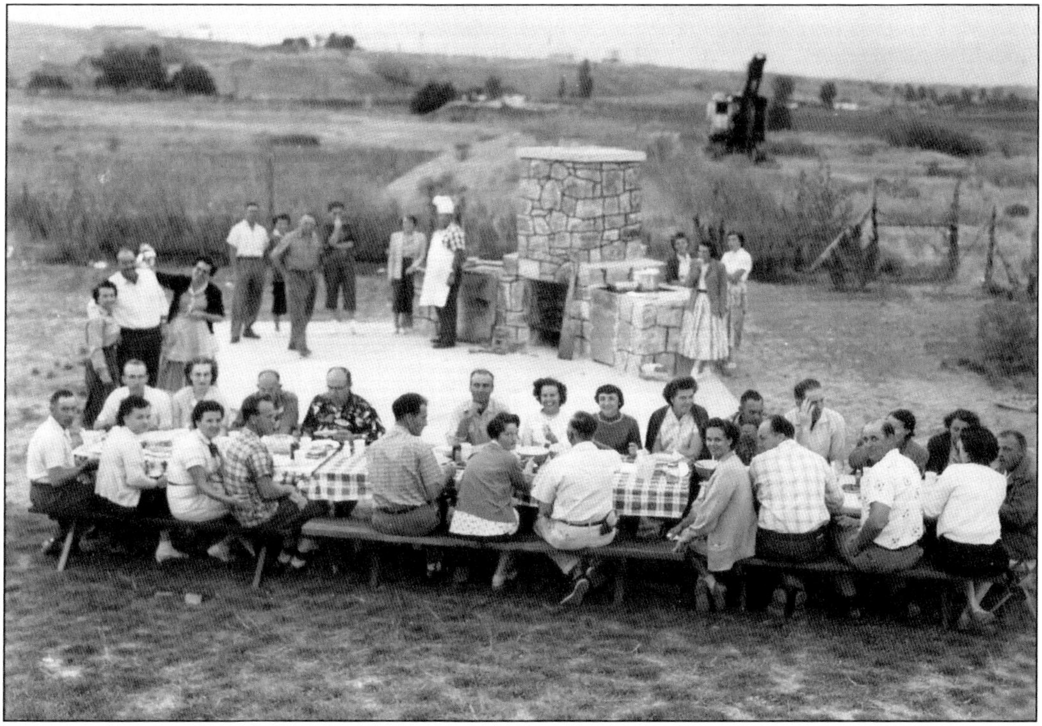

Ladies Club and Riverdale Park, c. 1956. Organized in June 1947 under the name Les Amies Gayes, the Riverdale Ladies Club was comprised of enterprising young married women devoted to service in the community. With only 30 members allowed, there was always a waiting list to join. Together with their husbands and the Lions Club, the club built this rock fireplace at Riverdale Park. (Photograph by Donald Child; courtesy of Lee Child.)

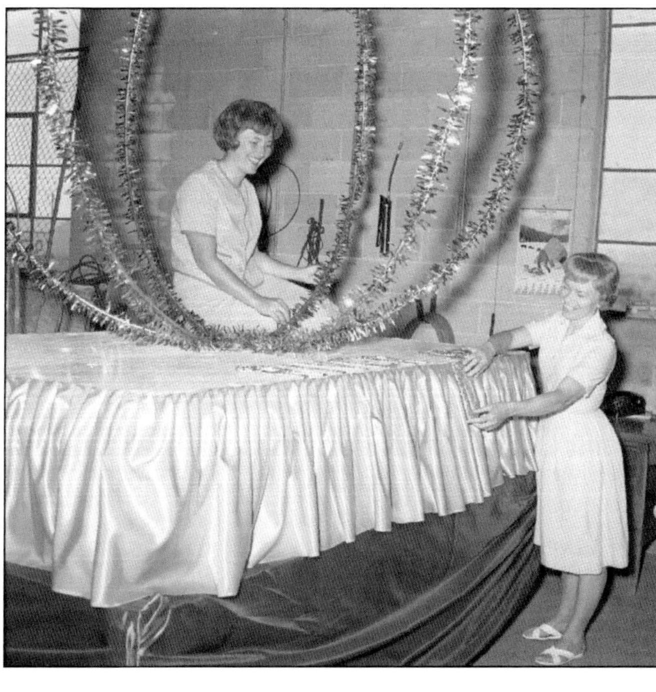

Ladies Club, 1964. Riverdale Ladies Club members paid dues of 25¢ per month and enjoyed special speakers at monthly meetings. Each year, they sponsored a project to improve the community. The club started a queen contest in 1954, the Miss Riverdale pageant, and a baby contest in 1956. Here, Doris Sanders (left) and Elva Hawkley are putting the finishing touches on the Miss Riverdale parade float. (Courtesy of Weber State University Special Collections.)

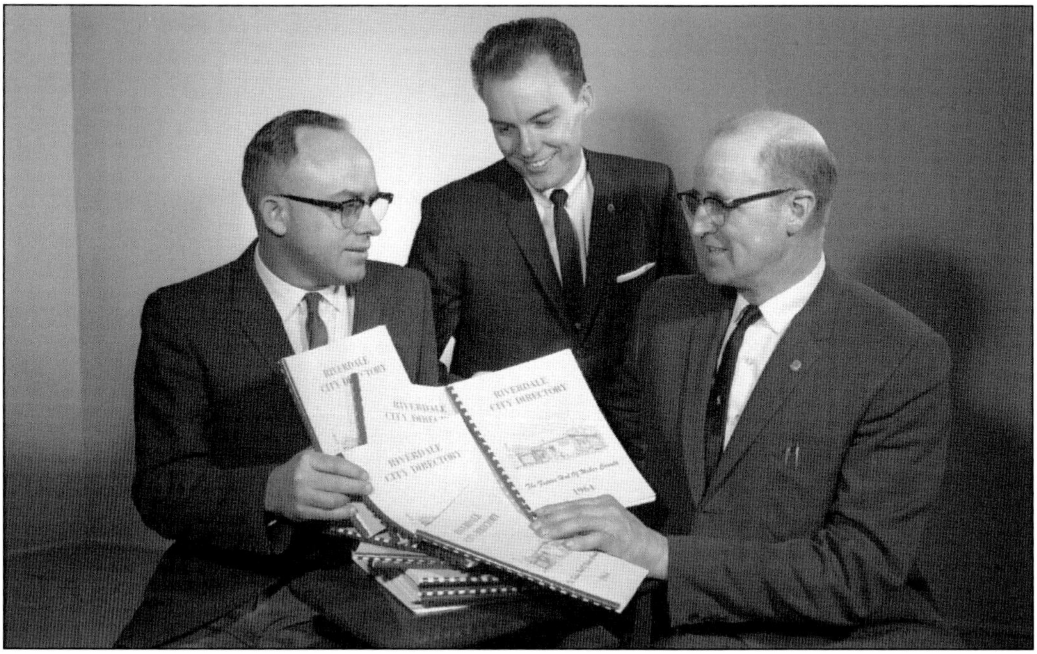

RIVERDALE LIONS CLUB, 1964. On June 30, 1954, the Riverdale Lions Club was formed at the Apollo Club with 40 charter members. In 1964, the Lions compiled a Riverdale city directory, displayed here by club members. The cover had an illustration of the Riverdale Municipal Building and the tagline "The Future Hub of Weber County." From left to right are Dahl Crabtree (president), Gordon Christensen (secretary), and Ted Anderson (first vice president). (Courtesy of Weber State University Special Collections.)

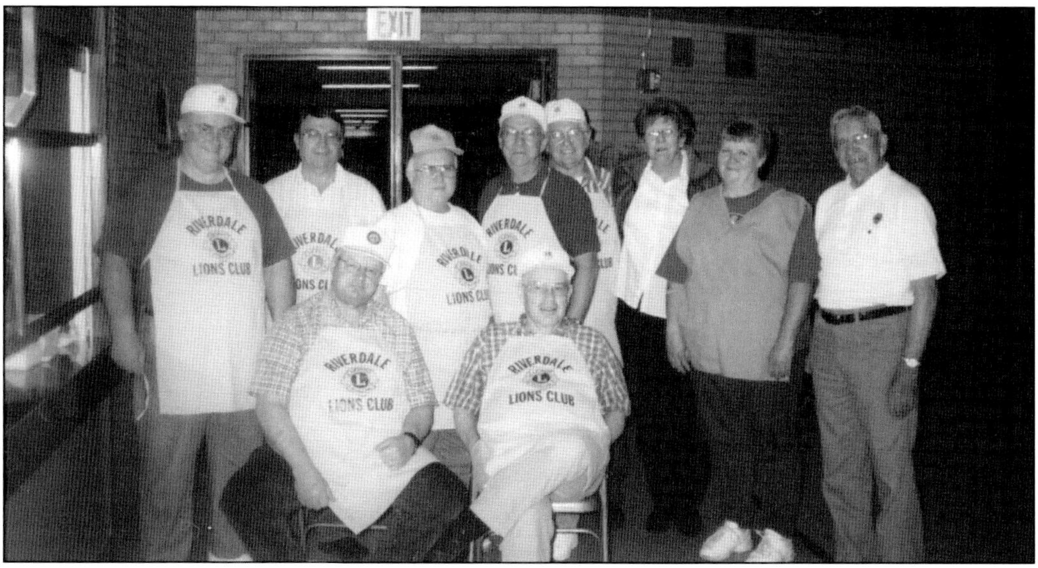

RIVERDALE LIONS CLUB, 2002. Involved in efforts to enhance the community, the Riverdale Lions Club holds an annual spaghetti dinner fundraiser at Riverdale Elementary School and breakfast at the annual Old Glory Days celebration. The Lions played an instrumental role in developing Riverdale Park, providing schoolchildren with eyeglasses, and other efforts in the community. (Courtesy of Riverdale Lions Club.)

Blanche and Grant Gibby. The Gibbys loved Riverdale from the moment they moved to the community. The city honored them for their contributions to the annual Fourth of July celebration. Previously, the celebration included only a parade and Boy Scout flag ceremony. Blanche went before the city council and asked them to expand the celebration. Working together, the Gibbys, city council, Riverdale Ladies Club, church leaders, and others added a choir, speaker, demolition derby, children's parade, ball game, booths, and a fireworks display to the day's events. (Courtesy of Janet Gibby Cox.)

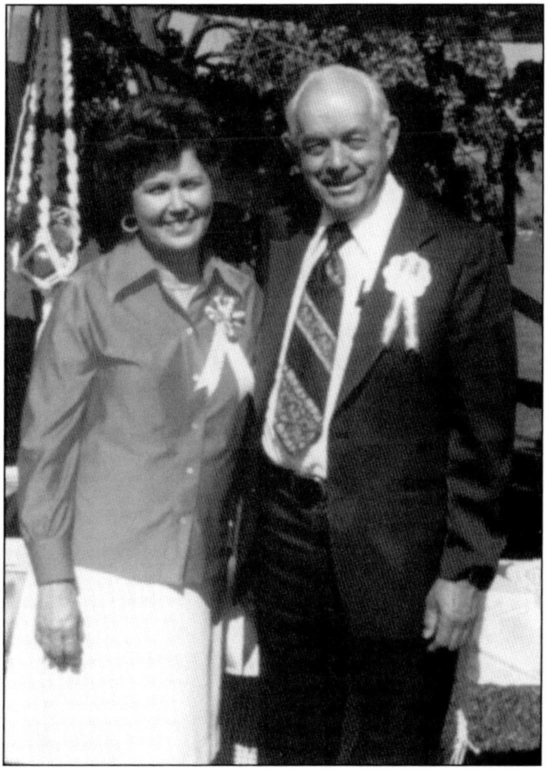

Donald and Donna Child Family. Donald Child captured many moments, events, and people in Riverdale through his camera lens. This book includes some of his photographs. He is pictured here with his family. From left to right are Steve, Lee, Donald, Donna, Ranae (baby), and Connie. (Courtesy of Lee Child.)

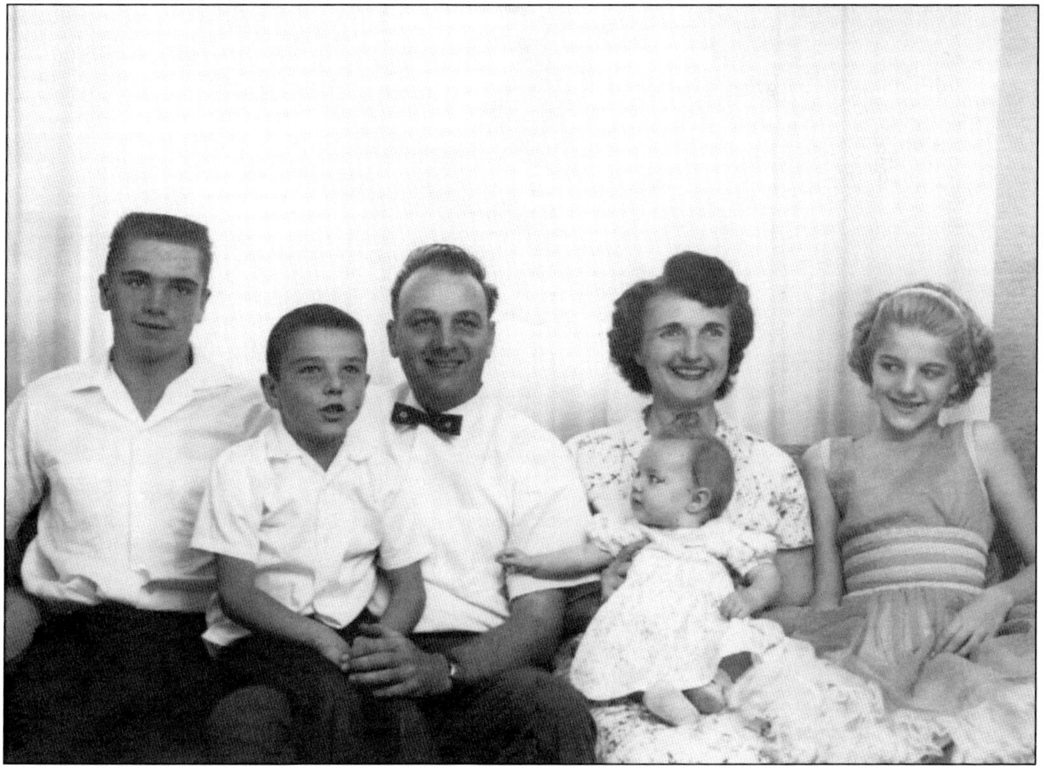

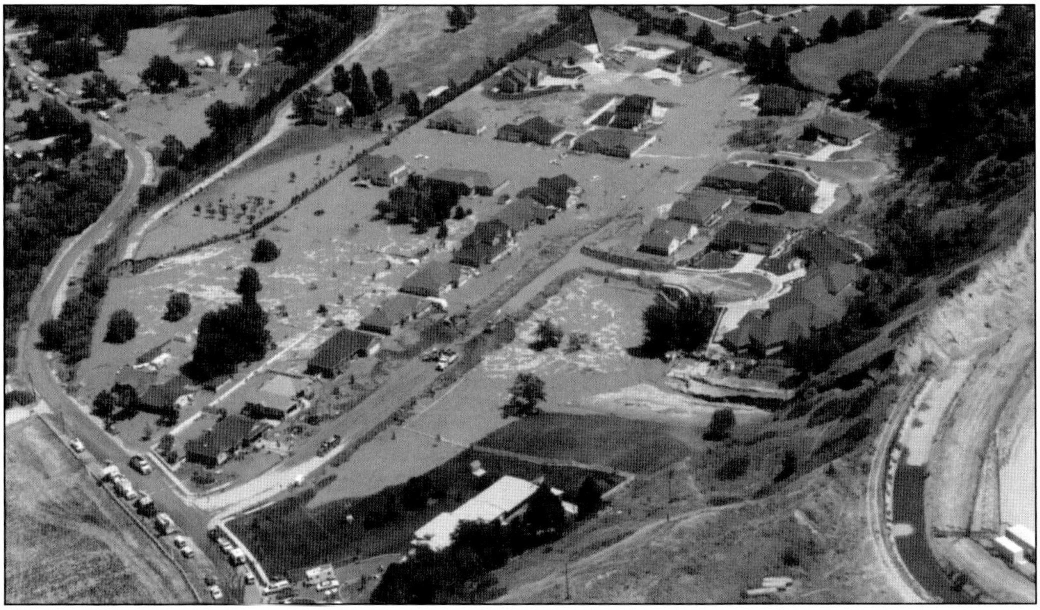

RIVERDALE CANAL DISASTER, 1999. On July 11, 1999, at approximately 12:08 p.m., a portion of the nearly 100-year-old Weber-Davis Canal broke at the top of a 110-foot-high bench. Mud, water, and debris rushed down the hillside, carving out a canyon. Officials shut off water to the canal, but the water that remained in the canal continued to flow for five and a half hours after the break. (Courtesy of Riverdale City.)

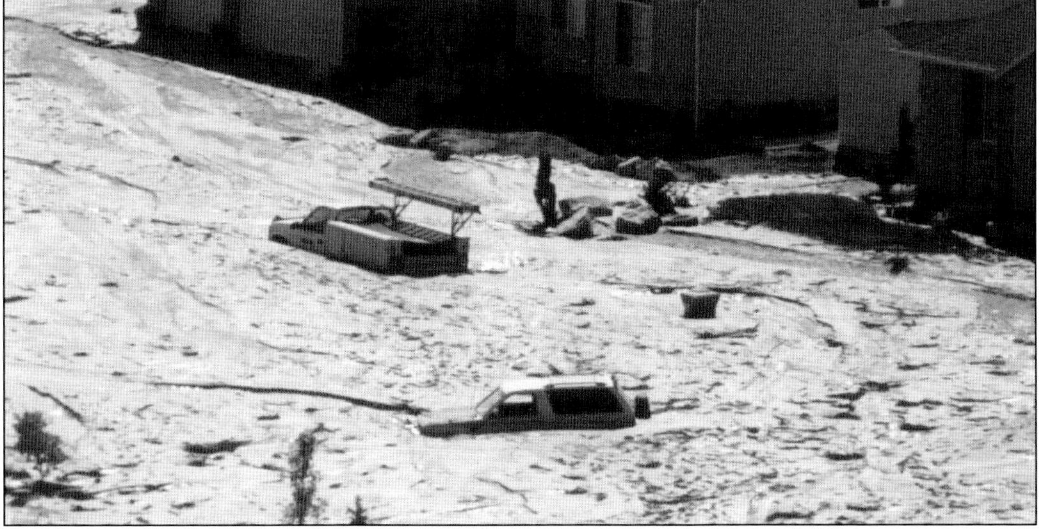

CANAL FLOODWATER AND MUD, 1999. The mud and water buried the Pinebrook Subdivision and filled 72 homes and yards with approximately 350,000 cubic yards of thick mud. The 63 acre-feet of water spread throughout the subdivisions below, creating a lake at Golden Spike Park. Over 140 properties were damaged, but there were no serious injuries or deaths. Cleanup efforts began immediately through the assistance of Riverdale City, the Red Cross, the LDS Church, and the Swanson Family Foundation. Thousands of volunteers of all ages assisted in a variety of ways, and hundreds of businesses donated materials and money. The volunteers were a testament to the great community spirit in Riverdale and surrounding communities. (Courtesy of Carl B. Cook.)

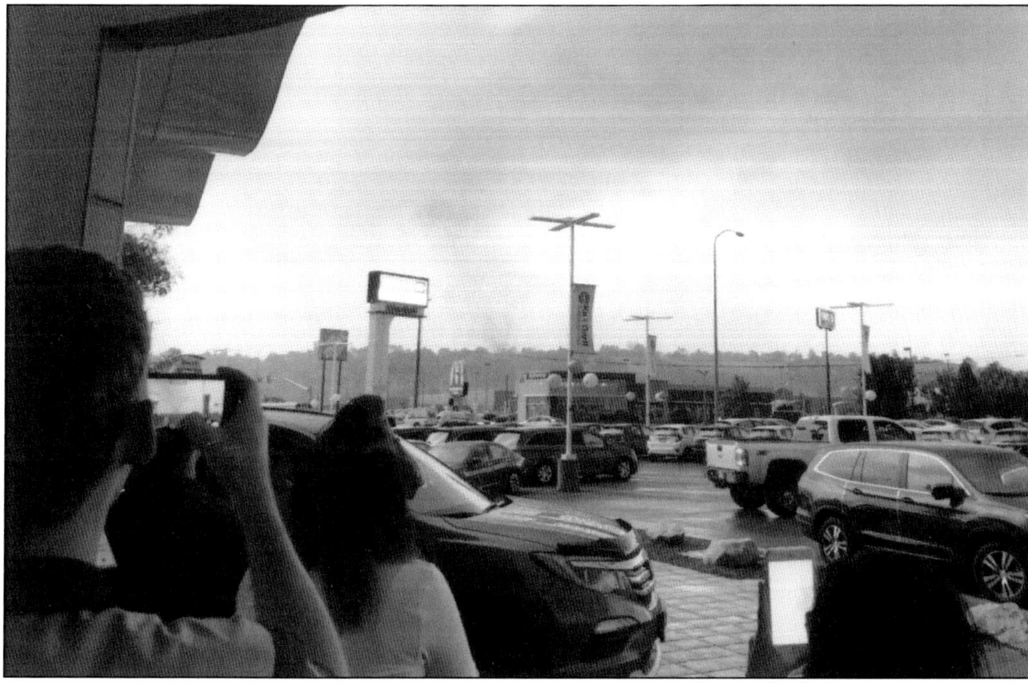

Riverdale Tornado, 2016. During a storm on September 22, 2016, a rare F1 tornado touched down in Riverdale and Washington Terrace. In this image, witnesses take photographs from Riverdale Road as the tornado passes through the south side of Riverdale. The storm uprooted trees, damaged several homes, and completely destroyed one home. (Author's collection.)

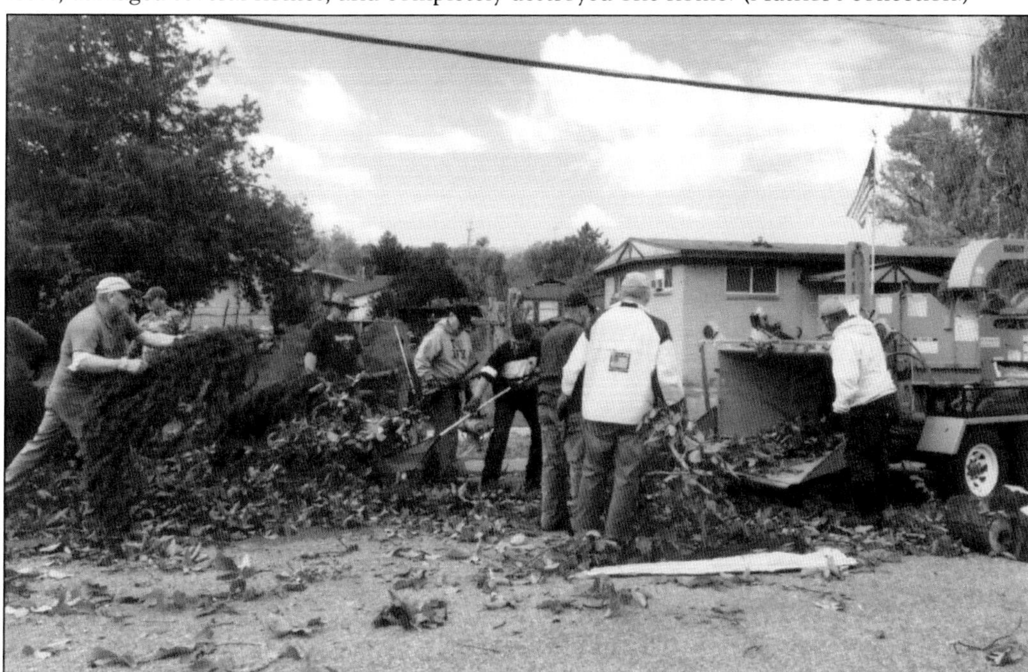

Tornado Cleanup. Volunteers clean up debris after the 2016 tornado. Time and time again, the community bands together in the face of good and adversity. (Courtesy of Andee Sanders.)

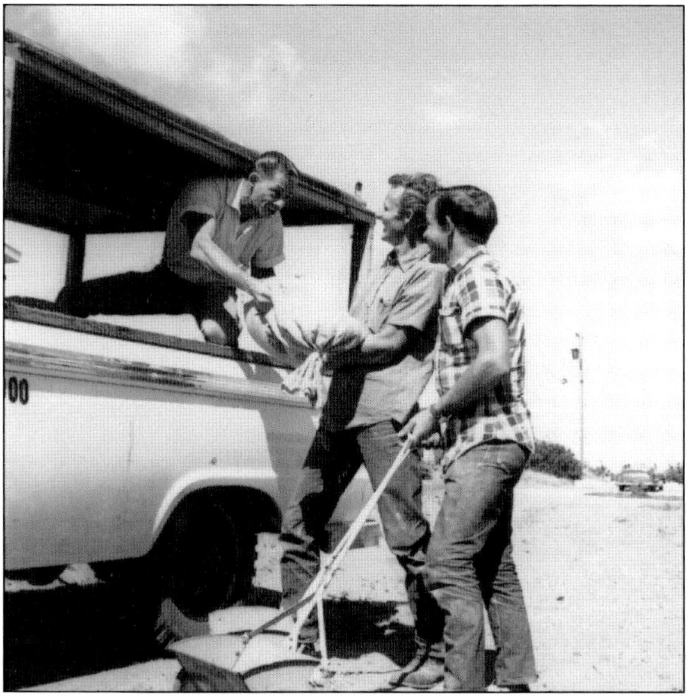

RIVERDALE JAYCEES. The Riverdale Jaycees worked together to serve the community as a group of men aged 21 to 36. The Jaycees built school bus shelters for Riverdale students when the school was destroyed by fire, raised money for needy families at Christmas, painted city hall, and displayed the city's first community Christmas tree, among other projects. Here, the Jaycees' chairman, Norman Leishman (left), works with fellow members to create the Riverdale Jaycee Tot Park in the Tibbits Subdivision on the east bench of Riverdale. (Courtesy of Norman W. Leishman.)

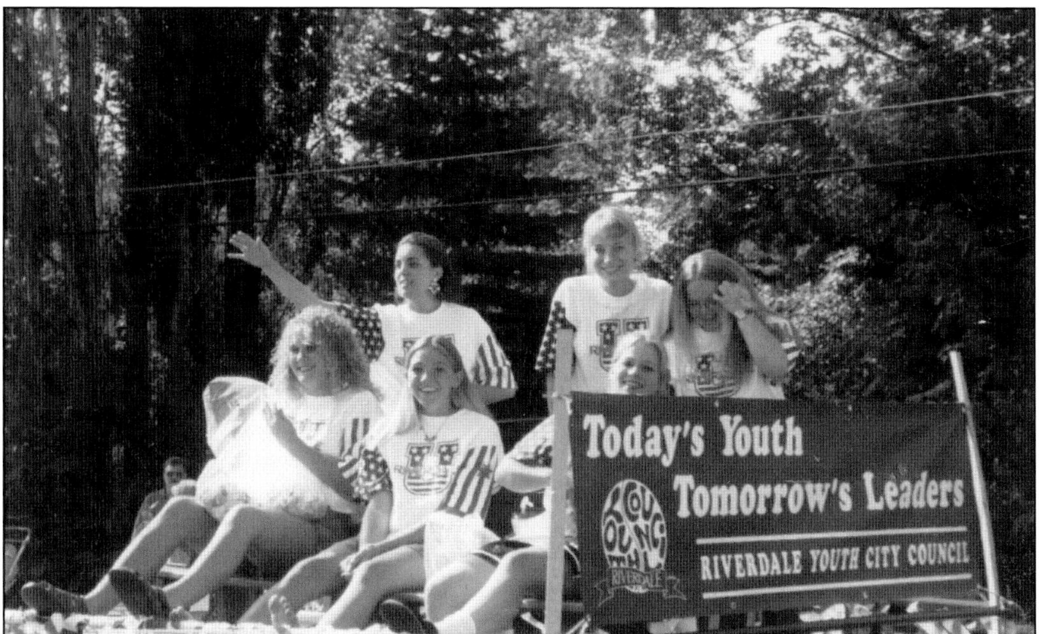

RIVERDALE YOUTH CITY COUNCIL, 1996. The Riverdale Youth City Council is a service organization for youth ages 14 to 18. Civic leadership experience is gained through planning activities, including the annual Easter egg hunt, Old Glory Days sunrise service, and a community Halloween party. In this parade photograph, from left to right are (first row) Ariana Pugmire (Sears), Alleson Jones, and Angel Simmons; (second row) Wendy Hansen, Katie Meldrum (Ellis), and Anne Hansen. (Courtesy of Melanie Stone Hansen.)

Nine

A Good Time
Movies, Music, and Old Glory Days

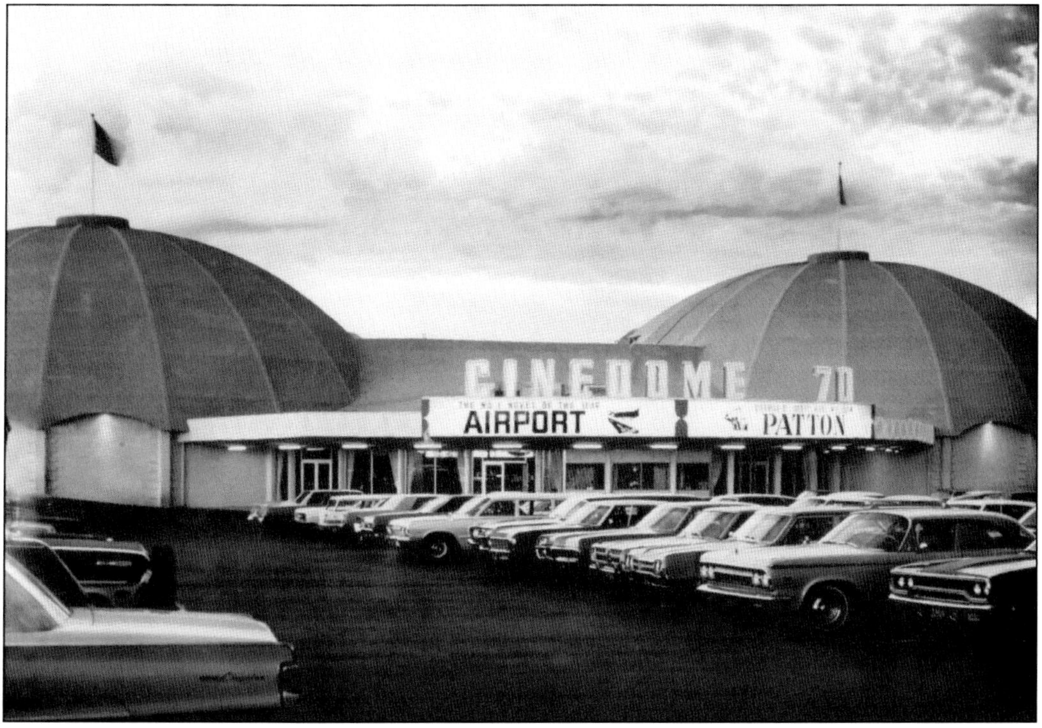

The Cinedome 70 Theater, 1970. On the land that was previously Pomona Orchard, a futuristic, twin-dome theater was opened in May 1970. The Cinedome 70 was built and owned by Darrell Tullis, Ray Hansen, and Roy Tullis and was perched upon Riverdale's west bench at 1481 West Riverdale Road. The domes each had a 110-foot diameter and were 60 feet tall. The theater featured seating for 1,600 in plush rocking chairs (800 for each 70-foot-wide curved screen), 35mm and 70mm movie projection (the first 70mm-capable theater in Northern Utah), an eight-track sound system with surround-sound capability, and a modern electric air-conditioning and heating system. During its 30 years of operation, customers watched iconic movies here including *Airport*, *Jaws*, *Grease*, *E.T. the Extra-Terrestrial*, and the original Star Wars trilogy. The theater closed in 2001, and the property was sold in 2004. The Cinedome was demolished on October 18, 2010. (Courtesy of Nancy and Mark Tullis.)

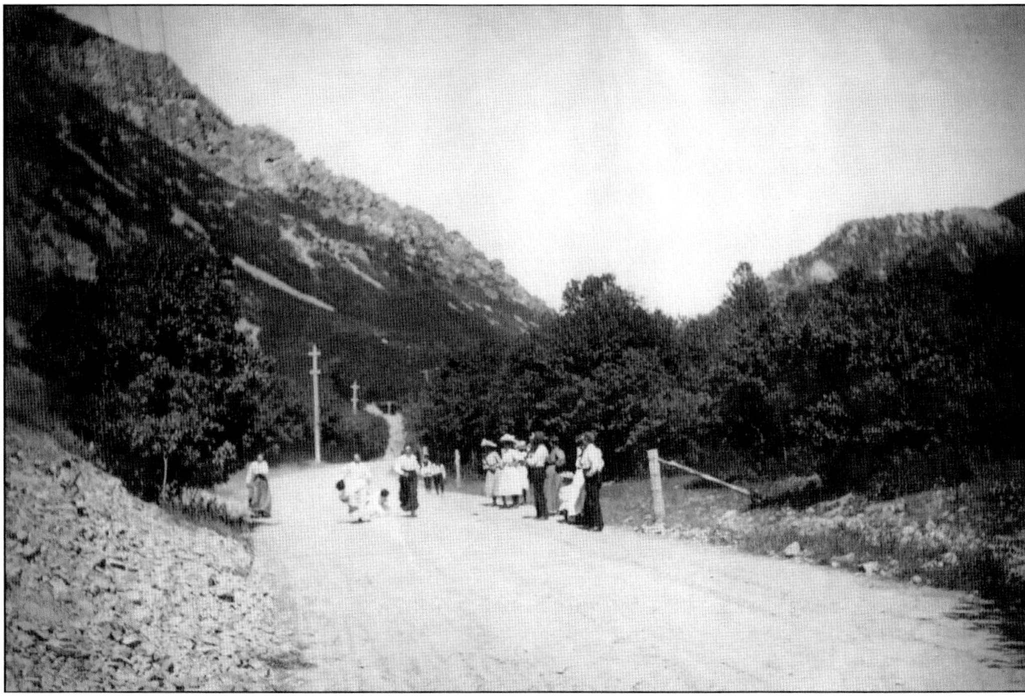

Ogden Canyon Outing, c. 1912. Ogden Canyon, a short drive from Riverdale, served as an ideal place for picnics. This photograph of a Riverdale Ward outing shows a group of women having a race. Riverdale residents also enjoyed trips to Lagoon, which once had a dance pavilion. (Courtesy of the Lucille Child Judkins family.)

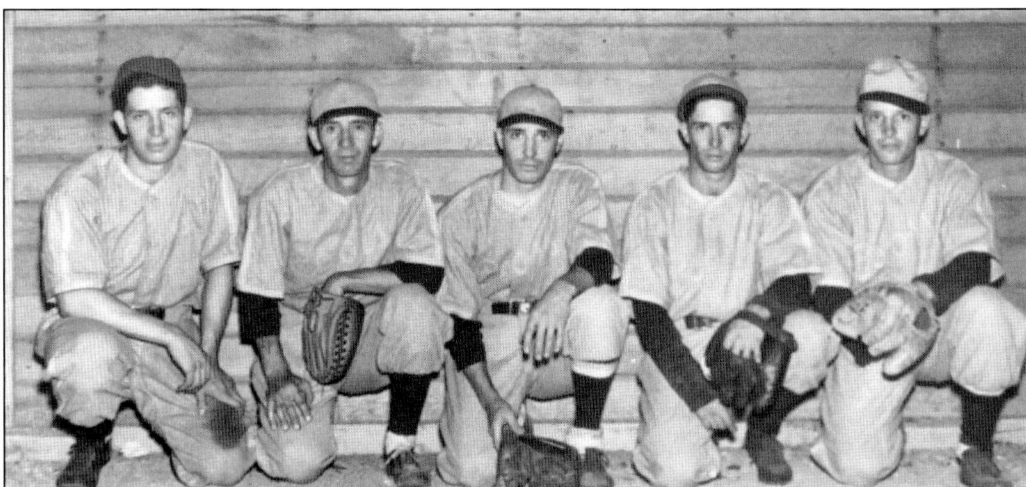

Farm Bureau Baseball Team, 1940. The five Zito brothers played on Riverdale's semiprofessional team in the Weber County Farm Bureau Baseball League. The team played at John Affleck field, once located on Wall Avenue in Ogden. Lou Zito, a legend of his time, pitched a record 24 strikeouts during a 1938 state tournament game. From left to right are Ted "Teddy" Zito (infielder), Tom Zito (catcher), Bill Zito (pitcher), Joe Zito (outfielder and catcher), and Lou Zito (pitcher). (Courtesy of Connie Fuller.)

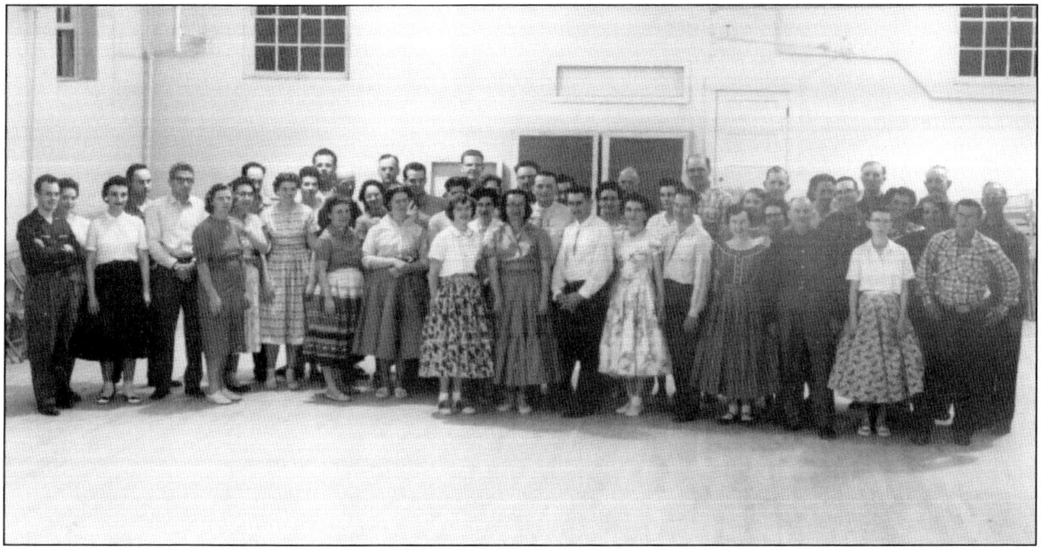

RIVERDALE SQUARE DANCE CLUB, C. 1955. A popular activity, square dances were held every Friday night. The event served as date night for many couples. This photograph, taken in the cultural hall in the basement of the old Riverdale Ward meetinghouse, includes Cleo Thompson, Woodrow Thompson, Edis Henderson, Ileen Henderson, Olive Thompson, Delbert Pike, Marva Pike, Ezra Bingham, Helen Bingham, Ruth Bradley, Wendell Bradley, Kenith Allen, Cleoma Allen, Edith Brough, Sedley Brough, Cleo Brough, ? Stephens, Phyllis Cevering, Afe Cevering, Lucille Stephens, Virginia Anderson, Ted Anderson, Roy Stephens, Leatha Myers, Martha Davis, Neal Myers, Howard Ellis, Hal Davis, Vernessa VanNoy, William "Avon" VanNoy, Blanche Gibby, Grant Gibby, Beth Tesch, and Wilford Tesch. Dick Derry called the dances. (Courtesy of Kathleen Cevering.)

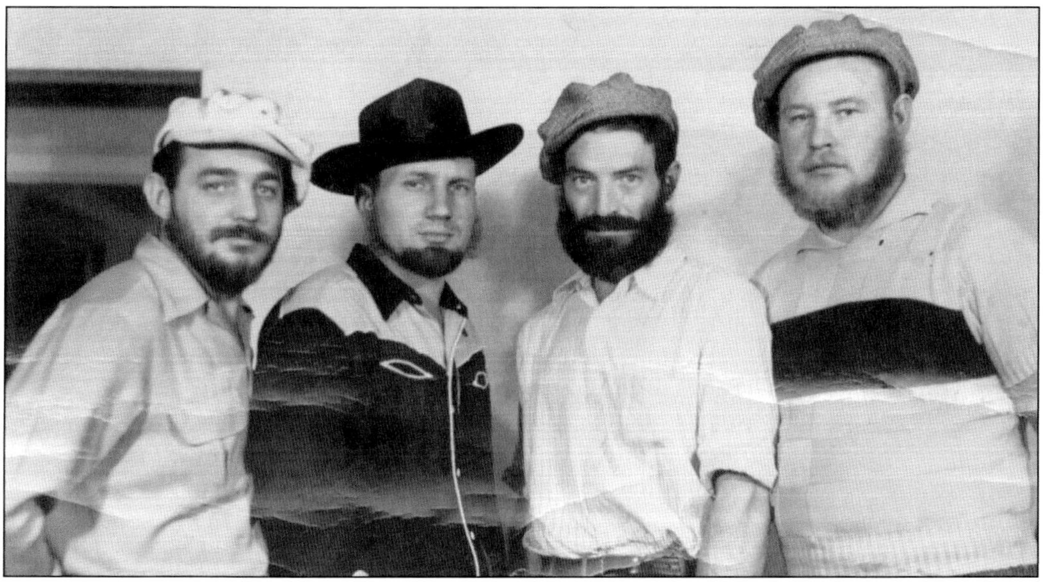

PIONEER DAY BEARD GROWING CONTEST, 1950S. In the early days of the community, residents celebrated Pioneer Day on July 24 to commemorate the arrival of the Mormon pioneers to the Salt Lake Valley. As part of these celebrations, men participated in beard-growing contests. In this photograph are, from left to right, Scott Bills, Alex "Swede" Carlsen Jr., Lyle Farrer, and Garth Stephens. (Courtesy of Riverdale City.)

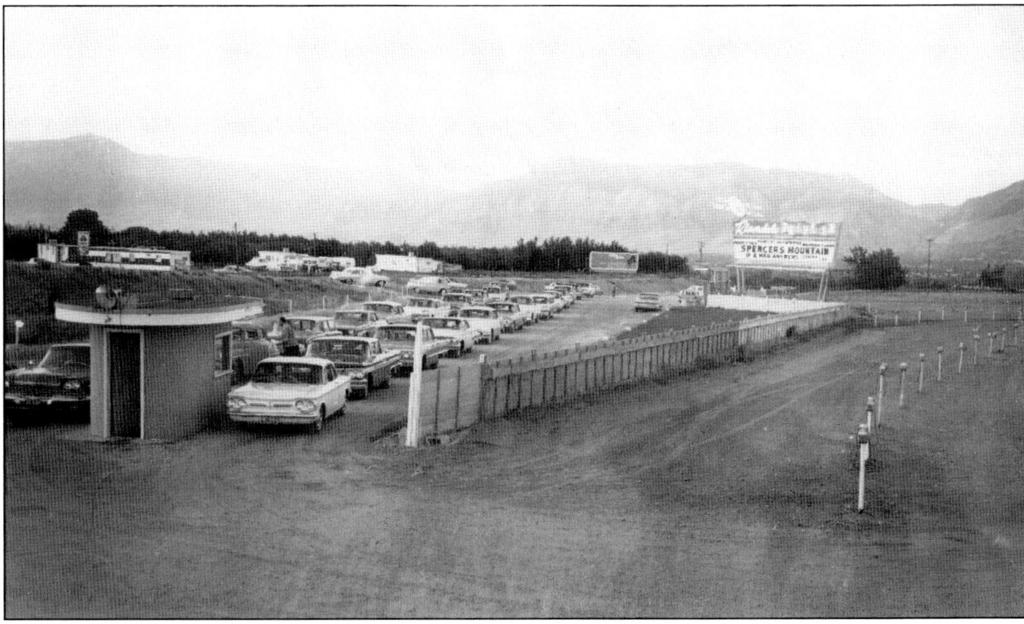

RIVERDALE DRIVE-IN THEATER, 1963. The Riverdale Drive-In opened on May 23, 1947. Owned by Roy Tullis and other partners, the drive-in featured one screen until 1973, when a second screen and radio-based sound system were added. The Riverdale Drive-In closed in 1985. It was located at 1551 West Riverdale Road, the current location of Cherry Creek Apartments. (Courtesy of Nancy and Mark Tullis.)

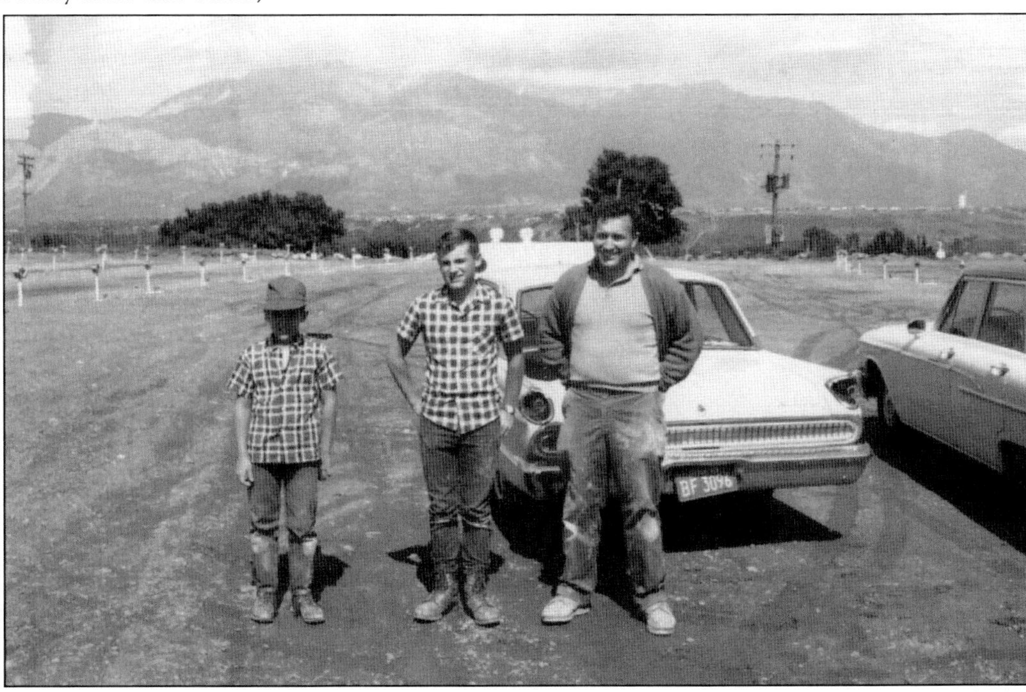

RIVERDALE DRIVE-IN THEATER, 1963. With the Wasatch Mountains in the background, this setting served as a great place for an outdoor theater. From left to right are Randy Jacobs, Breon Jacobs, and Darrell L. Tullis. (Courtesy of Nancy and Mark Tullis.)

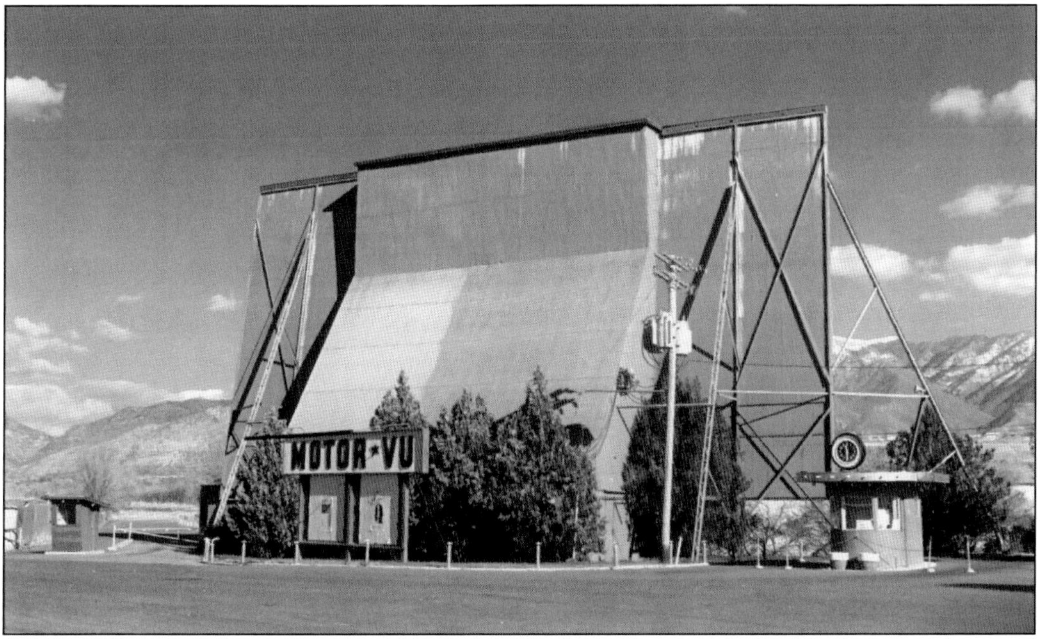

Motor-Vu Drive-In, c. 1960. The Motor-Vu Drive-In held its grand opening on June 18, 1947. This photograph shows the original screen and entrance to Motor-Vu, which was on the west side. To entertain children before movies began, owners installed a playground, several rides, and a mini streamliner train called *Motor-Vu Express.* (Courtesy of Brent Coleman, Motor-Vu Drive-In.)

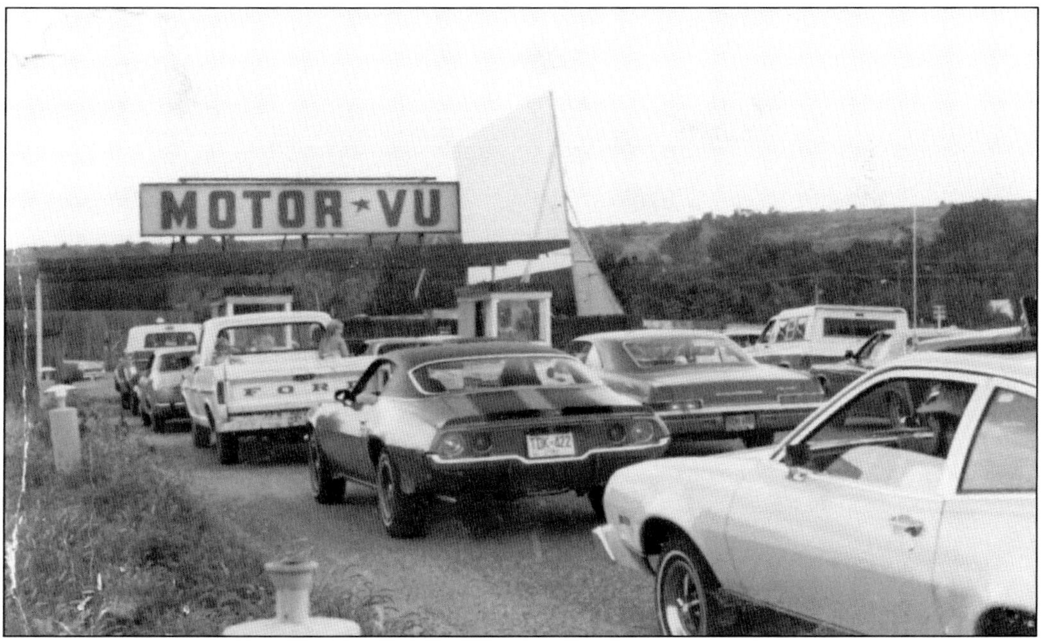

Motor-Vu Drive-In, 1971. In 1952, Howard Coleman started work as a lot boy at the Motor-Vu Drive-In and became the manager in 1963. He and his wife, Betty, purchased the drive-in in 1979, and it is currently owned by Howard's sons Brent, Bruce, and Dale. This photograph shows the current entrance to the drive-in. A popular swap meet is held here on Saturdays and Sundays. (Courtesy of Brent Coleman, Motor-Vu Drive-In.)

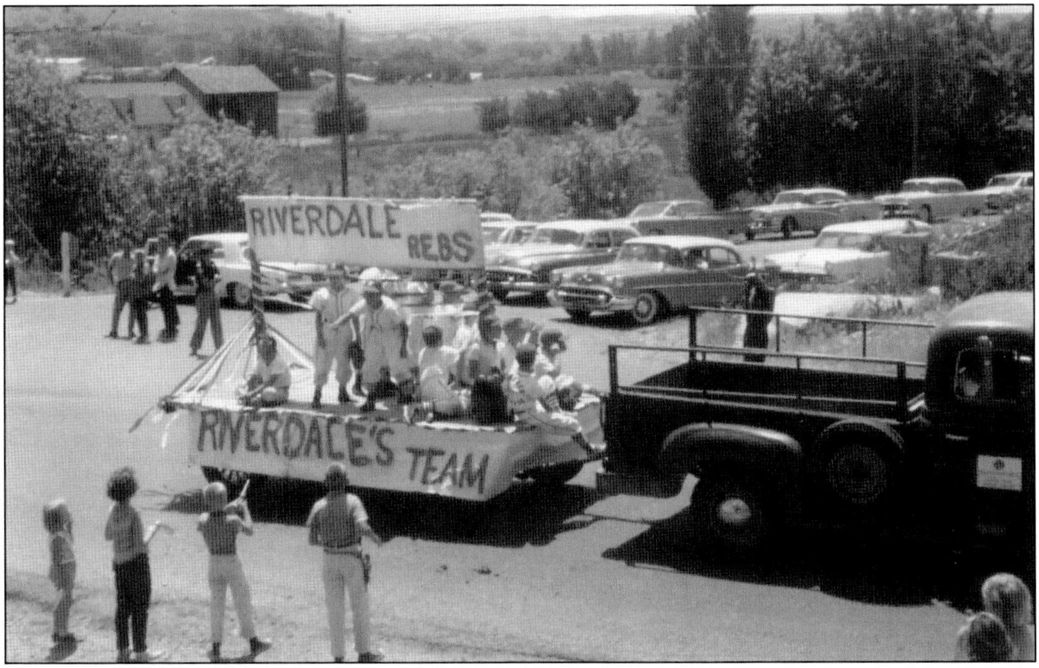

Boys Baseball Team. The Riverdale Rebs are participating in a parade on 4400 South. Riverdale offers a number of recreational sports for youth, including volleyball, flag football, basketball, soccer, baseball, T-ball, softball, tennis, and archery. (Courtesy of Gail and Doris Sanders.)

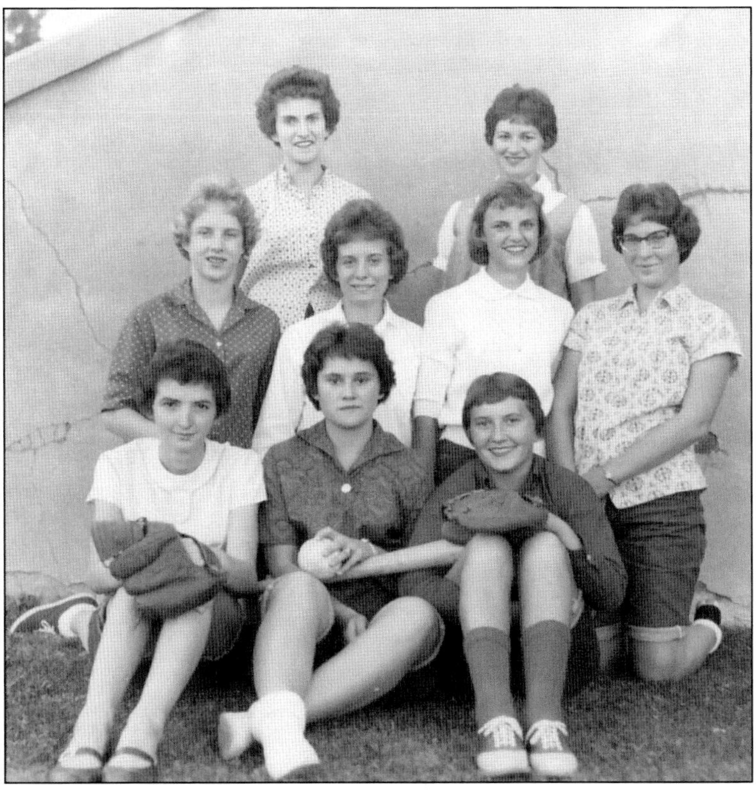

Girls Softball Team. From left to right are (first row) Karen Henderson, Cathy Thompson, and Karen Knight; (second row) Merle Crabtree, Karen Hamblin, Connie Dee, and Jane Davis; (third row) Claudia Stimpson and Irene Sears. (Photograph by Donald Child; courtesy of Lee Child.)

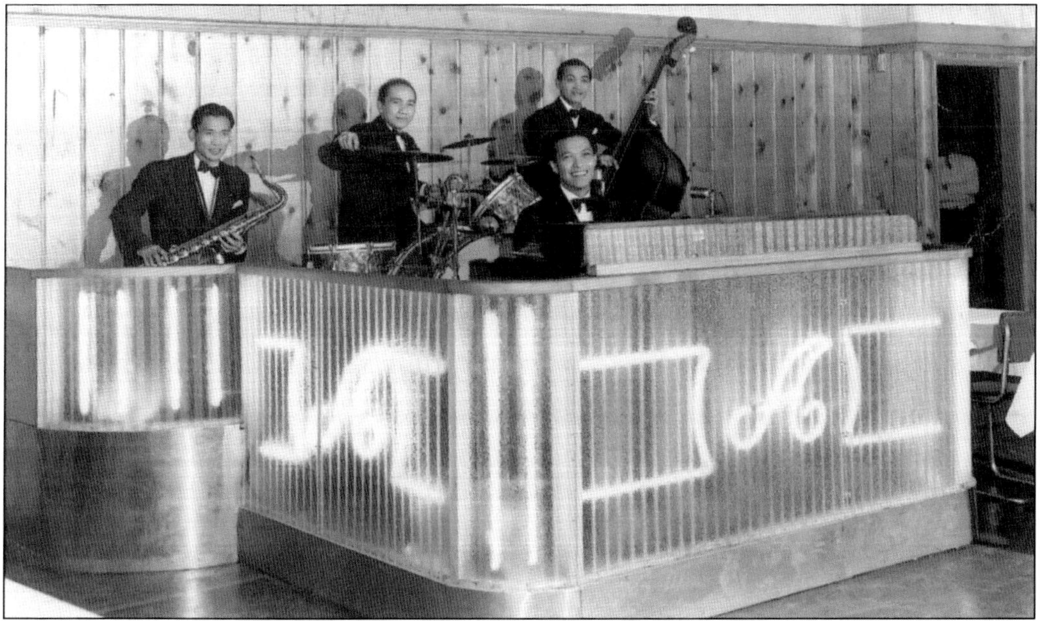

Apollo Club, 1948. The Apollo Club, a unique place for dining and dancing, was located west of Riverdale School. Owners Lou Bryan and William Zito opened the club on December 21, 1940. Friday and Saturday nights featured a swing band. Fermin Santos, a prominent local musician and civic worker, later purchased the popular nightclub. The band in the photograph played at the Apollo Club until its closing around 1961. From left to right are Mariano Cabrales (saxophone), Fred Javier (drums), Fermin Santos (piano), and Benny Surel (bass). (Courtesy of Anita Cabrales Draney.)

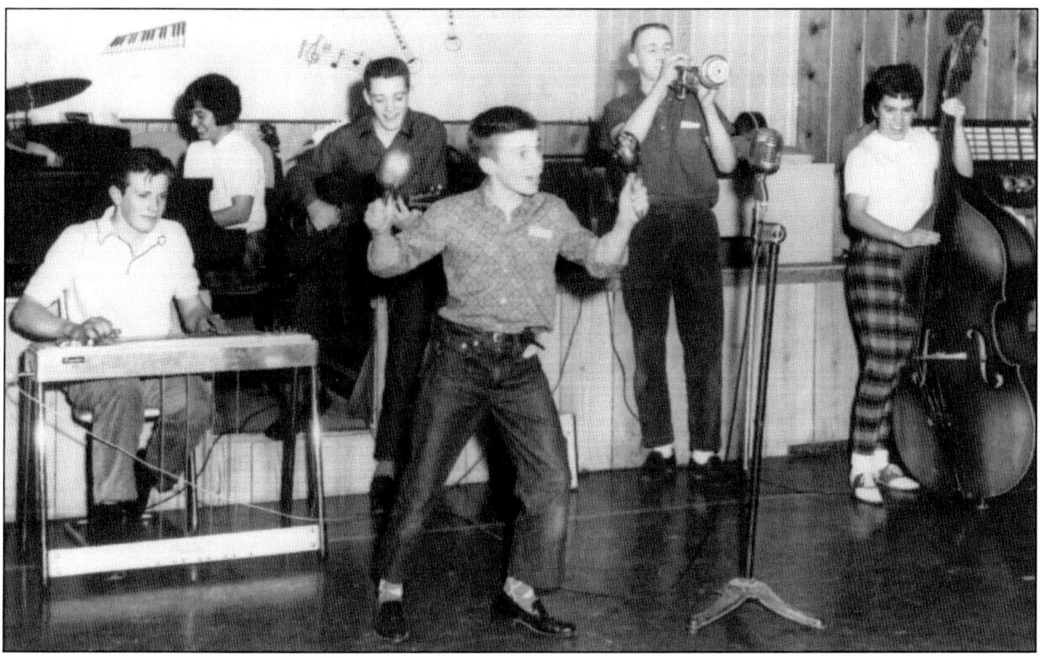

Apollo Club, 1961. This photograph was taken at a church dance at the Apollo Club. From left to right are Johnny Hull (steel guitar), Anita Cabrales (piano), Cordell Hull (guitar), Jarrell Fay Hull (singing), Dennis Hull (trumpet), and Mary Ann Cabrales (bass). (Courtesy of the Hull Family)

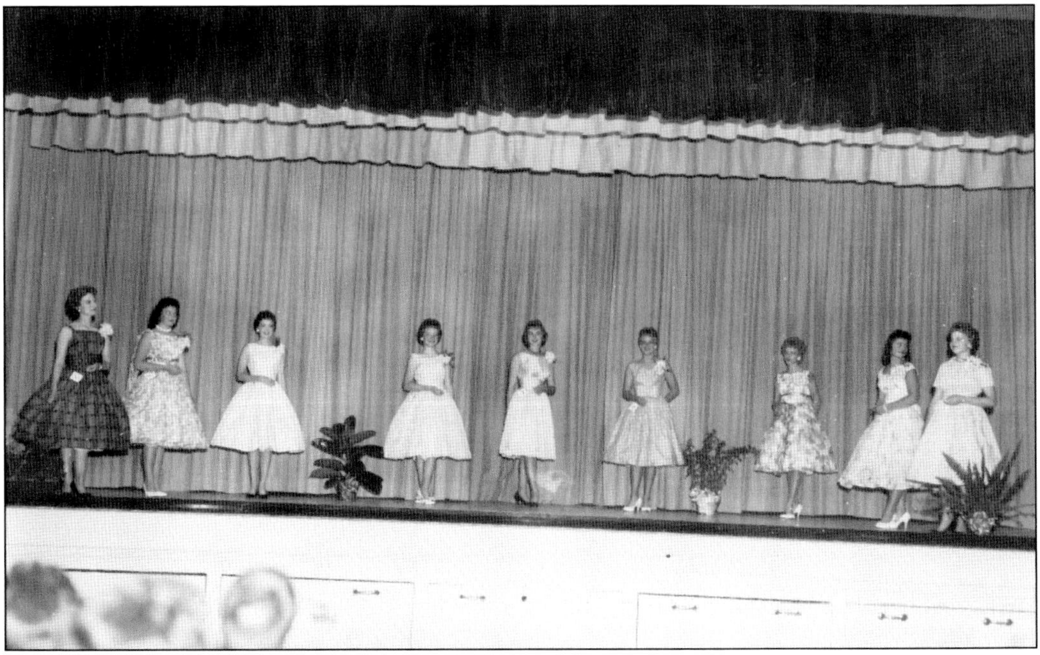

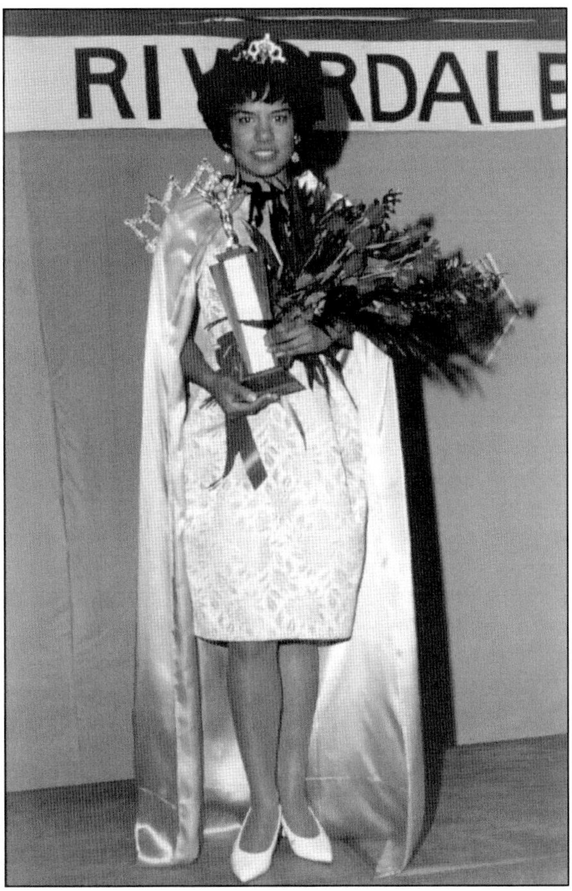

Miss Riverdale Queen Contest, c. 1960. The Riverdale Ladies Club organized a beauty pageant in the 1950s for the Fourth of July celebration. Open to single girls between the ages of 16 and 21, each girl was judged on talent and beauty. Judges selected one queen and two attendants. (Courtesy of Riverdale City.)

Miss Riverdale Mary Ann Cabrales, 1963. Mary Ann Cabrales was crowned Miss Riverdale at age 16 in 1963. Other Miss Riverdale winners included Betty Bingham (1954), Vickie Allstead (1958), Carma Hull (1960), Brigitte Buckway (1961), Linda Tesch (1964), Connie Fuller (1965), Sherry Ellis (Ferrin) (1966), Betty Oberbroekling (Wilson) (1967), Ellen Thompson (1968), Kathy Bond (1969), Penny Thompson (1970), Connie Hoopes (1971), Jan Martin (1972), Shelly Helm and Diane Doliwa (1975), Sharrie Call (1976), and Kelly Smith (1986). (Courtesy of Mary Ann Cabrales Woodbury.)

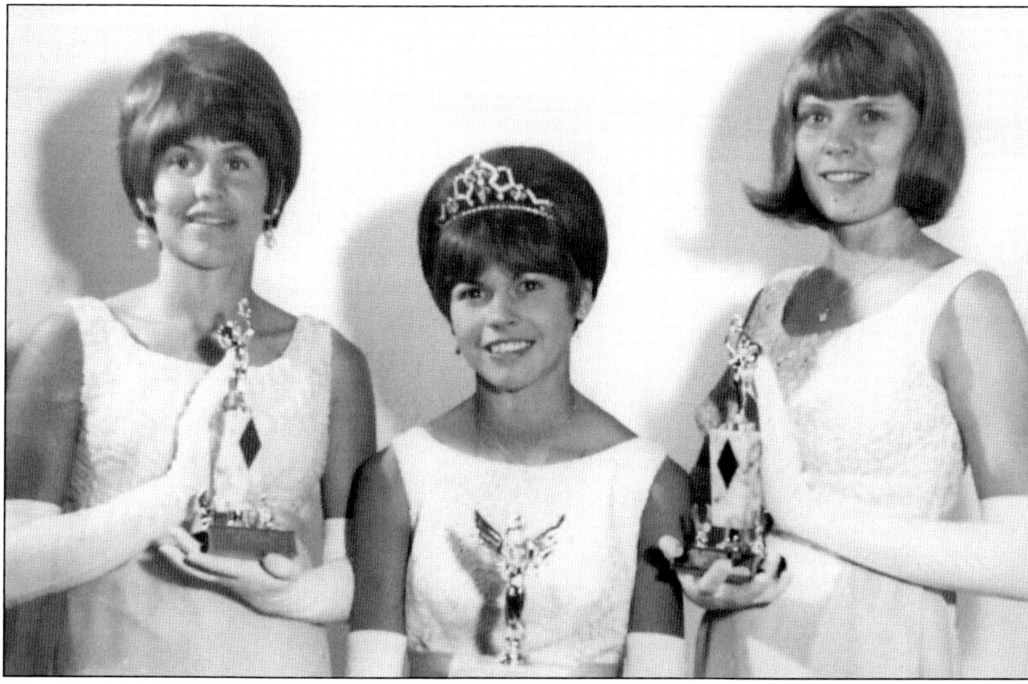

MISS RIVERDALE SHERRY ELLIS, 1966. Miss Riverdale 1966 was Sherry Ellis (center), seen here with her attendants Jolene Stimpson (left) and Lorna Cragun. Over the years, the contest was held at the church, school, and the Cinedome 70 theater. (Courtesy of Sherry Ellis Ferrin.)

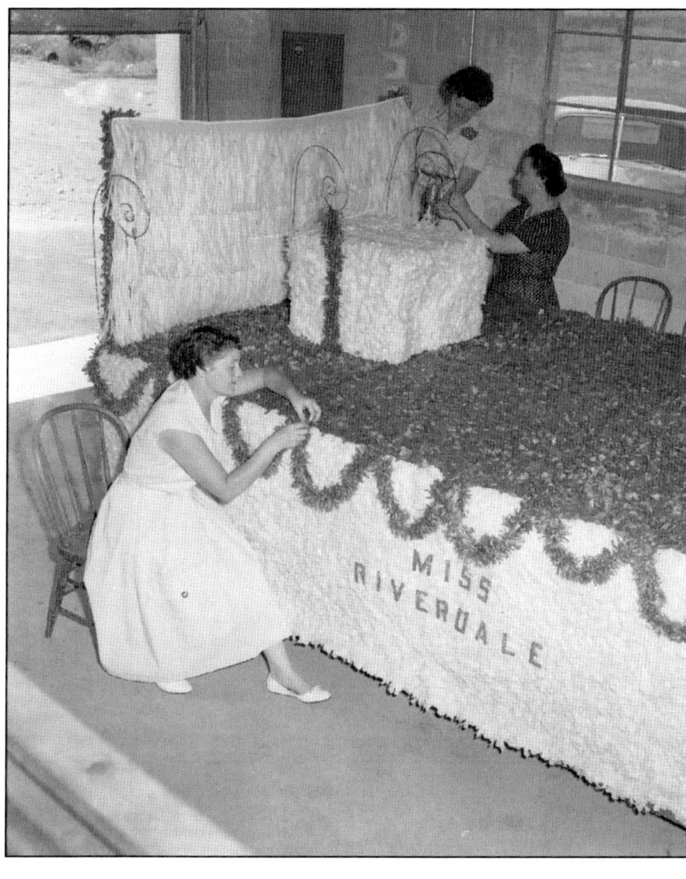

MISS RIVERDALE FLOAT, 1960. Irene Farrer (seated), Ruth Parker (back left), and Dorothy Nebeker (back right), members of the Riverdale Ladies Club, are putting the finishing touches on the float for the Ogden Pioneer Days parade. Miss Riverdale and her attendants rode in the Ogden and Riverdale parades. (Courtesy of Weber State University Special Collections.)

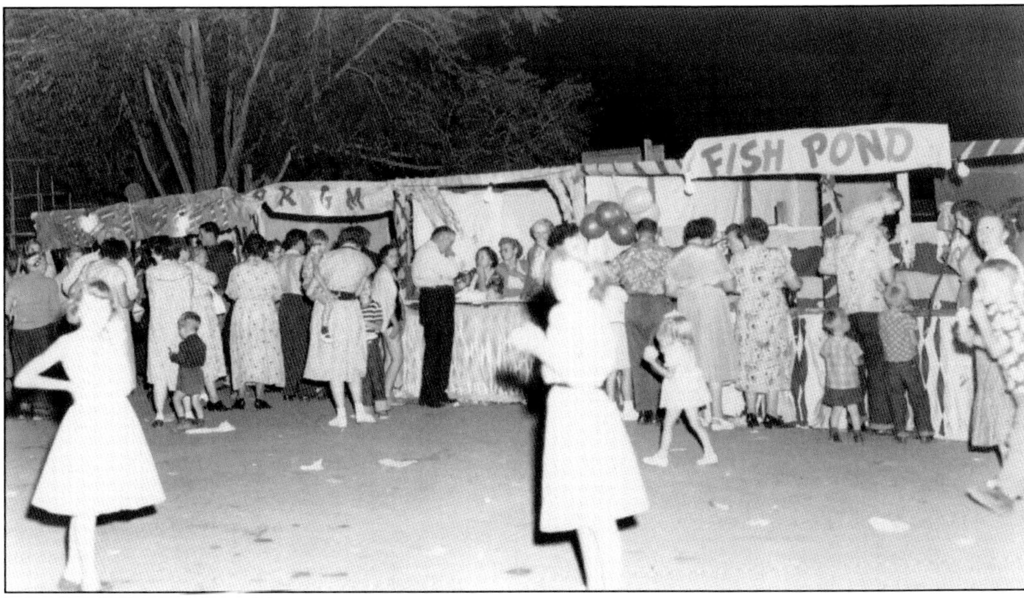

Fourth of July Celebration. Since 1955, Riverdale has come together on Independence Day in a celebration called Old Glory Days. This photograph shows booths and attendees at the celebration. (Courtesy of the Lucille Child Judkins family.)

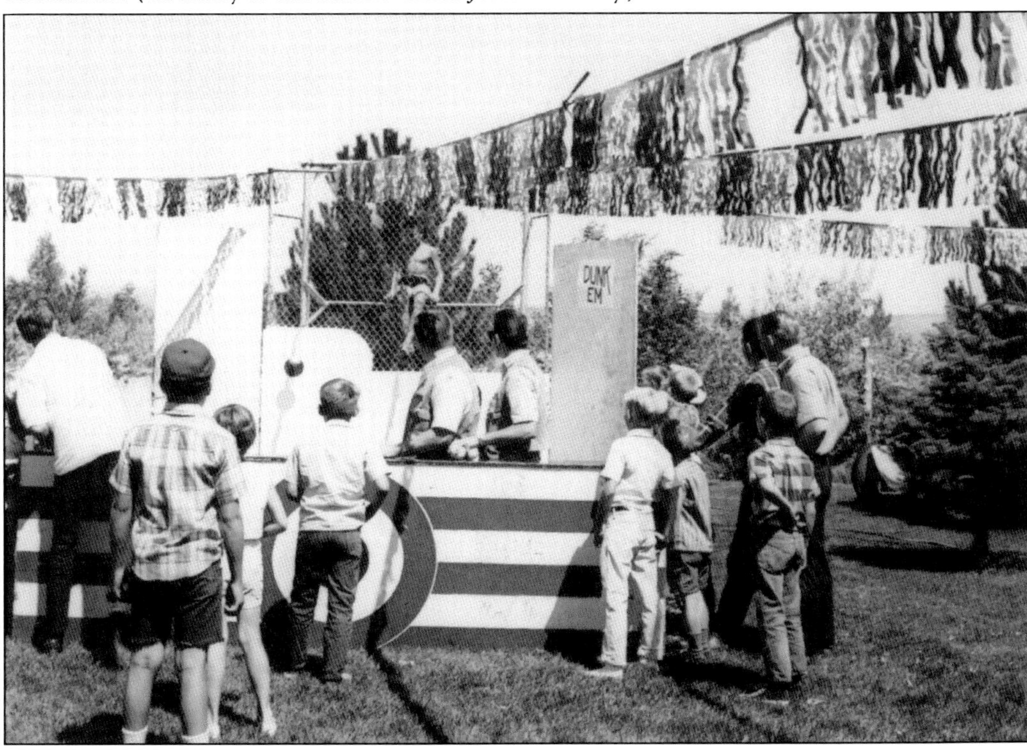

Dunk Tank. Old Glory Days has involved many activities over the years, including a flag ceremony, a choir singing patriotic songs, demolition derby, parades, ball games, concession stands, vendor booths, fish scramble, nickel grab, a drawing to win a pony, greased-pig competition, dunk tank, and fireworks. (Courtesy of Norman W. Leishman.)

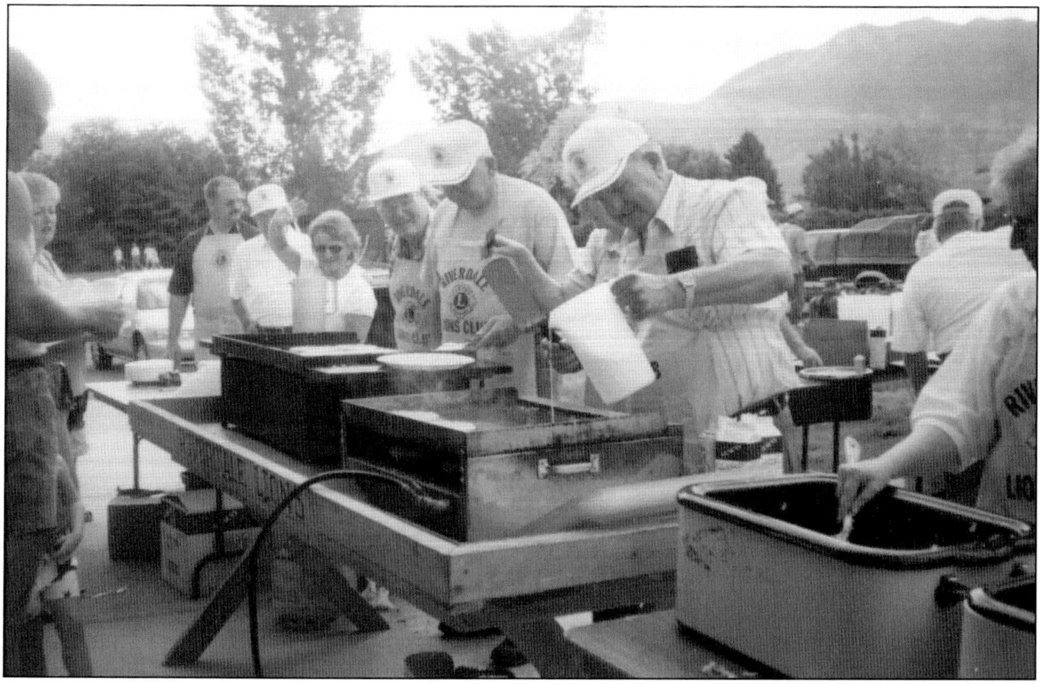

LIONS CLUB BREAKFAST. Following the sunrise service and flag-raising ceremony, the Lions Club serves an annual fundraiser breakfast at Riverdale Park. A breakfast of pancakes, eggs, sausage, and orange juice is cooked and served by the Lions. (Courtesy of Riverdale Lions Club.)

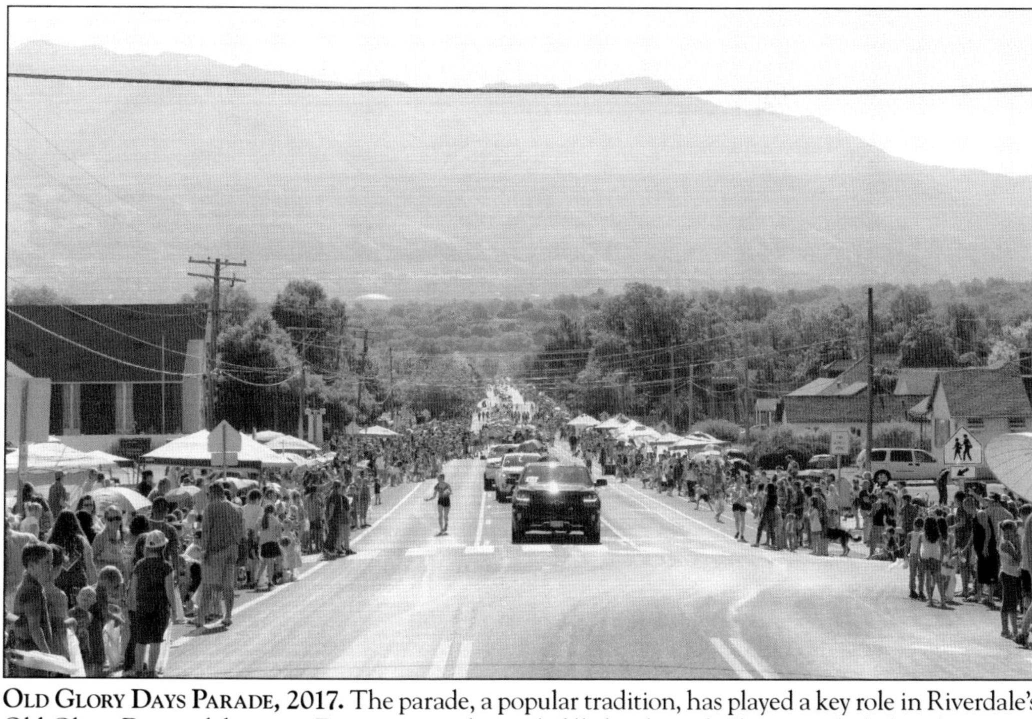

OLD GLORY DAYS PARADE, 2017. The parade, a popular tradition, has played a key role in Riverdale's Old Glory Days celebration. Festivities at the park fill the day, which is concluded with a grand fireworks display. (Author's collection.)

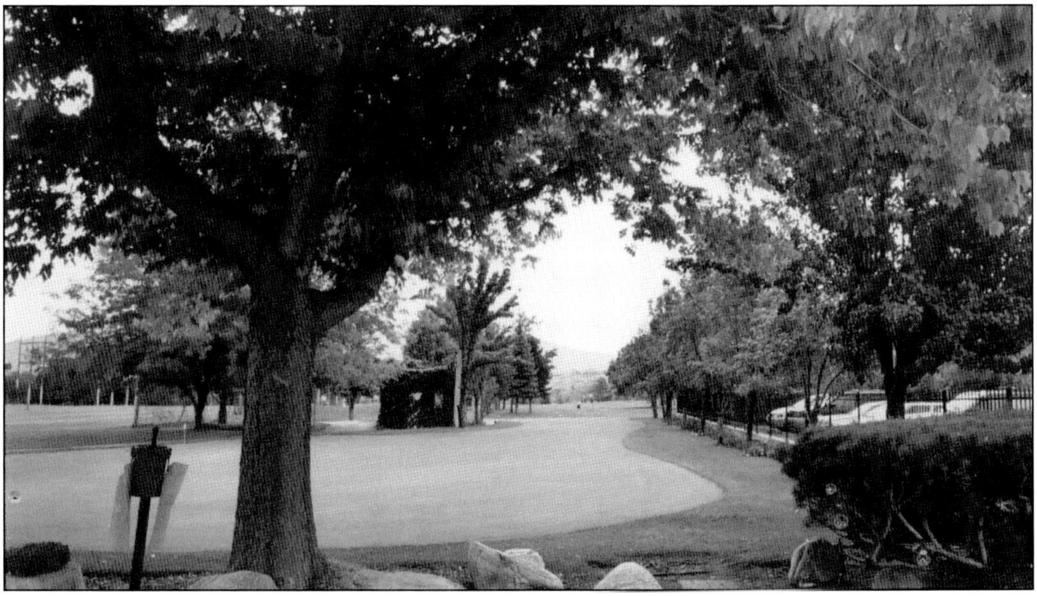

Schneiter's Riverside Golf Course. Originally a part of the Ritter family homestead, Ernie Schneiter Sr. opened this golf course on April 18, 1961. The course was skillfully designed to show the natural beauty of the hills, Weber River, ponds, and woods. Prior to the golf course, ponds here had been used for ice-skating in the winter. (Courtesy of the Schneiter family.)

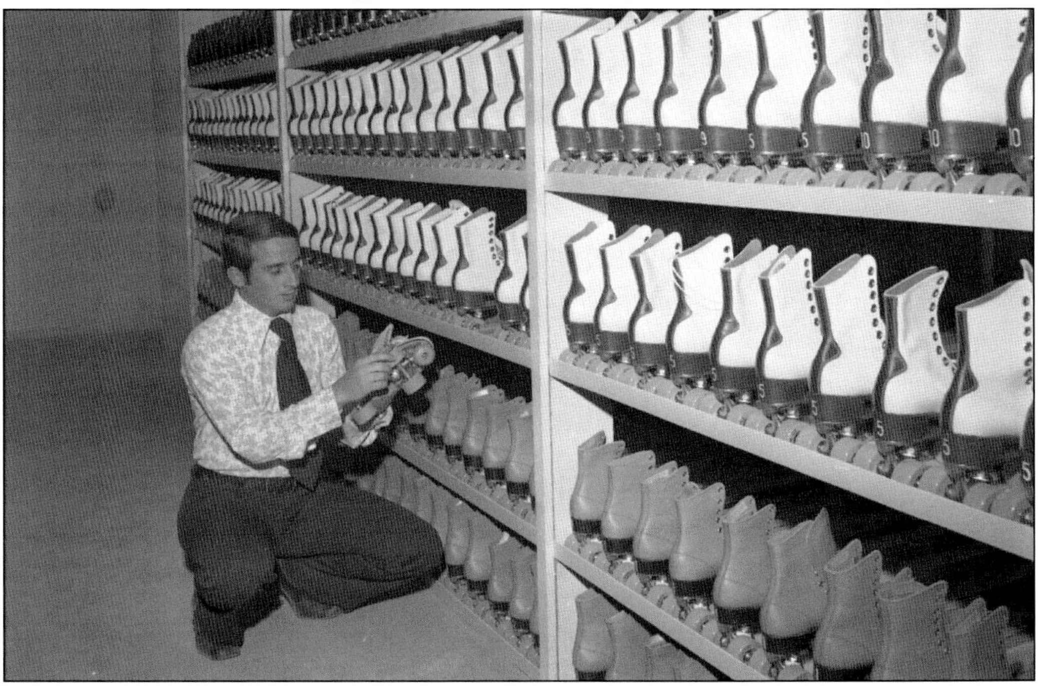

Classic Skating, 1973. The Classic Skating roller rink opened December 27, 1973. Operated by Henderson Enterprises, the rink was located at 4181 Riverdale Road. Mark Henderson, seen here, managed the rink. In addition to Classic Skating, Classic Waterslides (still in operation), and Classic Mini-Golf entertained many during the summer months. (Courtesy of Weber State University Special Collections.)

Ten

RIVERDALE

THE CITY TODAY

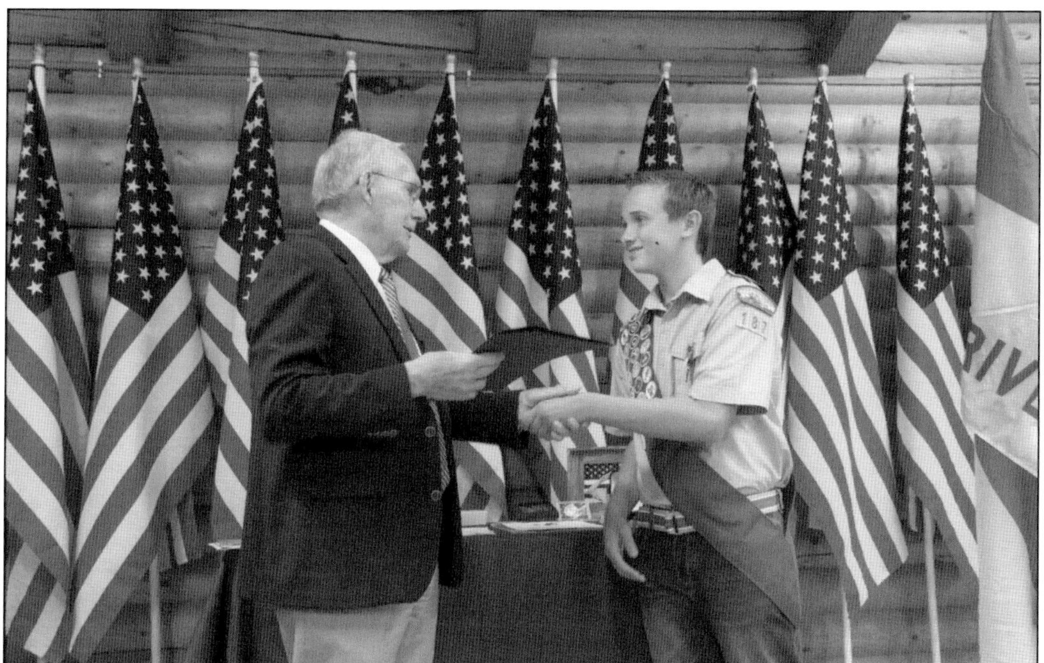

MAYOR SEARLE. Elected in 2014, Mayor Norm Searle has been active in the community and very involved in making Riverdale a great place to live and do business. Mayor Searle is seen here congratulating Garritt KC Roberts at his Eagle Scout Court of Honor on November 12, 2016. (Courtesy of Tara Roberts.)

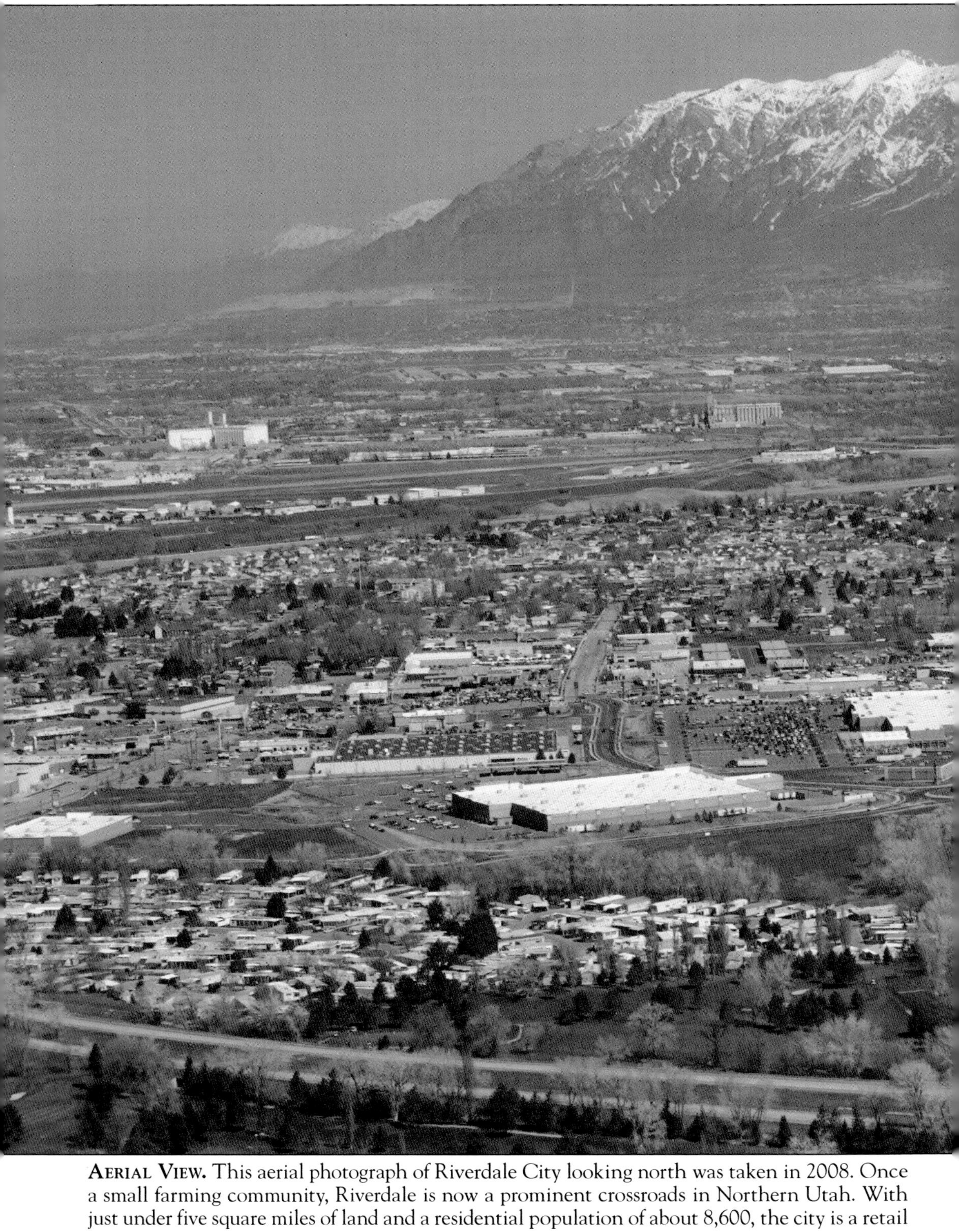

Aerial View. This aerial photograph of Riverdale City looking north was taken in 2008. Once a small farming community, Riverdale is now a prominent crossroads in Northern Utah. With just under five square miles of land and a residential population of about 8,600, the city is a retail

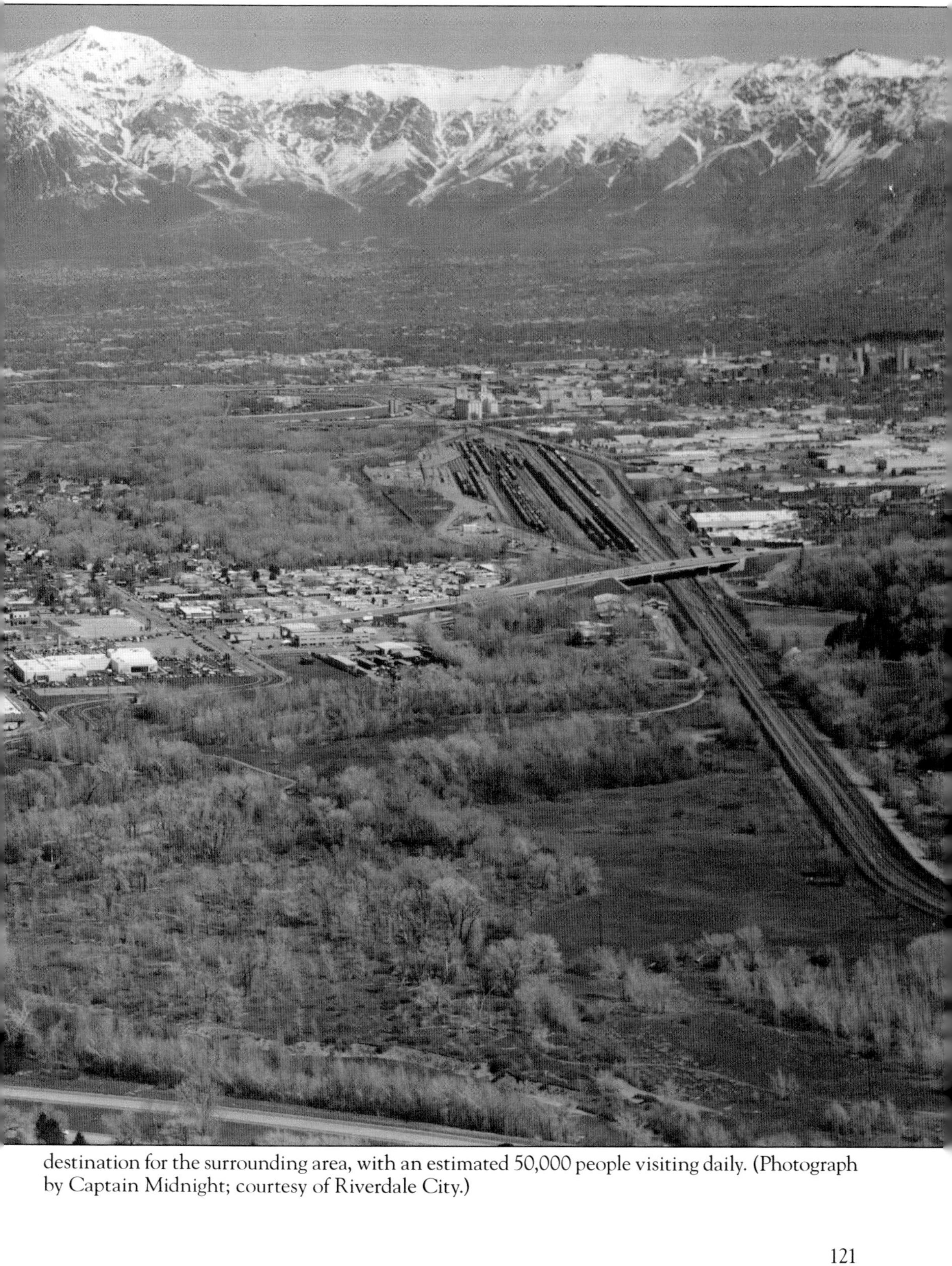

destination for the surrounding area, with an estimated 50,000 people visiting daily. (Photograph by Captain Midnight; courtesy of Riverdale City.)

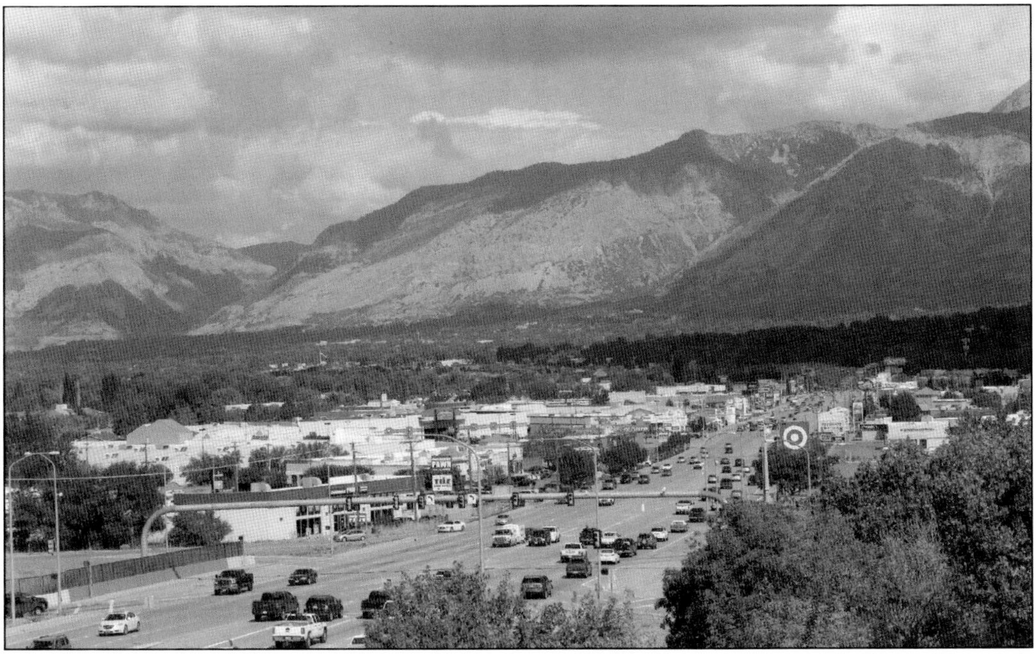

RIVERDALE ROAD, 2017. Once only farmland, Riverdale Road has grown into a busy three-mile stretch of highway that changed the character of the city. Up to 50,000 visitors shop, dine, and enjoy the amenities in Riverdale each day. Riverdale Road has changed and grown several times and continues to play an important role in Riverdale. (Author's collection.)

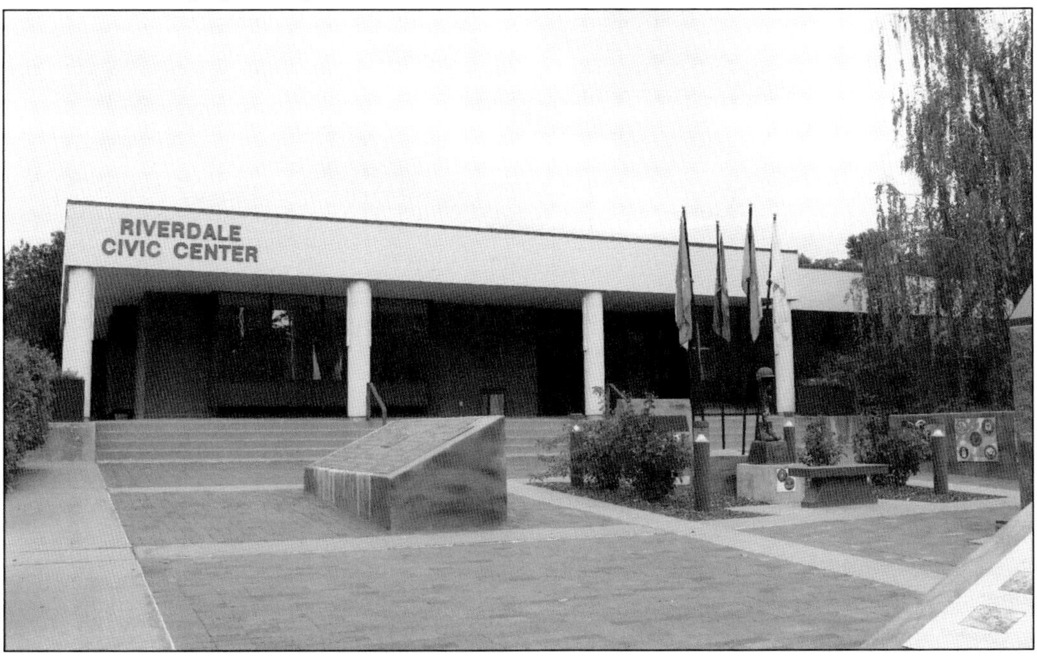

RIVERDALE CIVIC CENTER. Constructed in 1985, this building is the center for city government. It houses the city council chambers, administrative offices, and the city court. The civic center sits adjacent to the police station and is near the public works building. In 2010, the city dedicated the Riverdale Veterans Memorial in front of the civic center. (Author's collection.)

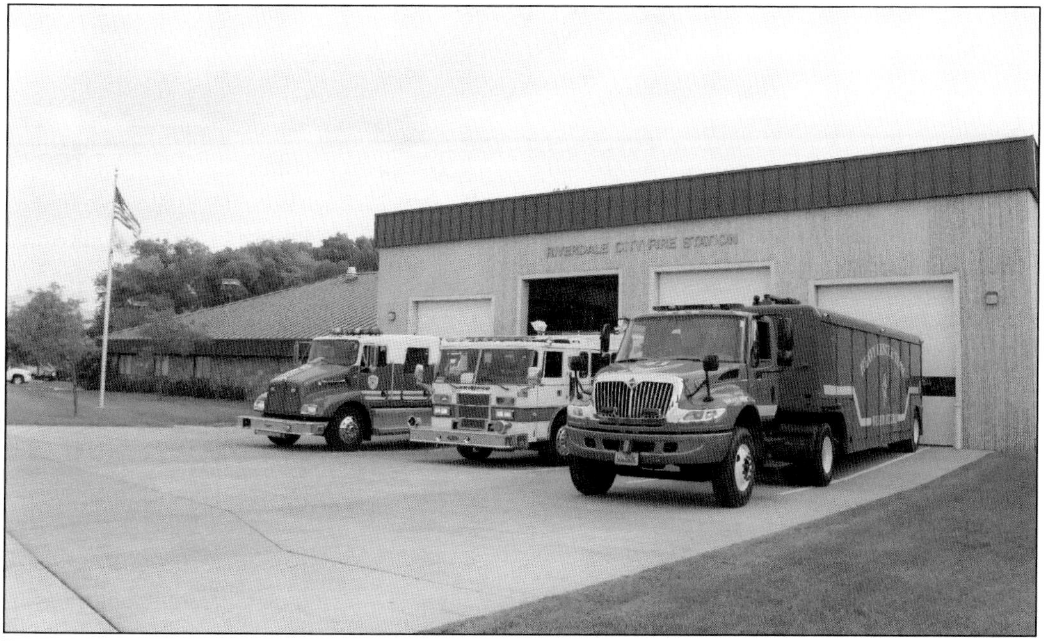

RIVERDALE FIRE STATION. Built in 1998, Riverdale's fire station is located at 4334 Parker Drive. The 11,000-square-foot building has seven bays for fire and emergency vehicles, a kitchen, recreation room, and sleeping quarters. The fire department employees a fire chief, an administrative assistant, and nine full-time and 14 part-time firefighters. Frequently involved in community and school events, Riverdale's firefighters provide excellent service to the community. (Author's collection.)

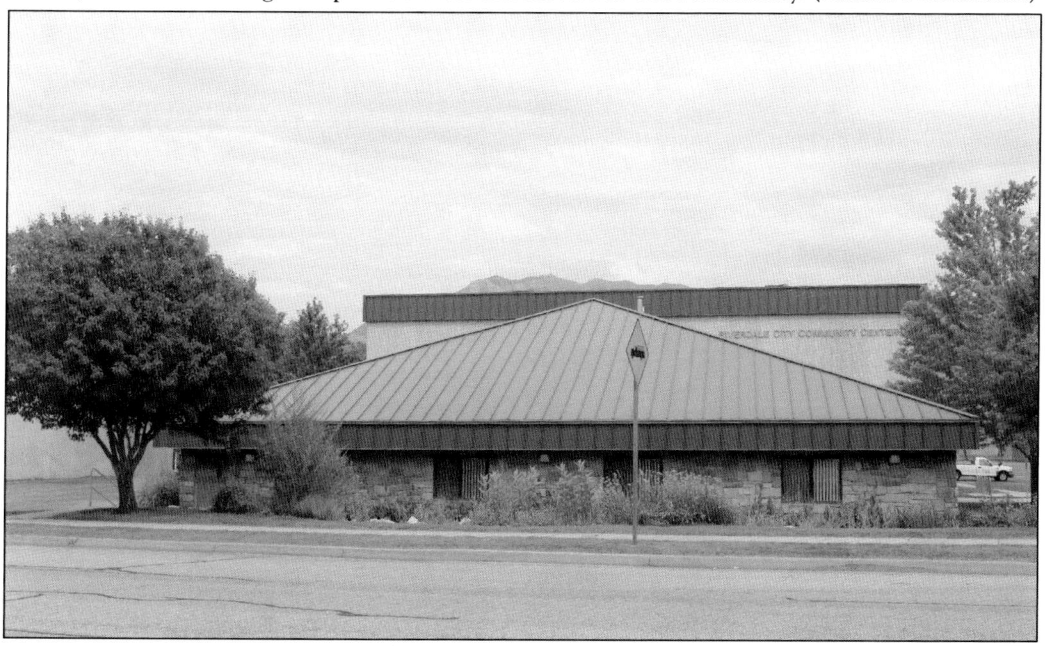

RIVERDALE COMMUNITY CENTER. The 18,000-square-foot Riverdale Community Center was built in 1998 on land where a pea vinery once stood. The center has a full-size gymnasium, exercise room, kitchen, and two large meeting rooms. Here, residents enjoy basketball, pickleball, ping pong, and group fitness classes. It also serves as a meeting place for the community. (Author's collection.)

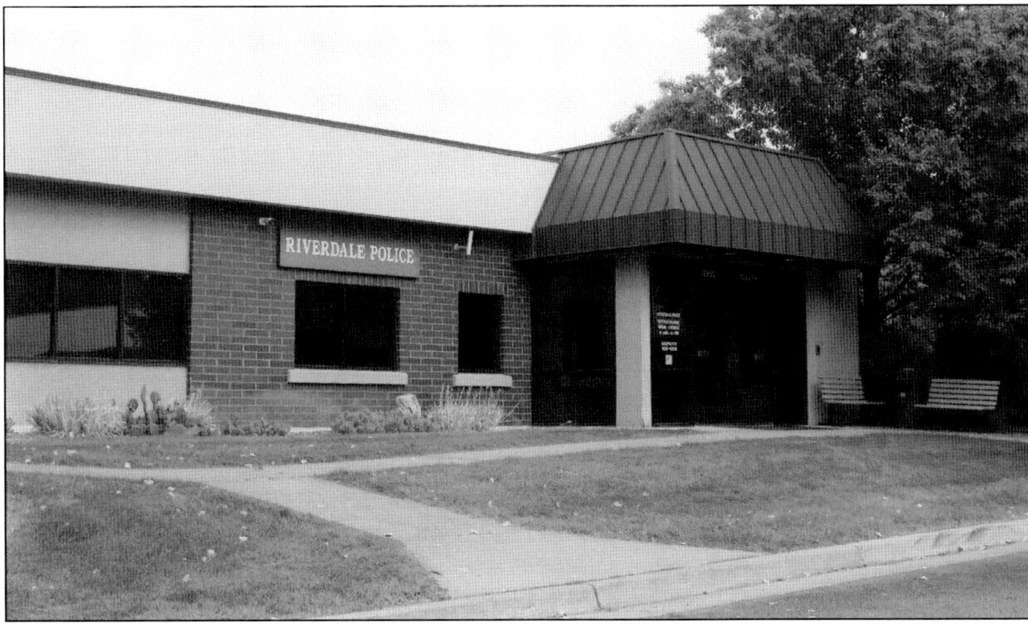

Riverdale Police Station. Dedicated on December 13, 1994, the law enforcement complex is located near the civic center. Riverdale's police force has grown from one to 18 officers, including an animal control officer, two administrative staff members, three crossing guards, and a police service dog. Despite having a relatively small residential population, Riverdale businesses attract tens of thousands of visitors each day, necessitating the services of the Riverdale Police Department. (Author's collection.)

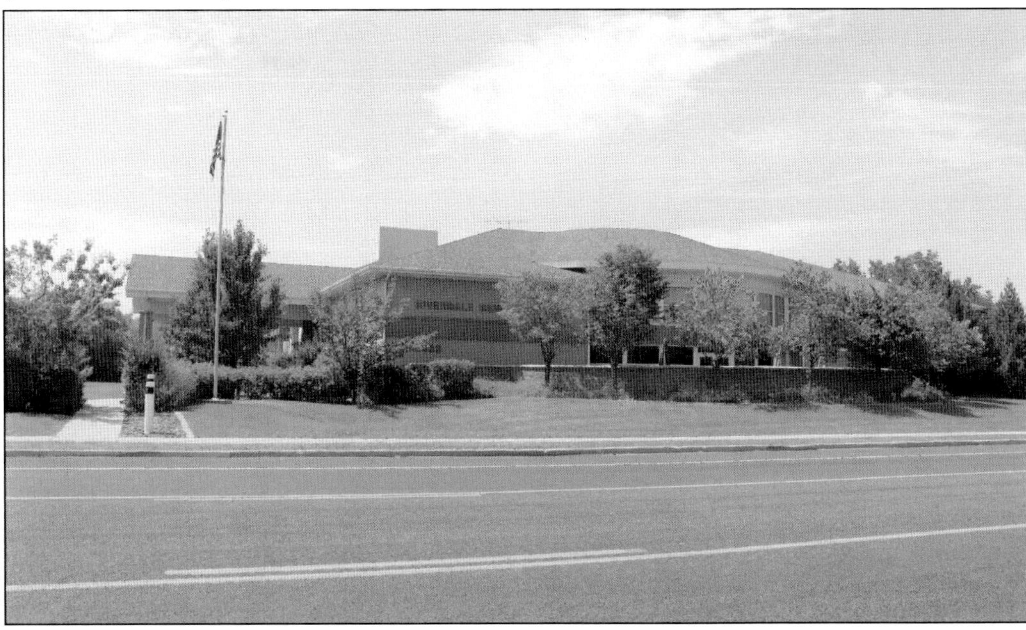

Riverdale Senior Center. Opened in July 2005, the Riverdale Senior Center is a place where seniors can gather with old friends and make new friends. The facility offers a variety of activities, classes, holiday events, and opportunities for involvement in humanitarian projects. Here, seniors also enjoy a small library and lunch that is served daily. (Author's collection.)

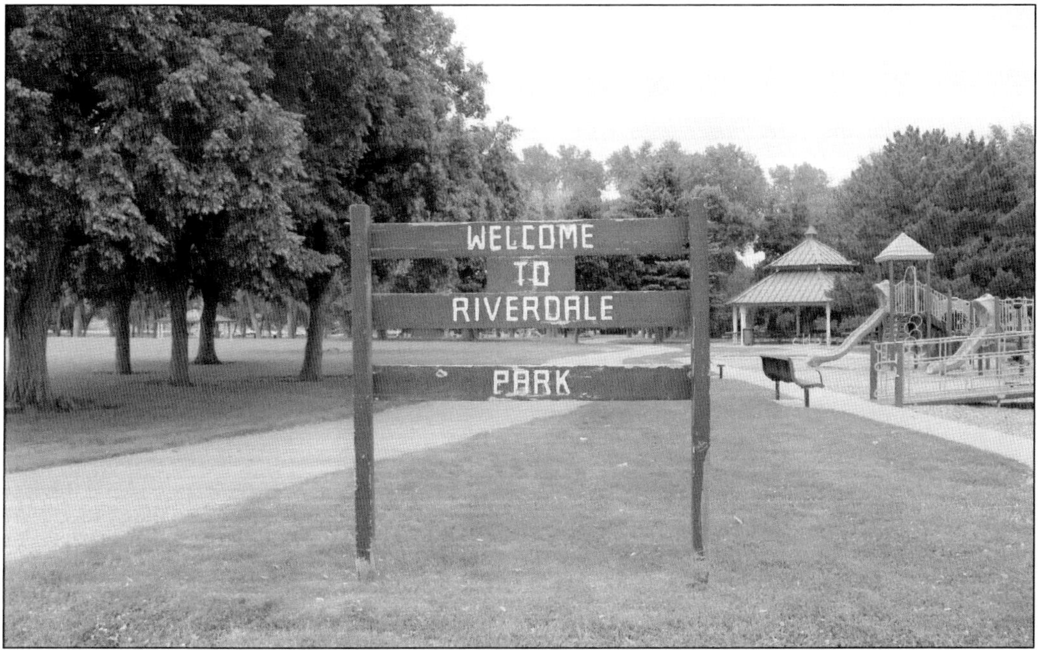

RIVERDALE PARK (UPPER). Riverdale Park is located north of Riverdale Elementary School and adjacent to the community center and fire station. The upper (southern) section features a large pavilion, playground, a baseball/softball diamond, tennis courts, walking path, and a large open field. (Author's collection.)

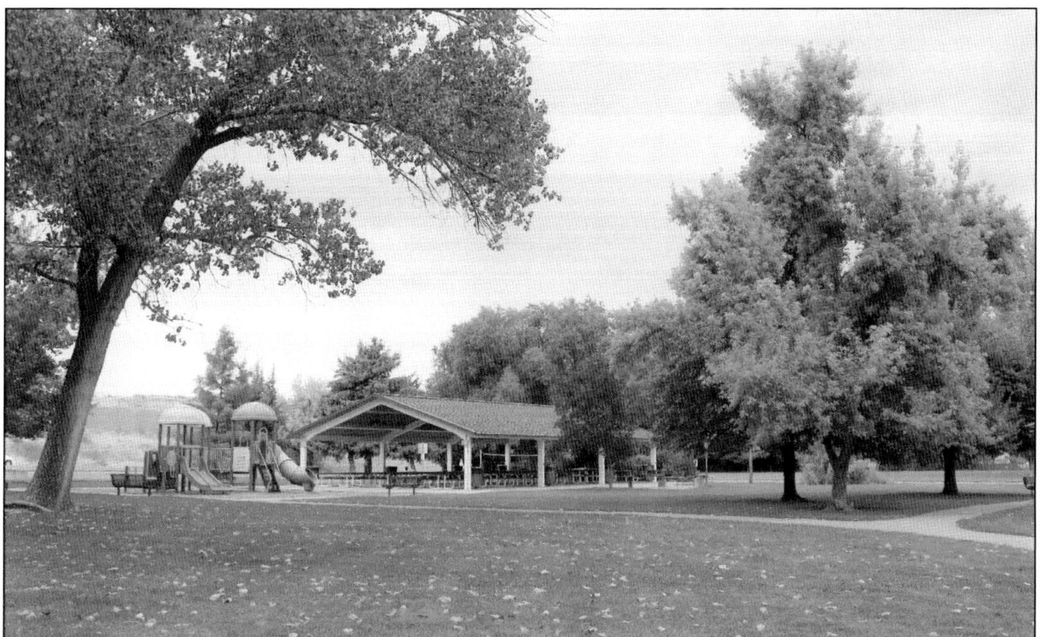

RIVERDALE PARK (LOWER). The lower (northern) section of the park is more wooded, with several pavilions, two playgrounds, a splash pad, sand volleyball court, and a walking path. Once a natural gravel pit, today the popular park hosts activities for Old Glory Days and attracts visitors from all over the area. (Author's collection.)

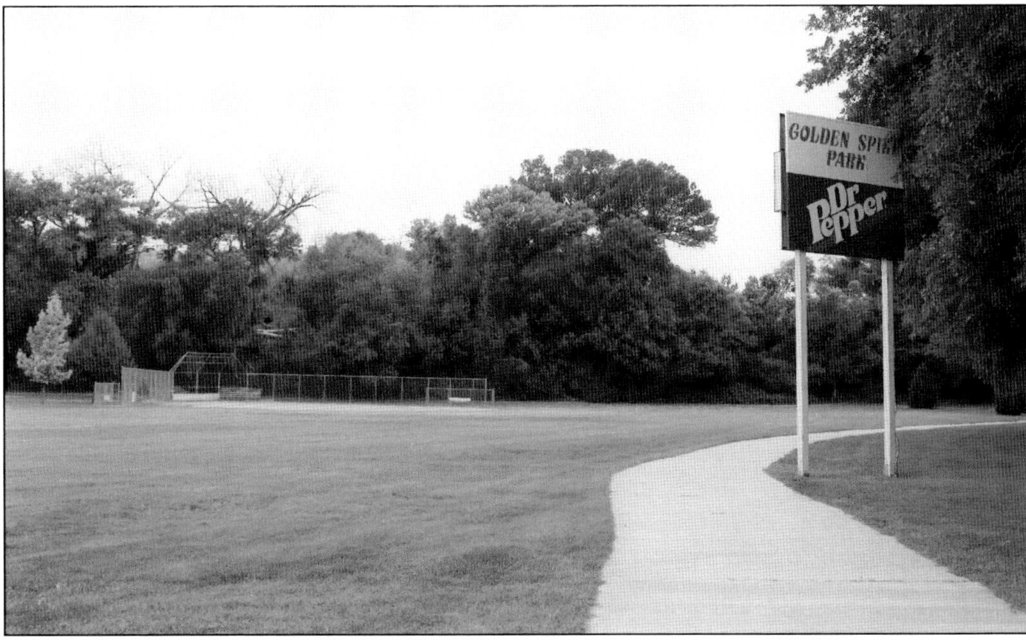

Golden Spike Park. Golden Spike Park, located at 1150 West 5000 South, features a large pavilion, playground, two baseball diamonds, a large open grass area, and walking trail. The name for the park was suggested by the Golden Spike Empire Vintage Car Club. The park filled with water during the canal disaster in 1999. (Author's collection.)

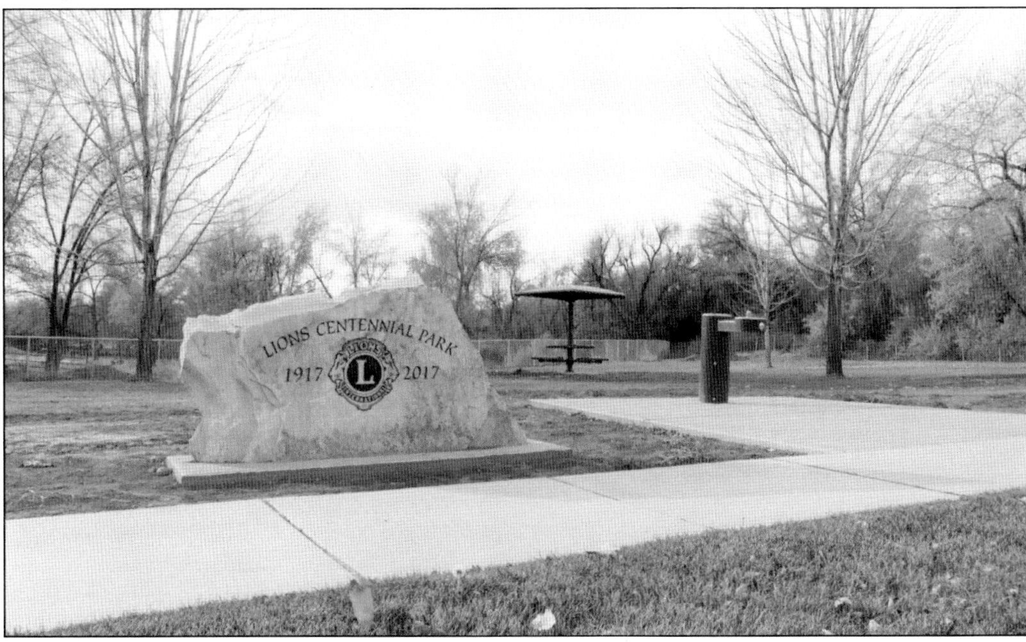

Lions Centennial Park. This small park commemorates the 100th anniversary of the founding of the Lions Club and is on the site of the first log schoolhouse in Riverdale. Formed in 1954, the Riverdale Lions Club plays an important philanthropic role in the city. The Lions sponsored this park to provide more green space in the city. A ribbon-cutting ceremony for the park was held on October 23, 2017. (Author's collection.)

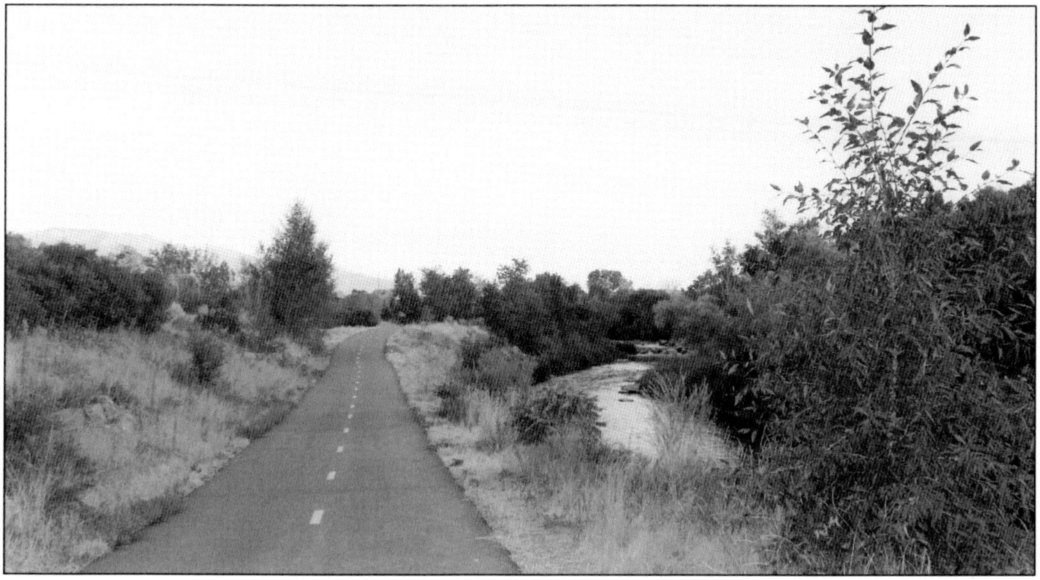

Weber River Parkway Trail. In 1994, Riverdale Greenway Association co-chairs Nancy Brough of the city council and resident David E. Blackner worked to create a river walkway trail. Officially opened on July 4, 1997, the Riverdale section contains a portion of the 12-mile Weber River Parkway Trail, a beautiful paved trail that parallels the Weber River. The trail begins south of the civic center and connects to the Ogden River Parkway Trail on the north, all part of the 27-mile Centennial Trail loop. The trail is used for walking, running, biking, and other activities. It also provides access to the disc golf course and Riverdale Bike Park. Protected lands around the trail include cottonwood forests and wetland areas. (Author's collection.)

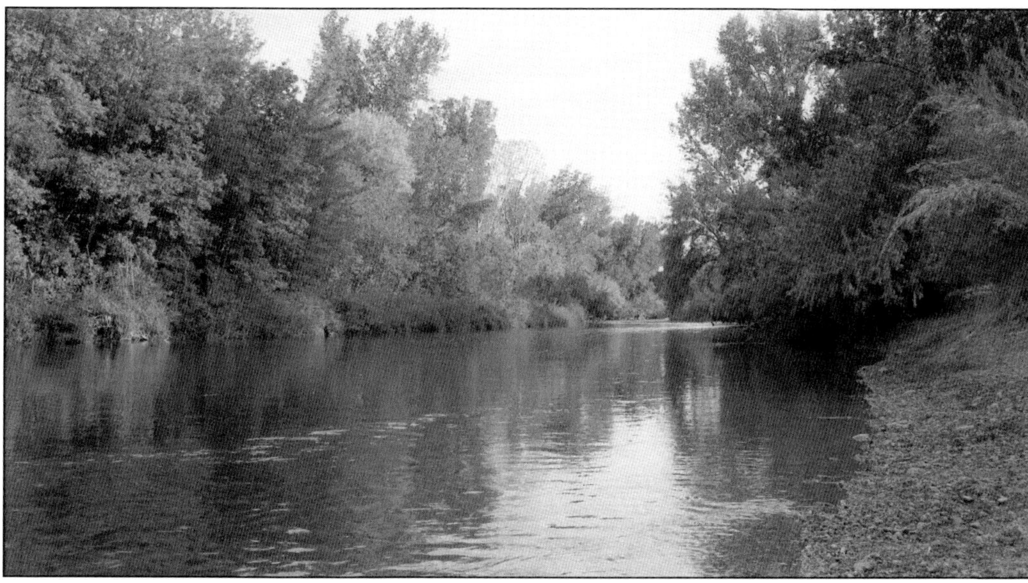

Weber River. The Weber River has always played an important role in Riverdale. Early settlers used it to irrigate crops and to power the mill, and as a site for baptisms. The river has provided recreation in the form of ice-skating, tubing, kayaking, and swimming, and as a great place to skip or throw rocks. Despite all the changes Riverdale has seen, from the early days of Stringtown to the bustling city of today, the river has remained a constant. (Author's collection.)

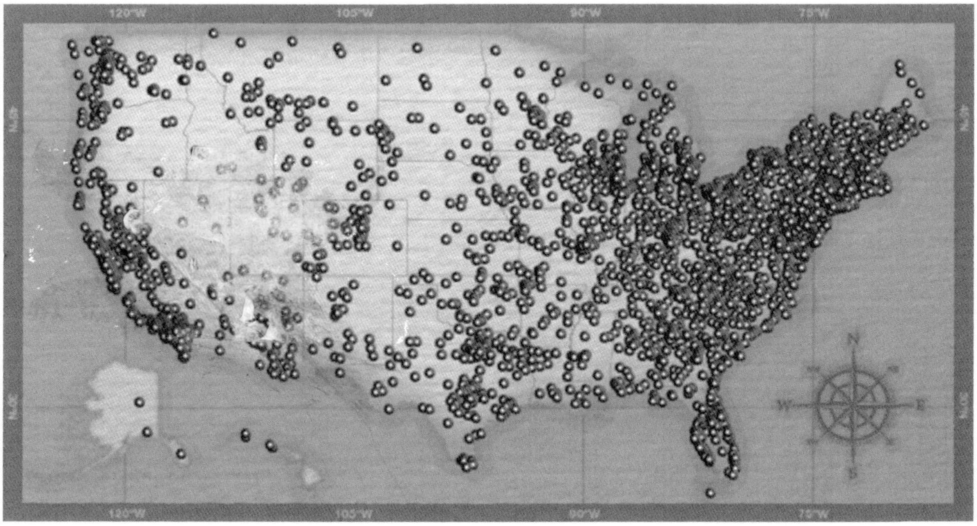